Humanistic Pedagogy Across the Disciplines

Amy E. Traver • Dan Leshem
Editors

Humanistic Pedagogy Across the Disciplines

Approaches to Mass Atrocity Education in the Community College Context

palgrave
macmillan

Editors
Amy E. Traver
Department of Social Sciences
Queensborough Community College, CUNY
Bayside, NY, USA

Dan Leshem
Harriet and Kenneth Kupferberg Holocaust Center (KHC)
Queensborough Community College, CUNY
Bayside, NY, USA

ISBN 978-3-030-06958-2 ISBN 978-3-319-95025-9 (eBook)
https://doi.org/10.1007/978-3-319-95025-9

This Palgrave Macmillan imprint is published by the registered company Springer Nature Switzerland AG
The registered company address is: Gewerbestrasse 11, 6330 Cham, Switzerland

This book is dedicated to the tireless efforts, insight, and creative courage of our Queensborough Community College (QCC) colleagues: students, faculty, and staff. It has been a pleasure learning from and with you. Also, to our children Raenen, Mayrav, and Yotam for whom we do the work we do.

Acknowledgments

This volume is the result of a true team effort on the parts of many faculty, students, and staff at Queensborough Community College (QCC) and the Harriet & Kenneth Kupferberg Holocaust Center (KHC). Proceeding chronologically, we would like to thank the Challenge Grant from the National Endowment for the Humanities (NEH), which provided matching funds to our generous donors' contributions and allowed us to establish the KHC/NEH Endowment Fund to maintain the Colloquium Series in perpetuity. Of course, many people at QCC helped implement these grant programs, starting with President Diane B. Call and Vice President of Institutional Advancement Rosemary Zins. We would also like to thank the team that developed the proposal and helped grow the concept over the first several years, including QCC faculty members Drs. Sarah Danielsson, Susan Jacobowitz, and Emily Tai in addition to former KHC Executive Director, Dr. Arthur Flug. More broadly, we are grateful for the staff of the KHC, especially Assistant Director Marisa Hollywood, who helped plan, implement, and manage the budgets for most of the series represented in this book.

A special acknowledgment is due to the faculty coordinators who led the NEH grant over its initial years and who, through their efforts, helped shape what it has become. Equally important are the many colloquia speakers—including scholars, directors, policymakers, and genocide and mass atrocity survivors—who generously contributed their time, experience, and expertise to the college and our larger community. Additionally, we are thankful for the QCC faculty who aligned courses with the annual

Colloquia. Their inclusive approach to teaching and to generating learning communities was essential to the success of these past five years, and it will be equally so in future endeavors. Finally, we must recognize QCC's students, whose openness, active engagement, and creativity serve as the inspiration and foundation for all of our work.

Contents

Notes on Contributors

Azadeh Aalai, Ph.D., is an Assistant Professor of Psychology at Queensborough Community College (QCC), the City University of New York (CUNY). She is a social psychologist specializing in mass media depictions, the psychology of aggression, warfare, and genocide, and gender-related studies. She is also an adjunct for the M.A. program in Psychology at New York University. She was the recipient of a Kupferberg Holocaust Center/National Endowment for the Humanities (KHC/NEH) grant naming her the scholar-in-residence at the KHC for 2017–2018. She has also worked with the United States Holocaust Memorial Museum as a recipient of the Silberman faculty seminar exploring the themes of sex and gender during the Holocaust.

Rose Marie Äikäs, Ph.D., M.A., M.S.W., is an Associate Professor of Criminal Justice at QCC, CUNY. Äikäs has taught at the University of Helsinki-School of Law, Smith College-Graduate School of Social Work, Rutgers University School of Criminal Justice and Social Work, and in a New York State correctional facility. Her courses include Introduction to Criminal Justice, Criminality and Mental Illness, Social Work Research Theory, and Criminal Justice Policy Implications for Social Work Practice. Äikäs has international and domestic prison research experience, professional experience as a criminal justice and social work practitioner, and program development experience.

Kathleen Tamayo Alves, D.A., is an Assistant Professor of English at QCC, CUNY, where she teaches literature and composition. She holds an M.A. and a D.A. in English from St. John's University. Her research centers on eighteenth-century literature and culture, biopolitics, and literary history. She has presented and published portions of her book-length project—*Body Language: Medicine and the Eighteenth-Century Comic Novel.* She has also received a number of awards, including the CUNY Faculty Fellowship Publication Program Award, the CUNY Academy William Stewart Travel Award, and the Professional Staff Congress (PSC)-CUNY Summer Grant.

Aliza Atik, Ph.D., is an Assistant Professor of English at QCC, CUNY. She holds a Ph.D. from Stony Brook University where she won several awards for her scholarship, including an Andrew W. Mellon Dissertation Fellowship. Atik's research interests include Victorian studies, Jewish literature, and Arab/Israeli literature. Her article, "Calibrating the Female Body: Shame, Disgust, and the Recuperative Gaze in Amos Gitai's Kadosh," was published in *Shofar: An Interdisciplinary Journal of Jewish Studies.* Atik also works as an assistant editor for the peer-reviewed and Modern Language Association (MLA)-indexed journal *Victorian Literature and Culture.*

André Brégégère, Ph.D., is an adjunct Professor of Music at QCC, CUNY, and William Patterson University. He holds a Ph.D. in composition from the Graduate Center, CUNY, with a dissertation on the music and theoretical work of Henri Pousseur. His recent and ongoing scholarly work includes "Some Thoughts on Maximally Smooth Voice-Leading among Pcsets and Set Classes" (SMT Arlington 2017) and "The Serial Concept in Pousseur's *Votre Faust*" (*Oxford Handbook of Faustian Music*, OUP forthcoming). His music has been performed and broadcast in the United States and Europe, and released on the label New Dynamic Records. www.abregegere.com

Johannes Burgers, Ph.D., is an Assistant Professor of English and Digital Humanities at Ashoka University in New Delhi, India. His chapter reflects work done while an assistant professor at QCC, CUNY. His research focuses on intersections of race science, sexuality, and modernity in a transnational context, specifically the influence of anti-Semitism on literature. His articles on this topic have been published in *The Journal of the History of Ideas*, *Jewish Studies Quarterly*, and edited collections. His book manuscript investigates the relationship between anti-Semitism and modernism in the work of Marcel Proust, James Joyce, Gertrude Stein, William Faulkner, and Robert Musil.

Julia B. Carroll, Ph.D., is a Professor of English, developmental English, and English as a Second Language (ESL) at QCC, CUNY. She has co-authored multiple peer-reviewed articles focused on teaching reading and writing skills to multilingual learners utilizing curriculum related to the Holocaust, genocide, and mass atrocity. She is also a practitioner of Academic Service-Learning (ASL), and her research in this area has been published in the following three journals: AAC&U's *Diversity and Democracy*; *Teaching English in the Two-Year College*; and *Basic Writing eJournal.*

Steven Dahlke, D.M.A., is an Associate Professor of Music at QCC, CUNY. He holds a D.M.A. in vocal performance, choral music, and music education from University of Southern California (USC) with highest honors and his M.M. from Manhattan School of Music. Dahlke has published and presented in the areas of Choral Music Education, ASL, and Global Diversity Learning. He has soloed with the Oregon Symphony Orchestra, Seattle Symphony Pops, Portland Youth Philharmonic, Portland Baroque Orchestra, and Aspen Music festival, among others. He conducts musical theater and is co-director of Jazz Hands Children's Theater, advancing kinesthetic and empathic communication.

Melissa Dennihy, Ph.D., is an Assistant Professor of English at QCC, CUNY. Her research focuses on multiethnic US literature, community college pedagogies, and the teaching of writing and literature. Dennihy's work has been published in *Pedagogy*, *Teaching English in the Two-Year College*, *MELUS*, and *Southern Studies*, as well as numerous essay collections.

Barbara K. Emanuele, M.A., is an adjunct Lecturer of English at QCC, CUNY. She has served as an educator and an administrator in CUNY for over 20 years. Her focus is on composition instruction to students in an urban setting.

Franca Ferrari-Bridgers, Ph.D., is an Assistant Professor of Communication at QCC, CUNY. She holds a Master's degree in Hispano-American languages and literatures (Università Statale, Milan, Italy, 1995); a Master's degree in linguistics (Freie Universitaet, Berlin, Germany, 1998); a Ph.D. in theoretical linguistics (New York University, 2005); and a Master's degree in experimental psychology (Brooklyn College, 2015). Ferrari-Bridgers' research interests are in the field of linguistics, psycholinguistics, listening assessments, pedagogical research in high-impact practices, and higher education in prison.

Aviva Geismar, M.F.A., is an Assistant Professor of Dance at QCC, CUNY. Geismar is also the Artistic Director of Drastic Action, a contemporary dance company that has performed extensively in New York City, throughout the United States, and in Germany. Geismar's 2016 education and performance project "Dis/Location (Fort Tryon)" explored the immigrant experience in the largely immigrant neighborhood of Washington Heights, New York City. In February 2018, her choreography was presented on "Soaking Wet" at the West End Theater. Geismar holds an M.F.A. from University of Wisconsin-Milwaukee and a B.F.A. from New York University.

Susan Jacobowitz, Ph.D., is an Associate Professor of English at QCC, CUNY. She earned her doctorate at Brandeis University. Her research areas include second-generation experience including literature, graphic texts and performance art, intergenerational transmission of trauma, and conflicts and challenges of Jewish identity. Her scholarship has been published in Australia, the United States, Germany, Brazil, Israel, and India.

Cary Lane, Ph.D., is an Assistant Professor of English at QCC, CUNY, where he teaches freshman composition and developmental education courses. Lane's research interests include examining how arts-based teaching approaches and campus cultural centers affect learning outcomes in writing courses. Lane served as curator-in-residence at the KHC, where he curated two exhibitions and integrated exhibit content/themes into pedagogy across the disciplines. Lane received his B.A. in studio art from the University of Rochester, his M.F.A. in art theory and practice from Northwestern University, and his Ph.D. in postsecondary and adult education from Capella University.

Mirna Lekić, D.M.A., is an Assistant Professor of Music at QCC, CUNY. A pianist, she is active as a recitalist, chamber musician, and educator. Her recent publications include two critically acclaimed recordings: a debut solo album titled *Masks* (Centaur Records 3519), and *Eastern Currents* (Romeo Records 7320), a disc of contemporary chamber music. Lekić is a graduate of the Eastman School of Music, the Mannes College of Music, and the Graduate Center, CUNY. *www.mirnalekic.com*

Dan Leshem, Ph.D., is the former Executive Director of the KHC at QCC, CUNY. He holds a Ph.D. in comparative literature from Emory University. His dissertation, *The Language of Suffering: Writing and*

Reading the Holocaust, argues for the necessity of ethical approaches to interpreting Holocaust testimony. While at Emory, he served as Program Manager of the Holocaust Denial on Trial (HDOT) website. Between 2010 and 2015, Leshem served as Associate Director for Research at the USC Shoah Foundation and adjunct Assistant Professor of Comparative Literature at the University of Southern California.

Benjamin Lawrance Miller, M.F.A., is an Assistant Professor of English at QCC, CUNY, where he teaches composition and creative writing. He holds an M.F.A. in writing from CalArts and a B.A. in philosophy from Boston University. Most recently, he has published creative work in *Entropy*, *BLYNKT*, and *Literary Orphans*. He is the co-author of "What Trump Gets Right and Wrong About Conspiracy," an editorial in *Inside Higher Ed*.

Danny Sexton, Ph.D., is an Assistant Professor of English at QCC, CUNY. His fields of study and research are Victorian literature and culture, postcolonial literature, science fiction, gender and sexuality, masculinity, and race. He has presented at numerous conferences and published articles on race, gender, and Victorian and postcolonial literature. Three principles guide his teaching philosophy: (1) teaching "up" to students, (2) changing the *way* students think, and (3) creating an atmosphere of respect that honors the various cultural and ethnic backgrounds of his students.

Amy E. Traver, Ph.D., is an Associate Professor of Sociology at QCC, CUNY. Her research interests include student success in community colleges, as well as intersections of adoption, race/ethnicity, and gender in American family life. Her most recent publications include articles in *Teaching Sociology*, *Internet and Higher Education* (with Volchok, Bidjerano, and Shea), and *Qualitative Inquiry* (with Duran), in addition to the co-edited volume (with Perel Katz) *Service-Learning at the American Community College* (Palgrave Macmillan 2014). Traver was the faculty coordinator of the 2015–2016 NEH/KHC Colloquium Series at QCC, and the 2016–2017 scholar-in-residence at QCC's KHC.

Kathleen Wentrack, Ph.D., is an Associate Professor of Art History at QCC, CUNY. She holds a Master's degree from the University of Amsterdam and a Ph.D. from the Graduate Center, CUNY. Wentrack's recent publications include "1970s Feminist Practice as Heterotopian: The Stichting Vrouwen in de Beeldende Kunst and the Schule für kreativen Feminismus" in *All Women Art Spaces in the Long 1970s* (Liverpool University Press 2018). Wentrack is a contributing editor to *Art History Teaching Resources* and the peer-reviewed journal *Art History Pedagogy and Practice.*

CHAPTER 1

Introduction: Humanistic Pedagogy Across the Disciplines—Approaches to Mass Atrocity Education in the Community College Context

Dan Leshem

As the drive for universal Holocaust education became a widespread phenomenon in the late 1970s, there were many provocative discussions in public forums about how, what, when, and why such content should be taught. Early debates sought to establish a core curriculum or canon of texts, what qualifications instructors should have, and whether Holocaust memory should remain solely within the realm of disciplines such as history and Jewish studies, or if they have a broader and more universal context. This very important, early discussion largely settled around a fixed solution: *The Diary of Anne Frank* would be taught in middle schools, Elie Wiesel's *Night* would be taught in high school, and post-secondary Holocaust education would largely be the domain of history and literature departments. In addition, instruction at all levels would be heavily supplemented by survivor testimony, ideally through in-person rather than video testimony.[1] For the past 40 years, in other words, Holocaust victims and

D. Leshem (✉)
Harriet and Kenneth Kupferberg Holocaust Center (KHC), Queensborough Community College, CUNY, Bayside, NY, USA

A. E. Traver, D. Leshem (eds.), *Humanistic Pedagogy Across the Disciplines*, https://doi.org/10.1007/978-3-319-95025-9_1

survivors, through the moral, ethical, and humane immediacy of their first-person accounts, have been our most effective Holocaust educators.

Considering the age of remaining survivors, it is with pragmatic—yet unresolved—anxiety that Holocaust educators and center directors search for a solution to the following question: How will we teach the Holocaust in the absence of any direct witnesses? Although largely silent and ignored for years after the war, Holocaust survivors have become its most effective and transformative educators over the past several decades. The impact of their presentations to students of all ages is palpable in their audiences' intellectual and emotional reactions, not only in the immediate moments after the sharing of Holocaust testimony but weeks and even months later in course evaluations and assignments. While the fallibility of survivor memory has been oft noted—especially in terms of details such as dates and precise locations—the truths that they tell are different from those available in contemporaneous documents, photographs, and even diaries. They speak to the human experience of global, national, and local suffering at the hands of other human beings and, at times, the destruction of human beings. Crucially, they speak about their own experiences, in the first person, transforming all their listeners into what has been called "secondary witnesses" (Assmann 2006, 269). Through their narratives we become witnesses to both "inhuman" atrocity and human resilience.

Survivors have also provided a moral compass for Holocaust education by being among the first to advocate that scholars turn away from debates of the uniqueness of the Holocaust and toward the holistic inclusion of a full spectrum of instances of genocide and mass atrocity, especially in the twentieth and twenty-first centuries. This shift in emphasis—which does nothing to diminish the importance of the Holocaust nor obscure those elements of its development, execution, and aftermath that were sui generis and are therefore genuinely unique—is crucial for ensuring the future of Holocaust education, developing the potential to recognize and interrupt societies that are moving toward genocide, and deriving lessons for ourselves and our students about how to become agents of societal change. All of these concerns are at the heart of the humanities curriculum.

Without a doubt, survivor voices—in society in general and in the classroom in particular—have propelled the scholarship and teaching of genocide, mass atrocity, and human rights into a central focus of humanities education. In a sense, Holocaust survivors have taught us *how to hear* survivors of other genocidal experiences and sensitized us to the traumatic impact of mass atrocity that ripples geographically and generationally from a local context to a global audience. One must bear in mind, however, that Holocaust survivor testimony resonates so profoundly in the United States due to a variety of social, cultural, historical, and religious factors, and might resonate very differently or not at all with students from different educational backgrounds such as recent immigrants from Africa, Asia, and Central and South America. This is not to say that these regions have no specific and local history of genocide and mass atrocity, but rather that a lack of prior exposure to the history of the Holocaust might leave students from these regions at a loss to understand the importance American culture ascribes to the Nazi genocide. For these reasons as well, the expansion of the focus of traditional Holocaust education to a more global understanding of the causes and consequences of genocide and mass atrocity allows students to enter the discussion from the atrocities most proximal to their background and experiences. In other words, if the Holocaust is to be discussed and taught globally, it must be understood in a global context utilizing a Humanistic Pedagogy—teaching practices that emphasize students' sustained engagement with the most profound challenges of human *being*, such as humanity's tendency to create massively violent societies as well as remarkably resilient individuals and cultures.

The NEH/KHC Colloquium Series at Queensborough Community College

Humanistic Pedagogy in the Community College Context

Community colleges have long been at the forefront of transformational pedagogical innovations. In fact, community colleges were fertile ground for the development of Holocaust and genocide pedagogy, giving rise to the first Holocaust courses and centers in the late 1970s and early 1980s.[2] Queensborough Community College (QCC) of the City University of New York (CUNY) is home to the Harriet and Kenneth Kupferberg Holocaust Center (KHC), one of the first college-based Holocaust resource centers in the country. The KHC launched in 1983 following years of collecting teaching and learning resources and developing classroom-based practices appropriate to post-secondary education. Over the intervening decades, it has grown into an archive of Holocaust artifacts, a library of over 6000 volumes, an exhibition space that has featured over 30 originally researched exhibits, a center for student learning through internships and fellowships, and a programmatic hub that each year hosts more than 30 events for the campus community and general public.

Significantly, community colleges are an ideal place to establish and test Humanistic Pedagogical practices, in particular. Community colleges are primarily teaching institutions that serve the neediest students—those who have been underserved by underperforming secondary schools, the newest immigrants, and those closest to the poverty level. In order to reach these student bodies in ways that will sustain a lifelong commitment to the ideals of a humanistic education, community college instructors typically leverage their research training and teaching interests to innovate post-secondary pedagogy, often engaging in experimentation designed to meet the needs of ever-evolving student populations. This is especially true at QCC, where, as of the latest statistics, over 400 full-time faculty members—80% of whom have terminal degrees—along with additional part-time and contingent instructors serve 16,000 students who hail from over 129 countries and speak nearly 70 non-English languages at home (QCC Office of Institutional Research and Assessment 2016). Many QCC students themselves came to this country as refugees if not asylum seekers. As is typical with community college students, many QCC students are also "non-traditional" in that "when compared to their baccalaureate-seeking counterparts, who are frequently considered the norm in higher education, (they) are more likely to be older, working, parenting, low-income, female, of color, and of first-generation college and/or American status" (Traver and Katz 2014). Since community colleges are open-enrollment institutions, many QCC students also have developmental education needs in math, reading, and/or writing, in addition to their English language learning challenges. In other words, QCC, like most community colleges, is a teaching and learning laboratory where research-trained faculty work innovatively to provide transformative educational opportunities to students from diverse ethnic, educational, class, linguistic, and cultural backgrounds. These Humanistic Pedagogies, and the transformative learning they support, will become increasingly relevant and even essential at four-year colleges and universities as student expectations evolve along with student populations.

The Initial Hypothesis

For these reasons—to explore possible futures of Holocaust and genocide education in a world without Holocaust survivors and to meet the evolving demands of diverse student populations in higher education—the KHC sought funding from a National Endowment for the Humanities (NEH) Community College Challenge grant in 2010. NEH intended the grant opportunity to identify and fund six national demonstration programs that would develop best practices in incorporating campus-based cultural centers into the humanities curriculum across the disciplines. College-based Holocaust centers around the country consistently struggle to engage faculty around their pedagogical content and approach. This proposal innovated that model by recruiting and supporting faculty to be the thought partners who would themselves create the pedagogical content based on the mission and holdings of the KHC. It envisioned broad, interdisciplinary engagement by faculty throughout the college who would align their ongoing courses with one or more of the colloquium events to deepen their students' learning in classes across campus. Peer-to-peer collaboration—between the faculty coordinators of each annual colloquium and their colleagues within and outside of their departments—would allow instructors to test the value of their pedagogical innovations through integration with other faculty and courses across campus.

The KHC's successful proposal and institutional fundraising created an endowment to support an annual faculty-led colloquium—each year's series of events, programs, and working groups builds on insights and lessons learned from previous years and designs new approaches based on experimentation, reflection, and assessment. In order to recruit the most interested and capable members of QCC's diverse faculty to lead each colloquium, the KHC issues an annual Request for Proposals (RFP).[3] As relatively few QCC faculty see an a priori relationship between the subject matter they research or generally teach and the Holocaust, the Executive Director of the KHC consults with potential applicants as they construct their proposals, helping them to make connections and assess the applicability between their course focus and related research, artifacts, exhibits, and testimony of the Holocaust, genocide, and mass atrocity. These proposals are evaluated by a team of external scholars and practitioners according to a strict rubric that emphasizes student and instructor engagement across the disciplines. After receiving the award notification, recipients typically set to work creating a trifold calendar of events—for wide distribution across campus and through the Center's mailing list—and identifying potential instructors from across the disciplines who agree to (1) align one or more courses to at least one of the colloquium events; and (2) create a substantive curricular assignment or activity to incorporate the topic of the colloquium into whatever course they teach. What struck the NEH reviewers as the most novel aspect of the KHC proposal was that it did not propose to create more Holocaust or genocide courses but to encourage instructors to incorporate this content into existing courses across campus. To date, instructors from English, history, psychology, criminal justice, dance, and many other disciplines have aligned existing courses with the annual colloquium series of events and lectures, challenging their students to confront the core lessons of violence and produce thoughtful responses in light of course curricula.

The First Five Annual NEH/KHC Colloquia

The KHC held its first Colloquium Series, "Genocide, Justice, and Human Rights," in the 2012–2013 academic year. This inaugural colloquium, led by Associate Professor of History Dr. Sarah Danielsson, was structured around two pivotal and problematic issues that have been of concern for genocide scholarship and memorialization: the nexus of human rights and genocide, and the nexus of justice and genocide. The colloquium series featured lectures and film screenings, and it started and ended with short conferences that highlighted these two issues.

The following year, the 2013–2014 Colloquium Series, "The Holocaust in a Global Context: Connections Across the Community College," led by Associate Professor of English Dr. Susan Jacobowitz, sought to address global genocide and Holocaust remembrance from a social justice perspective, create interdisciplinary collaborations, and feature faculty development. Participants—including full-time faculty, lecturers, and adjuncts—were invited to think broadly about connections between discrimination, persecution, and prejudice in the context of the Holocaust. Events included the performance of the one-man play, *The Soap Myth*, and lectures on varied topics from Holocaust testimonies to consideration of the impact of mental illness and physical disabilities during World War II and in our contemporary society. This series built on the previous year's efforts by adding a reading and conversation group for the instructors who had aligned their courses with the colloquium. During informal conversation sessions, participants shared course design ideas, pushed each other to consider new and innovative assignments and activities, and developed a reader that was used, and continues to be used, in affiliated courses.

"Testimony Across the Disciplines: Cultural and Artistic Responses to Genocide," the 2014–2015 Colloquium Series led by Assistant Professor of English Dr. Cary Lane and Assistant Professor of Music Dr. Steven Dahlke, was a large-scale, interdisciplinary pedagogy project that explored the Holocaust, genocide, and organized hate through a creative, arts-based, and student-centered approach. In this program, students from eight separate academic disciplines studied with professors, genocide scholars, embedded librarians, Holocaust survivors, and witnesses of mass atrocities from around the world. After a year of study, students responded with their own cultural and artistic "testimony," reflecting on their learning through a capstone exhibit of original performances, art exhibits, documentary filmmaking, painting, poetry, creative writing, exhibition curation, singing, and dance. By capping the year with student artistic, critical, and performance-based responses in a gallery exhibition at the KHC and through an evening of performances at the Queensborough Performing Arts Center, this colloquium series and its evaluation data demonstrated the power of pedagogy to achieve learning outcomes, social impact, and behavioral change.

Spanning the 2015–2016 academic year, "Gender, Mass Violence, and Genocide,"—led by Associate Professor of Sociology Dr. Amy Traver—consisted of eight events that were tightly linked to a newly established field of research in genocide scholarship: gender-sensitive studies of mass violence and genocide. The eight events that constituted the series had two foci: (1) how gender structures and mediates experiences of mass violence and genocide; and (2) how attention to gender can aid efforts to predict, prevent, and reconcile experiences of mass violence and genocide. Traver built on the previous year's inclusion of evaluation data to incorporate a layered, IRB-approved assessment protocol into the colloquium design, which generated very compelling data about pedagogy and student reflection and their impacts on student learning. Working with a team of four assessment-trained QCC faculty and one student researcher, she analyzed students' aligned assignments to find evidence of learning based on the Association of American Colleges and University's (AAC&U) Global Learning VALUE rubric (AAC&U 2016). One of the team's most significant findings was that the colloquium series increased student understanding of global crises but did not necessarily give them the tools to *apply* what they had learned.

The 2016–2017 NEH/KHC Colloquium Series, "Fleeing Genocide: Displacement, Exile, and the Refugee"—led by Assistant Professors of English Drs. Aliza Atik and Kathleen Alves and Assistant Professor of Music Dr. Mirna Lekić—explored a topic of contemporaneous urgency and engaged with current and contentious discourses. Building on the previous year, this series added nuance to the assessment process by asking faculty contributors to identify and tie course activities to specific outcomes and "real-world" applications. Relying on a multidisciplinary speaker series—from organizations such as the International Rescue Committee and the United Nations Department of Peacekeeping Operations—and a canon of essential texts both primary and theoretical, the Colloquium moved students beyond abstract compassion into an investigation of the reality of genocide and the trauma of displacement.[4] This approach bridged events of war and genocide from far-flung spaces to the local and familiar, provided an affective complement to the issues presented in the lectures, and encouraged students to respond to the concept of abstract compassion and the call for global inclusivity. The Colloquium culminated with music and stories presented by the coordinating faculty drawn from their own personal and familial experiences as refugees and as victims of persecution during the Japanese occupation of the Philippines.

The Future of the NEH/KHC Colloquium Series

Following the completion of the initial five-year grant period and building on its pedagogical innovations, the KHC and the NEH have worked to modify the program structure slightly to ensure that future colloquia meet the grant's goals of enriching humanities education at QCC by incorporating the resources and expertise of the KHC into courses across the disciplines. Based on our findings over the first five years of this program we have added several additional objectives to our RFP for future opportunities:

- demonstrate the contemporary relevance and urgency of issues surrounding the Holocaust, genocide, and mass atrocity;
- utilize student-centered pedagogy that—while building on accurate historical, anthropological, and social framing of historical atrocity—empowers students to view themselves as agents of social change;

- integrate more deeply KHC events, exhibits, and programs into the annual NEH/KHC Colloquium Series; and
- increase use of assessment and evaluation to understand the efficacy of our programming, facilitate continual improvement of our offerings to faculty and staff, and fulfill our mandate from NEH to demonstrate effective innovation.

It is hoped that the next five years will refine many of the broad discoveries that were made over the initial grant period, and that, through experimentation, evaluation, and incorporating the results, the NEH/KHC Colloquium Series will engage even more students and instructors across QCC.

The Current Volume

This volume examines discipline-specific and interdisciplinary approaches described by a cohort of 19 of the nearly 50 QCC instructors who participated in colloquia over the first five years of the grant. Rather than organize this volume according to the annual colloquia themes that are outlined above, the editors have chosen to structure the text according to four broad and overlapping pedagogical approaches that proved particularly effective for the annual faculty coordinators and their cohorts of participating faculty: arts-based, textual, outcomes-based, and social justice. We emphasize these approaches over the chronological development of the program because we anticipate an audience concerned more with praxis than the evolution of our program. Given that community colleges function as teaching and learning laboratories, we view these multiple approaches as capable of attracting and engaging diverse audiences with divergent learning processes, strengths, and interests.

Through their self-conscious and self-critical reflections, the chapters in this volume bring a distinct perspective to the dominant practices in Holocaust and genocide education in a number of ways: (1) they are concerned with developing new pedagogical models focused on experimentation and assessment; (2) they focus on novel associations and juxtapositions between the specificity of the unfolding of the Holocaust and other developments and insights into human thought, behavior, and development; and (3) they all emerged from an alignment with one or more of five annual colloquia that bring Holocaust, genocide, and mass atrocity education into courses across the humanities. In our experience, engaging with the complex, emotionally and intellectually fraught Holocaust, genocide, and mass atrocity content resulted in community college students' deeper course engagement and learning across the humanities. Yet, it is the belief of the editors that the transformative approaches discussed in this volume will resonate far beyond the world of community colleges to educators in all contexts, including schools, museums, memorials, and cultural centers.

The volume's first section presents four chapters that offer theoretical foundations and programmatic examples of each of the four featured approaches to mass atrocity education in the community college context. In Chap. 2, Dr. Lane reviews the pedagogical theories that led him, his co-coordinator Dr. Steven Dahlke, and his colleagues to explore the Holocaust, genocide, and organized hate through an arts-based approach. In Chap. 3, Drs. Atik, Lekić, and Alves review the role of textual and theoretical approaches that challenged students to become readers of the global refugee crisis through close study of primary and secondary texts of the Holocaust and other outbreaks of mass atrocity. In Chap. 4, Dr. Traver reviews the role of outcomes-based approaches, which tend to privilege Backward Course Design and utilize continual reflection, evaluation, and assessment to achieve their goals, in Humanistic Pedagogical practice. In Chap. 5, Dr. Susan Jacobowitz reviews the pedagogical theories that encouraged her, and her colloquium colleagues, to address and relate the Holocaust to ongoing human rights and social justice challenges of daily relevance to the lives of students. Each of these initial "approach" chapters introduce readers to, and encourage them to explore, several of the experience-based examples of these approaches that appear in the volume's second section.

The volume's second section contains reflective chapters that explore the design, execution, and outcomes of a course that was associated with at least one of the annual colloquia. They contain the discipline-specific purpose and approaches of that course, and many illustrate how high impact practices (HIPs), student-centered pedagogies, and structured reflection were used to amplify and deepen student engagement and learning. Each chapter also exemplifies two or more of the approaches outlined in the book's first section.

In Chap. 6, Dr. Azadeh Aalai describes her efforts to engage psychology students in consideration of the critical role that national and historical constructions of sex/gender play in genocidal policies and methods. By aligning her social psychology course with a 2015–2016 Colloquium

Series event, Aalai framed the Shoah in the larger context of the "psychology of evil," which helped to broaden students' reductive and, at times, incomplete knowledge of the subject. Additionally, by applying concepts specific to the discipline of psychology, she fostered students' capacity to understand how the Holocaust could happen, and how intersections of marginalized social identities—Jewish and Woman—impacted experiences of victimhood.

In Chap. 7, Dr. Rose Marie Äikäs describes a project linking her criminal justice course to the 2014–2015 Colloquium Series. In this course, students met with and interviewed formerly incarcerated women at Hour Children, a community service organization located in Queens, New York. After studying the Nazi approach to incarceration as a tool to reshape society by targeting and excluding certain populations from the state, Äikäs' students explored the challenges of reincorporation to society that confronted the surviving Jewish population after World War II. They then utilized this historical precedent, within a restorative justice framework, to understand some of the difficulties facing formerly incarcerated women.

In Chap. 8, Dr. Atik and Professors Aviva Geismar and Benjamin Lawrance Miller focus on a highly experimental, collaborative, interdisciplinary learning project that was aligned with the 2014–2015 Colloquium Series. Atik engaged her students in a struggle to move from passive and disinterested bystanders to active social agents implicated in the struggles of power and powerlessness; after which students in Geismar's "Theory and Practice of Modern Dance" translated Atik's students' writings into original performances for the capstone event of the series. Miller's students documented this interdisciplinary collaboration by creating a film that was publicly screened during the Colloquium's culminating exhibit and performance.

In Chap. 9, Dr. Johannes Burgers elaborates on the challenging confrontation between memory and history in literary narrative. In an upper-level English course centered on literary theory and aligned with the 2013–2014 Colloquium Series, Burgers provided his students with the critical language of cultural memory theory to examine a broad range of Holocaust literatures. Students in his course reflected on the intersections of truth and language, exploring the ways in which discursive context mediates subjective interpretations of historical events. After speaking with a Holocaust survivor and examining artifacts from the KHC, Burgers' students wrote about the complex connections between memory, society, material culture, and the self.

In Chap. 10, Dr. Julia B. Carroll outlines her use of a peer-to-peer collaborative project that paired English Language Learners (ELLs) with Education 101 students in consideration of genocide and multiculturalism within the context of the 2015–2016 Colloquium Series. Significantly, this project showed how Academic Service Learning (ASL) and student identity can inform efforts to teach mass violence and genocide. Carroll concludes with evidence of the project's impacts on ELL's second language acquisition, self-esteem, and knowledge of genocide and multiculturalism.

In Chap. 11, Dr. Dahlke describes his choral music class project, "Musical Responses to the Holocaust," as an example of Backward Course Design. Dahlke reviews the project's varied learning activities, alignment with the 2014–2015 Colloquium Series, and integration of ASL. He also adds to the literature on teaching the Holocaust through music, which has tended to focus on songs of resistance or the period more broadly, to reveal that musical performance is yet another way for students to work and think through this history.

In Chap. 12, Dr. Melissa Dennihy underscores the value of student-centered, distributed leadership models guiding student engagement with the Holocaust, genocide, and mass atrocity. Through her participation in the faculty working group of the 2013–2014 Colloquium Series, Dennihy created and refined a unit for her introductory literature course before introducing it to her spring-semester students. As implemented, Dennihy's class considered the necessarily partial perspective presented in any given text or exhibit before engaging in a high-stakes multimedia and multi-genre project in which students assumed the role of a curator of a museum on genocide or mass atrocity.

In Chap. 13, Professor Barbara K. Emanuele outlines a learning activity that examined first-year composition students' critical consumption of media and met English 101 learning objectives through the textual analysis of hate propaganda. Emanuele's students learned to negate the intention of hate speech by deconstructing hateful text and images from both Nazi Germany and other contexts in the twenty-first century. Modeling the use of peer-editing activities, library resources, the KHC, and teaching support programs, her chapter provides a strong model for how to engage students and faculty in Humanistic Pedagogy in Holocaust, genocide, and mass atrocity education.

In Chap. 14, Dr. Franca Ferrari-Bridgers grounds her public speaking students' skill development in their learning of North American Indigenous

Peoples' history. By connecting to an event in the 2015–2016 Colloquium Series, she provided her students with access to a historical and social sciences forum where they could learn about mass violence directly from experts in the field, apply what they learned to evaluate what has happened and is happening to indigenous peoples in the United States, and understand the conceptual framework and realities of genocide. Ferrari-Bridgers' chapter concludes with evidence of how her students' perceptions of the experiences of North American Indigenous Peoples changed as a result of their participation in the series.

In Chap. 15, Dr. Lekić and Dr. André Brégégère write about "Echoes of Exile," a program where student performers, listeners, and writers considered issues of cultural genocide and human displacement through chamber, vocal, piano, and jazz selections. Through participation in this program, which was associated with the 2016–2017 Colloquium Series, students came to see music as a language that could preserve differences, work out questions of tension and release, and create—through sound—a sense of home. Participating students and instructors used the musical composition process as a vehicle for understanding, discourse, and empathy.

In Chap. 16, Dr. Danny Sexton explains how he used the KHC and a connection to the 2016–2017 Colloquium Series to build on students' readings of essays on oppression, freedom, civil disobedience, and empathy. Using a problem-based learning activity, Sexton engaged students in the creation of hypothetical programs that could assist refugees to the United States. Through engagement with an urgent topic of global relevance, students explored the ongoing implications of violence, genocide, and ethnic cleansing.

Finally, in Chap. 17, Dr. Kathleen Wentrack writes of her efforts to integrate the themes and events of the 2016–2017 Colloquium Series into her History of Photography course. Using a pre-/post-test methodology she demonstrates how this integration helped to increase students' appreciation for the role images play in our society while also expanding their understanding of the complexities of genocide, displacement, and the refugee experience. Her contribution adds empirical weight to conversations about the use of diverse learning techniques and sources in Humanistic Pedagogies.

Concluding Thoughts

Of course, these chapters raise issues of vital importance to consider in the context of the future of Holocaust and genocide education, including how much prior, specific knowledge instructors need to teach courses that incorporate consideration of Holocaust, genocide, and mass atrocity. At times, several of these chapters venture close to the trends of overgeneralization and overspecification that Schweber (2006) worries about in her essay "'Holocaust Fatigue' in Teaching Today." That is, certain approaches might tend toward stripping the Holocaust of some "of its particularities in order to emphasize its commonalities with other events in history" or, on the other hand, "making its (Holocaust education's) focus so narrow that the historical reality is distorted, minimizing its usefulness in combating racism specifically and 'idiocy' more generally" (Schweber 2006, 51–52). Each of the chapters in this volume is offered as an experiment in experiential learning, tracing the progression of the instructor's line of thought from conception to implementation to assessment of a particular approach to teaching Holocaust, genocide, and mass atrocity across the disciplines. If excessive generalization and specification are concerns, so to would be an excess of caution in ever approaching these amorphous boundaries. Faced with the urgent need "to make the material new, interesting, intellectually engaging, and emotionally affecting," the chapters in this volume push at conventional boundaries "to build on what students have previously learned rather than reiterating that which they already know" (Schweber 2006, 50).

In the decades following the Holocaust, we find ourselves faced with a future without firsthand witnesses or survivors and a diverse student body without personal or even conceptual connection to the events of the Holocaust or other genocides. In this context, Schweber's anxiety—shared by many scholars, curators, and educators—speaks to a growing need for creative and experimental, data-driven Holocaust and genocide pedagogies in the service of preventing ethnic conflict and genocide in the world. This volume furthers this conversation by presenting a unique and ongoing case study on what one community college has done over the first five years of a continuing experiment in innovative, assessment-driven, and interdisciplinary Holocaust, genocide, and mass atrocity education. Through a series of attempts to revitalize the debates from early decades of Holocaust education, this volume explores how, where, when, and why to teach Holocaust, genocide, and mass atrocity within and beyond the community college context.

It is in this spirit that we view the following chapters in Montaigne's sense of "Essais," as "attempts" or "trials." They describe and document a process undertaken by a community college, a Holocaust center, a faculty, and a student body to explore the efficacy of profound humanities content in the general education curriculum across the disciplines. Furthermore, they demonstrate that engaging students through Humanistic Pedagogies that draw on profound questions of human *being*—subjectivity and identity, trauma and perseverance—often results in transformative learning experiences. The qualitative and quantitative evidence presented in this volume offer compelling evidence that exposure to the moral and ethical complexity of Holocaust, genocide, and mass atrocity education among community college students results in great improvements in critical reflection and expression.

Although these experiments were initially conducted in the community college context, the editors believe that the methods, results, and insights derived from this exploration have much broader implications about teaching and learning with Humanistic Pedagogies in diverse contexts, including four-year colleges and universities, high schools, and community education/museum programs. This volume provides a model for campus-based and other cultural institutions on how to engage instructors and students in close and extended study of your mission, holdings, exhibits, and expertise. Since furthering Holocaust, genocide, and mass atrocity education is essential to the cultivation of humanistic values and human beings, we invite readers to replicate and further experiment with these approaches—perhaps through the use of a dedicated Libguide, maintained and hosted by QCC's Kurt R. Schmeller Library, which adds additional detail to the assignments, lectures, and findings of each chapter: http://qcc.libguides.com/neh.

Appendix: Sample Colloquium RFP for Academic Year 2018–2019

The KHC requests proposals for the NEH Scholar-in-Residence Program that provides a year of support for an instructional staff member at QCC to design a year-long series of activities united by a common theme relating to Holocaust, genocide, and mass atrocity.[5] The program budget will support course relief, summer funding, and a significant budget for guest speakers, events, and materials. While the In-Residence program can be shaped to individual faculty members' skills and interests, the resulting activities should be public, ongoing, interdisciplinary, and student-centered.

Proposed activities could include, but are not limited to, the hosting or development of the following:

- Seminars
- Guest lectures
- Exhibitions
- Films
- Curriculum development
- Professional workshops for community college faculty
- Conferences

In-Residence proposals should build upon existing KHC programs involving survivors, students, faculty, community members, KHC resources, and/or propose the acquisition or creation of new resources such as an artistic or historical exhibit. Proposers are encouraged to review the website of the KHC at http://khc.qcc.cuny.edu for information about past, present, and upcoming programs, collections, and resources.

For the 2018–2019 year, the KHC is especially interested in In-Residence proposals that touch upon the following planned exhibits and ongoing initiatives:

- Genocide at home and abroad
- The reemerging nexus of nationalism, antisemitism, and other forms of hate
- Restorative justice, reparations, and rebuilding communities
- The Holocaust in Italy and across the Mediterranean

Interested faculty should contact the KHC Executive Director. As in the past, proposals will be solicited, received, and appraised by an external review committee, which will consist of a minimum of three members, one being a Holocaust scholar and another being a community college faculty member or academic administrator (current or former). In addition to program content, proposals will be ranked according to their assessment design and their level of pedagogical innovation.

Project Description

Your *Project Description* should not exceed five single-spaced pages. If there are two or more Applicants/Scholars, please include an additional page containing a *Project Management Plan* describing how the incumbents will divide up the work load. The *Project Description* should describe the specific roles and responsibilities of each participating faculty member as well as plans for regular communication and coordination among project team members and with the KHC.

Your *Project Description* should include each of the following:

1. Description of theme and intellectual rationale
2. Relevance to the mission of the KHC and to the annual themes listed on the announcement
3. List and description of proposed events/programs along with proposed dates/months
4. How the proposed project will integrate KHC Resources into QCC Academic Programs
5. Description of how the project will impact multiple disciplines and reach students from across campus
6. Planned publication, curriculum development, dissemination plans, and/or project deliverables
7. Evaluation plan with measurable outcomes
8. Budget (with narrative explanations)

Biographical Summaries

Please include a biographical summary for all applicant(s), not to exceed two pages each. All summaries must include information on the faculty member's educational background, publications, classes taught, and other relevant professional activities in the format specified in the application forms.

Letters of Support

Please feel free to include any letters of support you may have for your project idea from colleagues, department chairs, or external partners.

Application Submission and Deadline

Complete applications should be submitted via e-mail to the Executive Director of the KHC. Complete applications will consist of the following:

- PDF file containing narrative sections of the proposal (*Project Description, Budget, and Biographical Summaries*)
- Excel file containing completed *Budget Form*
- Any additional materials such as Letters of Support, e-mailed as a scanned PDF file

Budget

A total of $45,000 is available.[6] Please note the following *sample* of allowable budgetary expenses:

- Faculty release time
- Faculty summer salary and fringe benefits on summer salary
- Honoraria for guest speakers and performers
- Travel costs for guest speakers
- Travel costs for faculty coordinator
- Materials for seminar participants (books and duplicated materials)
- Archival acquisitions (books, archival materials, and digital humanities resources)

Proposals *may not* include funds to pay for support staff, so the NEH Scholar-in-Residence applicants should carefully consider associated administrative tasks and how they will be handled. Funds *cannot* be used for lobbying or any type of political advocacy, nor can they be used for food/refreshments. Further, any outside organizations that become involved in the project should not be involved in political advocacy.

No full-time faculty may request more than one month of summer salary.

Please note that any archival acquisitions purchased with fund moneys must be stored at the KHC and will remain the property of QCC and the KHC after the completion of your program. (If relevant, costs associated with any necessary preservation and archival processing should be included in the budget.)

You may include other costs that do not fit in the categories included in the *Budget Form*. Please be aware that some types of costs, including the aforementioned support staff and food, are not eligible. Please contact the KHC Executive Director with questions regarding eligible versus non-eligible costs.

To whatever extent possible, please also itemize all costs within the narrative of your proposal. Provide a basis for calculation of your estimate.

Evaluation Criteria

- Does the applicant and/or co-applicant(s) have expertise in one or more humanities disciplines or approaches?
- To what extent is the proposed topic relevant to the mission, materials, holdings, and/or programs of the KHC?
- To what extent will the proposed topic serve to involve a variety of the humanities disciplines?
- To what extent is the proposed project student-focused? Will it impact a broad community of students across the QCC campus (particularly within the humanities)?
- To what extent do the proposed activities integrate the KHC and the humanities at QCC? (e.g., the number of faculty/courses involved, KHC resources utilized)
- What will be the quality and scope of any curricula/instructional materials to be produced within the year, and how will they be disseminated to QCC faculty and students, as well as the broader public?
- How confident are you that the project team will be able to carry out the proposed work?
- How clearly does the proposal articulate a plan for capturing and measuring the impacts of the program—through either assessing student learning or evaluating the program's quality/effects?
- Are the proposed timeline and budget reasonable and appropriate?

This opportunity is made possible by the support of the National Endowment for the Humanities Challenge Grant for Two-Year Colleges and the fundraising efforts of the Harriet & Kenneth Kupferberg Holocaust Center at Queensborough Community College.

Notes

1. The one pervasive exception to this paradigm was in college and university history courses for a variety of reasons, although even this exception has been eased over the past 15 years as a result of broader historiographical acceptance of testimony.
2. Especially Dr. William Shulman who opened the Kupferberg Holocaust Center in 1983 and Dr. Zev Garber of the Los Angeles Valley College who edited *Methodology in the Academic Teaching of the Holocaust*, in 1988 (Garber et al. 1988).
3. The RFP included several required elements including a narrative that argued for the topic's importance and timeliness, a full budget for the $50,000 annual funding devoted to each year's colloquium, letters of support from their departmental chairs, and a complete and specific annual program of at least six events with commitment letters from each speaker agreeing to a specific date. The RFP is included as an appendix to this introduction.
4. To view a list of these core texts, visit the Colloquium Libguide at http://qcc.libguides.com/KHRCA_Fleeing_Genocide2016-17.
5. Beginning in year six of the NEH Challenge Grant the role of faculty coordinator was renamed to NEH Scholar-in-Residence at the suggestion of the NEH.
6. Beginning in year six of the NEH Challenge Grant, $5000 of the annual endowment payment for each year was set aside to fund conference travel and presentations available on a first-come first-served basis for former NEH Scholars-in-Residence and faculty coordinators in order to encourage and facilitate the "national demonstration" aspect of the grant mandate from NEH.

References

AAC&U. 2016, July 21. Global Learning VALUE Rubric. Association of American Colleges & Universities. https://www.aacu.org/value/rubrics/global-learning. Accessed 10 Aug 2017.

Assmann, Aleida. 2006. History, Memory, and the Genre of Testimony. *Poetics Today* 27 (2): 269.

Garber, Zev, Alan L. Berger, and Richard Libowitz. 1988. *Methodology in the Academic Teaching of the Holocaust*. Lanham: University Press of America.

Library Guides: KHRCA Colloquia 2016–2017: Fleeing Genocide: Displacement, Exile, and the Refugee: Introduction. Queensborough Community College. http://qcc.libguides.com/KHRCA_Fleeing_Genocide2016-17. Accessed 21 Aug 2017.

Library Guides: National Endowment for the Humanities Challenge Grant: Home. Queensborough Community College. http://qcc.libguides.com/neh. Accessed 21 Aug 2017.

QCC Office of Institutional Research and Assessment. 2016. *2016–17 Fact Book*. http://www.qcc.cuny.edu/oira/docs/factbook-2016-2017/FactBook-2016-2017.pdf. Accessed 21 Aug 2017.

Schweber, Simone. 2006. 'Holocaust Fatigue' in Teaching Today. *Social Education* 70 (1): 48–55.

Traver, Amy E., and Zivah Perel Katz. 2014. *Service-Learning at the American Community College: Theoretical and Empirical Perspectives*. New York, NY: Palgrave Macmillan.

PART I

Approaches to Mass Atrocity Education in the Community College Context: Theoretical Foundations and Programmatic Examples

CHAPTER 2

Arts-Based Approaches to Mass Atrocity Education

Cary Lane

In this chapter, I review the pedagogical theories that led me, and my colleagues, to practice mass atrocity education through an arts lens. I explore foundational ideas in higher education, provide examples of arts-based/creative educational approaches to the study of genocide, and summarize several large-scale, student-centered, arts-based, interdisciplinary pedagogy projects that integrated campus cultural resources for the purposes of genocide education, including the 2014–2015 National Endowment for the Humanities (NEH)/Kupferberg Holocaust Center (KHC) Colloquium Series, "Testimony Across the Disciplines: Cultural and Artistic Responses to Genocide," for which I was faculty coordinator. In doing so, I demonstrate how creative approaches encourage understanding, synthesis, and response to genocide-related content; how art practice can—and should—be used as a research platform for topics of mass violence; and how campus cultural centers provide pivotal resources for researching and presenting arts-based deliverables.

C. Lane (✉)
Department of English, Queensborough Community College, CUNY, Bayside, NY, USA
e-mail: CLane@qcc.cuny.edu

A. E. Traver, D. Leshem (eds.), *Humanistic Pedagogy Across the Disciplines*, https://doi.org/10.1007/978-3-319-95025-9_2

Introduction

To best understand how creativity and arts-based teaching can improve genocide, Holocaust, and mass atrocity education at the community college, it is necessary to examine foundational theories of adult learning, as well as corresponding best practices in Holocaust education. The theory and practice of teaching adults (including college students) is known as andragogy (Knowles 1980), and it centers around one central variable that differentiates educating children from adults: experience. According to Knowles (1980), adult students bring years of rich cultural, political, and social experiences to the college classroom, which help to foster curiosity, improve motivation, promote inclusivity, and increase student engagement. One key principle in Knowles's research is the idea that adults view their learning as self-directed and problem-centered, rather than content-centered. In short, college students perform best when they lead in their own understanding and response to challenging subject matter, and when they manage their own assessment. In terms of understanding and responding to the complexities of genocide and mass atrocity, adult learners have a distinct advantage because of their ability to handle the difficulty of the subject matter and their capacity to respond to it in multiple formats, including arts-based and creative modes.

Creativity is at the top of the revised version of Bloom's taxonomy of educational objectives for good reason (Anderson, Krathwohl, and Bloom 2001). Bloom and his team believe that creativity is achieved only by passing through the other less complex activities of remembering, understanding, applying, analyzing, and evaluating information. This is an essential point, because it is not by chance that the Holocaust—like other historical eruptions of genocide and mass atrocity—resists memory, understanding, and all forms of knowledge. In fact, given its alterity from the normal range of mundane experiences addressed in American college curricula, the Holocaust often generates silence, anxiety, and frustration for educators and students alike. It should be noted, however, that the difficulty of the subject matter does not absolve us from the important work of grappling and engaging in the rigors of understanding important historical aspects of Holocaust-related content.

In terms of its relation to Bloom's taxonomy, understanding and remembering historical content provides an essential baseline for upper-level thinking domains, such as analysis, synthesis, and creation. The process of creation (or being creative) also mitigates many of the issues associated with challenging subject matter by engaging students' diverse experiences and allowing them to emerge as leaders of their own learning. Additionally, allowing students the opportunity to be content creators in arts-based modalities ensures that visual and textual content are integrated—a symbiosis that appeals to students with diverse learning styles and intelligences (Gardner 1983, 1999).

One facet of adult learning theory that is central to the relationship between students' sensory experiences and learning—both prior to their encounter with genocide studies and in the context of that learning—is Jarvis's (1995, 2011) writings on adult learning processes. Like several of his predecessors (e.g., Dewey 1997; Knowles 1980), Jarvis believes that adults' experiences are directly tied to their learning; however, Jarvis (1995) advances prior theories on adult learning by asserting that learning *begins* with experience. Jarvis argues that learning is heavily tied to physiology and biology, and that experiences are directly related to sensory elements such as sound, touch, sight, smell, and feel. Consequently, learning becomes a more individualized process, relating to one's own experiences, sensations, existence, growth, and changes.

Together, Jarvis's (1995) and Dewey's (1997) theories on experiential learning, as well as Knowles's (1980) learner-centered theories on andragogy, form a foundation on which creative and visual approaches to mass atrocity education can be based. Accordingly, applying teaching strategies that allow adult students to lead, that contextualize course content using visual tools, and that utilize students' experiences will help learners relate to content, build curiosities, engage multiple intelligences (Gardner 1983), and ultimately facilitate transformative learning experiences (Mezirow 1991). Wlodkowski's (2008) writing on the importance of situational interest is essential in this regard. Simply put, if an adult learner is not interested in course content, assignments, or teaching practices, then they will not be engaged, nor will they find significant meaning in the learning process. Therefore, the purposeful and strategic use of creative and arts-based learning approaches—with its contextual and stimulative power—is a sound strategy for improving learning outcomes when studying the Holocaust or mass atrocity.

The International Association of Genocide Scholars (2017, 4) recognizes the essential role the arts play in understanding, researching, and reflecting on content related to genocide at the college level, stating that it is "incumbent" upon the academic community to incorporate the arts into the scholarly discussion of genocide and mass violence. They write about cultural and creative spaces dedicated to facilitating the study of genocide in the following way:

> Asking individuals to consider, digest and want to learn more about mass atrocity is a supreme challenge for educators, artists, and coordinators of public displays and memorials. These venues which reflect mass atrocity, however, are critical catalysts which hold up to the public a window of understanding and provide a vehicle to personal and genuine experience of the nature of genocide and mass violence through the lens of the cultural expression. Their power to affect the individual can often motivate awareness, contemplation and hence greater understanding of the complexities and legacies of mass violence and its relationship to the viewer. (International Association of Genocide Scholars 2017, 1)

At the community college, utilizing cultural centers, as well as creative modes of response and reflection, are potent means of bringing the study of genocide to vivid realization. The arts also have a unique power to evoke emotional response and promote interpersonal expression and empathy (Juslin and Sloboda 2011). Thus, cultural and artistic responses can deepen and intensify students' learning by both introducing and facilitating emotional, intergenerational, and intercultural connections.

Creative approaches to genocide education can also allow students to lead (and reflect on) their own learning process by becoming content creators, rather than simple consumers of knowledge. Furthermore, creative writing, music, dance, and visual arts can help to promote understanding through their universality and creative appeal. Arts-based learning activities such as poetry writing in response to readings about concentration camps, performing music composed by victims of the Holocaust, or photographing an actual Holocaust survivor can deepen students' understanding and promote empathy by offering an experience of history through the eyes of others. In turn, these activities promote students' ability to reflect with a more tactile awareness of subject matter that is "too often met with apathy, apprehension, or recoil" (International Association of Genocide Scholars 2017, 1). Queensborough Community College of the City University of New York (QCC)—one of the most diverse colleges in the United States—has learned to use creativity and arts-based approaches as standard practice. This turns Bloom's taxonomy on its head by empowering students to understand, analyze, and synthesize challenging genocide content through the creative process.

In terms of adult learning, creative and arts-based approaches to Holocaust, genocide, and mass atrocity education, when informed by foundational adult learning theory, and applied using best practices, can be of larger benefit to institutions of higher learning in that they:

- appeal to diverse and underprepared adult learners;
- are student-centered and student-directed;
- facilitate high-impact educational practices (HIPS);
- encourage collaboration across academic disciplines and departments; and
- help students respond to challenging and sensitive subject matter.

Arts-Based Approaches Appeal to Diverse and Underprepared Adult Learners

Creative and arts-based approaches to the study of the Holocaust, genocide, and mass atrocity are grounded in foundational education theory, especially those theories that focus on students who learn and think in diverse ways. Gardner's (1983) theory of multiple intelligences is one central theory that provides a framework for this initiative. While other foundational theories from psychologists such as Piaget (1972) generally focus on universal domains such as mathematical intelligence, Gardner's multiple intelligences theory aims to better examine the nature and structure of various intelligences using an array of symbolic systems, including linguistic, musical, and spatial. Developing multiple portraits of "symbolic competence" is the primary goal in his study of multiple intelligences, and includes the relationship and proficiency of each intelligence domain within cultural and societal frameworks (Gardner 1983, 23). One primary finding from Gardner is that *culture* plays a prominent role in what intelligences are featured, developed, fostered, measured, or valued. Since Gardner also establishes that contextually rich environments stimulate intelligences, it is advisable to supplement traditional, text-based, non-contextual teaching approaches with more motivating, cognitive-friendly methods that utilize cultural resources (i.e., student-directed, arts-based, high-impact teaching practices that are taught across—and between—multiple disciplines).

Another benefit of arts-based and creative approaches to genocide studies is that they help academically underprepared students, which is essential considering that 43 percent of learners enrolled in community colleges in the United States require some form of developmental coursework (National Conference of State Legislatures 2017), with significantly higher percentages locally. These students—especially those enrolled in urban community colleges—arrive with more socioeconomic disadvantages, a higher frequency of learning disabilities (Mamiseishvili and Koch 2012), and wider gaps in their academic literacies. Developmental education students include English language learners, graduates of underperforming secondary schools (Howell 2011), and adults returning to the community college after long educational hiatuses. The burden of developmental education also adversely affects financial aid, carries no credits, and delays—and often prevents—students from obtaining their degrees, so finding innovations that improve outcomes of developmental education students becomes even more essential to improving their likelihood of finishing college.

Unfortunately, developmental education students are frequently products of rote, lecture-based teaching and linear, text-based assessment methodologies—something Gardner (1999, 135) cites as "dangerous." However, research suggests that incorporating visual and creative learning strategies in the community college classroom is an effective intervention for improving academic literacies and expediting exit-from-remediation (Jacobs 2012; Elkins 2009; Stokes 2002; Sinatra 1983). To this end, Gardner asserts that linguistic systems, which were/are developed by humans in an effort to make sense of the world, may not appeal to the neurobiological structure of all learners. In fact, a large percentage of adult students are less capable of effectively decoding established linguistic (text-based) symbolism. The beauty of multiple intelligences, however, is that it appeals to diverse learners and allows strong intelligences to assist underdeveloped ones. When you combine this with Bloom et al.'s (Anderson, Krathwohl, and Bloom 2001) assertion that creativity forms the apex of information synthesis, as well as the motivational and experiential strengths of adult learners, a strong case can be made for the scaled use of creative, arts-based, student-directed approaches to mass atrocity education.

Arts-Based Approaches Are Student-Centered and Student-Directed

Student-centered teaching is informed by several educational theories and philosophies, including humanism, constructivism, pragmatism, psychology, and neurobiology (Gorzycki 2017), and is recognized most for putting the needs and the role of the learner first. While this places a large amount of responsibility on students to lead their own learning process (often in collaboration with fellow students), it also requires the instructor to relinquish control and willingly distribute leadership duties to students. In student-directed teaching, the instructor spends far less time speaking and lecturing, and much more time facilitating student-led initiatives that focus on the understanding, evaluation, analysis, synthesis, and creation of content (Gorzycki 2017; Anderson et al. 2001).

The benefits of student-centered teaching are numerous, including appealing to students' diverse learning styles, improving student engagement through personal reflection and activities, and increasing the relevancy of course content (Gorzycki 2017). The fusion of student-centered teaching with adult learning theory forms an enhanced set of best practices, which are supported by the following findings: (1) adult learners thrive when autonomy, self-direction, and use of diverse experiences are facilitated (Illeris 2002; Dewey 1997; Knowles 1980); (2) student motivation and engagement are increased (especially in male students) when choice is provided (Jacobs 2012; Perin 2011; Benson 1997); (3) the more flexibly modes of instruction are used, the more likely fixed (canalized) cognition and learning can be improved (Gardner 1999); (4) integrating content from multiple academic subjects improves comprehension and motivation by contextualizing content in dynamic and alternative ways (Kuh 2008); (5) content and curricula are best understood when accounting for diverse learning styles, varied socioeconomic backgrounds, and multiple cultural differences (Gorzycki 2017); and, (6) student-centered, high-impact approaches engage and unify all these characteristics with evidence-based success, especially for diverse adult learners with developmental needs (Kuh 2008).

Arts-Based Approaches Facilitate High-Impact Teaching

HIPs are evidence-based teaching approaches that increase student engagement, contextualize course content, and improve learning outcomes (Kuh 2008). According to Kuh (2008), HIPs appeal to college students from diverse backgrounds, heighten student engagement, and improve retention rates. Perhaps most notably, data on HIPs show that "underserved student populations benefit disproportionately from these opportunities, as compared to their more advantaged peers" (Kuh 2008, 2). One by-product of having creative, student-centered, genocide-related educational programs is that they provide excellent contexts for all ten HIPs, as outlined by the Association of American Colleges and Universities: (1) first-year seminars or experiences, which promote inquiry, collaboration, and information literacy exercises in an effort to build academic literacies; (2) common intellectual experiences, which integrate thematic content in courses or learning communities; (3) learning communities, which foster integration of courses and disciplines; (4) writing-intensive courses, which provide an increased platform and demand for writing and editing across the curriculum; (5) collaborative projects, which promote active learning among peer groups, as well as exposure to other cultures and perspectives; (6) undergraduate research, which gives students a head start on the process of both questioning and seeking out information to investigate answers; (7) diversity and global learning, which purposefully explores ethnic, cultural, and global issues, especially through service-learning projects; (8) service learning, which synthesizes course content with experiential approaches in real-world settings; (9) internships, an experiential learning modality that takes place in a work setting; and (10) capstone projects, which provide deliverables that integrate and showcase students' learning in a culminating project. The common thread among the ten articulated HIPs is that they all promote active learning, where students collaborate, reflect, write, synthesize, and engage in contextualized, student-centered modalities (Kuh 2008).

An additional advantage to teaching with HIPs is that they provide benefits for students from diverse and splintered populations (Carey 2012; Reinhart 2012; Kuh 2008). Contextual, integrated, multimodal approaches to college coursework appeal to students of diverse backgrounds because the content is relevant and because they create platforms for increased critical thinking and reflection (Reinhart 2012). Engagement is also promoted using different content/curricula among diverse student populations, creating environments and constructive learning opportunities for students with less exposure to diverse learning content (Carey 2012). One central recommendation made by HIPs researchers is that, in order for them to work best, HIPs must be consistently, frequently, and equitably used, as well as executed with diligence (McNair and Albertine 2012; Kuh 2008). This, in turn, takes dedication, planning, and budgetary commitment from college administrators and policymakers—what is termed "curricular intentionality" (McNair and Albertine 2012, 4).

Arts-Based Approaches Encourage Collaboration Across Academic Disciplines and Departments

Interdisciplinary teaching allows students to solve specific problems from multiple perspectives, to become knowledgeable of social, political, and cultural events that transpire globally, and to appreciate the interconnectedness of both academic content and the world (Newell and Miller 1983). According to Newell and Miller (1983, 2), "what distinguishes interdisciplinary study from simple eclecticism is that disciplines provide much more than pieces of a jigsaw puzzle that the interdisciplinarian need merely arrange in proper order." Rather, students learn from each discipline a distinctive way of looking at the world, and by studying different disciplines learn to confront their own biases and preconceived notions about the world. In terms of neurodiversity, applying creative and arts-based approaches in an interdisciplinary format is a natural way to appeal to diverse learning styles, facilitate student-centered approaches to teaching and assessment, and capitalize on the cultural diversity (experiences and backgrounds) of the student body.

Efforts to work across departmental boundaries and integrate campus cultural resources into curricula/instruction are also of significant benefit to students. Campus cultural centers such as art galleries, performing arts spaces, and historical centers are perfect conduits for experiential learning, student-directed programs, and capstones. Kuh (2008, 2) describes the format of this type of community-based learning thusly: "Many colleges and universities now emphasize courses and programs that help students explore cultures, life experiences, and worldwide views different from their own. These studies—which may address US diversity, world cultures, or both—often explore 'difficult differences' such as racial, ethnic, and gender inequality, or continuing struggles around the globe for human rights, freedom, and power. Frequently, intercultural studies are augmented by experiential leaning in the community and/or by study abroad." To enable the wider use of campus resources, college administrators must recognize the benefit of, and promote buy-in for, the integration of cultural centers in curricula across the disciplines. In the end, well-executed arts-based pedagogy projects require dedicated communication between administrators, directors of cultural centers, academic support staff, and participating instructors.

Arts-Based Approaches Help Students Respond to Challenging and Sensitive Subject Matter, Like the Holocaust, Genocide, and Mass Atrocity

For many students at the community college, their first academic exposure to genocide and mass atrocity is a challenging one; the content can be raw, emotional, and difficult to process—even for adults. This can be especially true during encounters with images, music, film, and poetry about mass atrocity. Kollontai (2015, 74) writes of this difficulty: "One of the key challenges for us as educators in presenting the topic of evil and suffering through the visual image, in whatever academic discipline, is how to communicate unspeakable events in the history of humankind in such a way that does not overwhelm and traumatise a student to the extent that it produces a sense of powerlessness or indifference that disengages rather than engages the student." On the other hand, and based on this fear, instructors can often overcorrect by approaching teaching, curricula, and assessments in a way that is too linear or formal due to the raw and sensitive nature of the content.

Considering the scope of cultural, experiential, and learning diversity at community colleges, it is critical that teaching methodologies provide enough flexibility to appeal to canalized learners. The use of cultural and artistic approaches to the study of mass atrocity is a helpful tool for this purpose, as they ensure that diverse learners express and reflect on challenging subject matter in ways that provide cognitive flexibility. There is also the possibility for students to *use* experiential and emotional components during their study of the Holocaust. The fundamental importance that emotions play in building strong and long-lasting learning cannot be overestimated (Damasio and Sutherland 1994). The study of creative writing, visual art, dance, or music can develop strong emotional connections to unfamiliar histories, cultures, and experiences—and by doing so, advance student interest in community action and involvement (Goldstein and Winner 2012; Hodges 2010). As an example, Freeman (2006), a professor of history at the State University of New York at Oneonta, provides student survey data from her experience using more images and film in a History of the Holocaust class. The survey found that the graphic nature of the images and films used strongly impacted students (despite being from a generation "used" to seeing violent images) and that students reported an increase in both their understanding of course content and their perceived ability to respond to course content.

These findings further indicate a deficiency in traditional best teaching practices and point to a central constraint in the effort to scale the use of visual literacy in postsecondary teaching of genocide: the outdated instructional paradigm within which universities teach. Simply put, teaching and assessing learning outcomes through traditional lecture/exam—or even Socratic teaching methods—hinders learning by its inability to teach beyond pure text and linguistic modalities. In fairness, the gravity and soberness in the content and themes of genocide studies makes the use of creative teaching approaches intimidating to many instructors. It is also important to understand that genocide curricula require rigor, and that text-based approaches are necessary to establish proper knowledge and understanding. However, the need for flexibility and adaptability in teaching methodologies of genocide-related studies are also essential for two main reasons: (1) they successfully appeal to students' cultural and neurobiological diversity; and (2) they engage and motivate students. Elkins (2009) argues that colleges are behind the visual literacy curve because of stale, conventional teaching methods, as well as archaic organizational policies. He asserts that embedding visual multiculturalism not only improves learning outcomes by developing visual literacy, but also serves the needs of a modern, diverse college population.

An Example of an Arts-Based, High-Impact, Student-Centered, Interdisciplinary Program that Studied Genocide, Organized Hate, and the Holocaust

One example of a large-scale, arts-based, student-centered, interdisciplinary pedagogy project responding to themes of genocide was the 2014–2015 NEH/KHC Colloquium Series at QCC. The series was coordinated by me, alongside co-Faculty Coordinator Dr. Steven Dahlke, an associate professor of music. Titled "Testimony Across the Disciplines: Cultural and Artistic Responses to Genocide," the series used art practice as a research modality (Sullivan 2015) for global learning initiatives and invited students to showcase their own cultural and creative responses to the Holocaust and mass atrocity. In this series, 300 students from six separate academic disciplines studied with 20 professors, 5 genocide scholars, 2 embedded librarians, and 12 Holocaust survivors. Together, participating faculty, visiting artists, survivors, visiting scholars, and students engaged in high-impact practices that were highlighted by interactive, intergenerational, and intercultural collaborations (Conway and Hodgman 2008).

Since QCC serves one of the most diverse counties in the United States, the series appealed to participating students' cultural and neurobiological diversity in six main ways: (1) by using art practice as a research platform (Sullivan 2015); (2) by using creativity as an inclusivity tool; (3) by using the arts as a collaborative, interdisciplinary teaching tool; (4) by implementing a distributed leadership model for the program, ensuring that the 300 participating students took a leading role; (5) by utilizing campus cultural and pedagogical resources; and (6), by capturing students' creative responses to genocide and showcasing them as a form of testimony. Additionally, students from each of the participating courses and disciplines were able to use a centralized, online library database ("LibGuide") as a research hub with access to embedded librarians throughout their research process.[1] To execute the series' mission, participating instructors willingly assumed secondary roles as facilitators and guides, rather than traditional instructors and lecturers. This enabled students to lead in their own learning process, be the sole content creators of the project, and provide all deliverables.

Here are several examples of work produced by students in "Testimony Across the Disciplines: Cultural and Artistic Responses to Genocide":

- Criminal justice students, through a service-learning project with Hour Children, a local community center that assists recently incarcerated women, presented a film documenting their experiences with restorative justice and community healing (as described in Chap. 7 of this volume).
- Developmental English students gave dramatic reenactments of plays and music written by Jews in the Terezín Ghetto.
- Photography and English language learners (ELLs) collaborated to interview, photograph, and write biographical narratives about 12 Holocaust survivors.
- English students wrote graphic narratives and works of prose in response to chosen artifacts from the Holocaust.
- Poetry students created ekphrastic poems that responded to contemporary art pieces with themes of mass violence.
- Developmental reading students explored empathy in the context of Middle East conflicts and used multimedia presentations to communicate how victims and perpetrators of mass violence promote or lack empathy.
- Painting students interviewed Holocaust survivors and created art that responded to their experience.
- Dance and English students collaborated to create a documentary film that communicated students' responses to surveillance and systems of power (as described in Chap. 8 of this volume).
- Creative writing students authored and read original spoken word and poetry as artistic responses to their study of genocide.
- Dance students choreographed and performed original dance pieces that artistically responded to political and cultural subjugation and dominance.
- The QCC Chorus collaborated with a local youth choir, the QCC Pop Choir, and a string quartet that specializes in playing music composed during the Holocaust (as described in Chap. 11 of this volume).
- Art history students curated a capstone exhibit of student responses to genocide.

As evidenced, students' creative work reflected the breadth of humanities disciplines at QCC, as well as the scholarly range of the visiting scholars and artists.

Fig. 2.1 Organizational model of an arts-based, student-centered, interdisciplinary pedagogy project featuring students' capstone projects responding to genocide and mass atrocity

The colloquium series' ten events (see Appendix) provided an inclusive and creative platform for students to study mass atrocity, collaborate with artists and scholars, confront their own biases, and do so from multiple perspectives, and through HIPs. They also served as open forums for the campus to explore cultural and artistic responses to genocide and for students to directly respond to their immersion. As such, each visiting scholar and colloquium participant structured their presentations as reflective, interactive workshops with the goal of developing students' creative responses to genocide (see Fig. 2.1). One example of an arts-based, student-centered event from the series was "Culture as Survival: Music and Theater in the Nazi Concentration Camps and Ghettos," led by Dr. Lisa Peschel of the University of York, England. A noted scholar of theatrical performances in the Terezín Ghetto during the Holocaust, Dr. Peschel shared recent findings from her project, *Continuity in Diaspora: Theatrical Performance in the Terezín Ghetto*. To facilitate more impactful learning, she divided students into small groups and provided each group with an excerpt of a script written in the ghetto. Students then created a brief dramatic performance of the excerpt that used framing devices (e.g., program notes, a brief spoken or performed introduction, running commentary on the script) to make the performance understandable to spectators who did not know the history of the ghetto. The colloquium ended with a presentation of the students' dramatic performances.

The colloquium series' lectures, collaborations, and projects culminated in two student-led capstone projects. The first capstone project was a student-created art and poetry exhibition at the KHC entitled, "Testimony Across the Disciplines: QCC Students Respond to Genocide Through Art and Writing." This exhibit was populated exclusively with QCC students' artistic responses to genocide. For example, Professor Susan Jacobowitz's students wrote their own graphic narratives responding to genocide after reading Art Spiegelman's *Maus* and Joe Sacco's *Safe Area Gorazde*. These student works were not only part of the capstone exhibition; they were also featured in the campus literary journal, *Duende*, and the campus newspaper, *Communique*. The capstone exhibition also featured collaborations between six different academic departments. One such interdisciplinary project was between Professor Jules Allen's advanced photography course and Dr. Julia B. Carroll's developmental writing course for English language learners. Working together, these students interviewed Holocaust survivors, wrote biographical narratives, and took formal portraits of the survivors, which were displayed side-by-side on the gallery walls.

It is important to note that the KHC served as more than just a location for the capstone exhibit. Given its stated mission to educate, research, and remember acts of mass atrocity, the KHC also played a vital role in facilitating students' learning. For example, students from QCC's Art & Design Department's Gallery and Museum Studies Program served as curators of the capstone exhibit. Through service learning, these students learned about maintaining a collection, researching museum content, planning and designing an exhibition, publicizing an exhibit, assisting visitors, and providing educational services to visitors. The students' curatorial endeavor was also enriched with a visit by Mr. Clifford Chanin, Director of Education at the National September 11 Memorial & Museum, who helped students understand the challenges and responsibilities of archiving and displaying artifacts related to mass atrocity.

Additionally, Scherezade Garcia, a professional artist from Parsons—The New School, and Dr. Edward Paulino, a visiting genocide scholar from John Jay College of Criminal Justice of the City University of

New York, provided curatorial students historical context and assistance with mounting an installation of "collected" memories on postcards, which hung on the gallery walls. The idea for this installation stemmed from another artwork where participants communicated their memories (or lack of knowledge) about the 1937 genocidal massacre in the Dominican Republic. Often referred to as the Parsley Massacre, thousands of Haitians, as well as Dominicans of Haitian descent, were murdered by Dominican troops in the border region of Hispaniola in October 1937 (Bishop and Fernandez 2017; Johnson 2003).

The program's second capstone project was a student performance at the QCC Performing Arts Center (QPAC) entitled "Testimony Across the Disciplines: QCC Students Respond to Genocide Through Music, Dance, and Poetry." At this event, students recited poetry and the spoken word that responded to their study of organized hate, dance students performed original choreographed pieces of interpretive dance, and the QCC Choir sang an original piece by Composer-in-Residence Eric Hachikian based on a Jewish prayer "Ani Ma'amin" in collaboration with the MOTÝL Chamber Ensemble. This collaboration followed a musical structure similar to an experience at the United States Holocaust Memorial Museum in Washington, DC, where the visitor follows a Holocaust victim's life throughout their visit. In the composition, various vocal performers became silent as the piece developed, leaving only a few survivors at the end. The MOTÝL Ensemble provided an additional layer of music to depict the increasingly horrific events that culminated in Hitler's Final Solution. Music professor Dr. Steven Dahlke rehearsed the choir, and dance professor Aviva Geismar's students choreographed and performed an original dance component to the piece.

As music was used as a form of expression by victims of the Holocaust, MOTÝL also performed "Music from Terezín," which included description of the musical and artistic pieces from Jewish prisoners at Terezín. Complementing this presentation was a student-created slideshow that used photographs, original watercolors, and children's drawings and poems to depict daily life in Terezín. This multimedia approach created a connection between the audience and the music's history, as well as tied the capstone event to themes and content in the series.

Student Responses to the Arts-Based Pedagogy Project

In all, the program provided a dynamic, creative, student-centered, and creative learning opportunity for participating students. Students reflected on their learning experience in an Institutional Review Board-approved post-survey, and many of these reflections indicated enthusiasm for this arts-based learning experience. One student who participated in Dr. Warsi's multimedia research project on the topic of empathy noted, "I had a chance to think more about empathy and its benefits to society." The same student also indicated that "the pictures" were the most motivating aspect of his learning process and that they "helped me understand." Another student, who served as a docent for the capstone art exhibition, said, "Adding more creativity in future courses will get my attention and make me more interested in different topics. I will study more deeply." A fellow student-docent indicated that the interdisciplinary work was particularly enriching for her: "Combining English with art helped provide a better understanding of the work." She concluded her survey by saying, "Culture helps students open their minds to see things from a different standpoint."

Other Examples of Arts-Based Approaches to Mass Atrocity Education

As outlined in this chapter, the arts have an integral role in advancing genocide education (Apol 2017; International Association of Genocide Scholars 2017; Kollontai 2015; Juslin and Sloboda 2011; Damasio and Sutherland 1994). In sum, teaching the Holocaust and organized hate within a diverse adult learning environment can be improved when: (1) students create (Anderson et al. 2001); (2) multiple intelligences are stimulated/utilized (Gardner 1983); (3) content is contextualized (Kuh 2008); and (4) students take a leading role in their learning (Jarvis 1995; Knowles 1980). To this end, there are several chapters in this volume that describe creative, dynamic pedagogy projects that used arts-based, student-centered, high-impact approaches to mass atrocity education at an urban community college.

Two of these chapters, in particular, overview how filmmaking was used to facilitate (and document) student learning about mass atrocity. In Chap. 7, Äikäs articulates how criminology students examined restorative justice through an academic service-learning project with Hour Children, a local program that empowers formerly incarcerated women. A short documentary film was created that featured students' interviews, interactions, and reflections about this complex, experiential learning experience, as well as their transition into stewards of social action. In Chap. 8, Atik, Geismar, and Miller describe a student-centered, interdisciplinary pedagogy project that documented—through film—dance and English students' collaborative exploration of Holocaust-related themes, such as discrimination, surveillance, and power structures. The students' film project was presented at the capstone NEH performance, "Testimony Across the Disciplines: Students Respond to Genocide, Through Music, Dance, and Poetry."

Additionally, two chapters in this volume analyze the dynamic use of musical approaches to mass atrocity education. In Chap. 15, Lekić and Brégégère detail several music-based assignments and reflections that focused on the capstone music concert, "Echoes of Exile," which was part of the 2016–2017 NEH/KHC Colloquium Series, *Fleeing Genocide: Displacement, Exile and the Refugee*. These creative assignments used the concert (as well as corresponding lectures and exhibits) as a musical platform for students to examine the global refugee crisis, including rising anti-immigrant sentiment and xenophobia. In Chap. 11, Dahlke describes data/outcomes from a music-based project titled "Musical Responses to the Holocaust," a pedagogy project that, through music, taught students about the Holocaust from the victims' perspectives. Then, the roles reversed and students taught the music (and its human rights concepts) to children of the Corona Youth Music Project, an academic service-learning partner organization.

Lastly, several of the chapters in this volume describe multimedia-based approaches to mass atrocity education. In Chap. 12, Dennihy outlines a scaffolded, student-centered project that introduced learners to Holocaust survivors and artifacts at the KHC, explored how various types of media communicate information/propaganda differently, and had students curate media in a simulated museum context. Similarly, in Chap. 13, Emanuele summarizes a creative pedagogy project where English students read and analyzed historical examples of vile hate speech/images, and then, using multimedia, reframed the hate speech in order to promote tolerance and understanding. In Chap. 17, Wentrack details a project where art history students analyzed photographs related to current world conflicts and the plight of refugees in order to examine the role that tragic images—including those of displaced people and refugees in crisis—have on society. In addition to creatively teaching course content, a unifying by-product of this project—and most of the arts-based projects detailed in this volume—was the enhanced development of students' empathy, improved understanding, and the ability to become engaged citizens.

Appendix: 2014–2015 NEH/KHC Colloquium Series, "Testimony Across the Disciplines: Cultural and Artistic Responses to Genocide"

Colloquium Event #1: Wednesday, September 17, 2014; 12 p.m.–2 p.m.:
"Culture as Survival: Music and Theater in the Nazi Concentration Camps and Ghettos"
Dr. Barbara Milewski, Swarthmore College
Dr. Lisa Peschel, University of York, England
Colloquium Event #2: Wednesday, October 22, 2014; 12:10–2 p.m.:
"Dance, Disability and the Holocaust"
Ms. Heidi Latsky, Founder, Heidi Latsky Dance
Introductory words by Dr. Amy Traver, Department of Social Sciences, QCC
Colloquium Events #3a–3d: various dates from September 2014–February 2015:
"Writing as Testimony: A Workshop Series on Responding to Genocide with Poetry, Graphic Narratives and Creative Writing"

1. Tuesday, September 23, 2014; 10 a.m.–12 p.m.:
   "Graphic Depictions of Genocide: Art Spiegelman, Joe Sacco and J.P. Stassen Take on Auschwitz, Bosnia and Rwanda"
   Dr. Susan Jacobowitz, English Department, QCC
2. Wednesday, October 8, 2014; 12 p.m.–2 p.m.:
   "Responding to Genocide: Creative Writing in Conversation with Art"
   Prof. Jodie Childers, English Department, QCC
3. Wednesday, November 5, 2014; 12 p.m.–2 p.m.:
   "Poetry of Conflict: The African-American Experience"
   Dr. Joel Kuszai, English Department, QCC
4. Wednesday, February 11, 2015; 12 p.m.–2 p.m.:
   "Facilitating Written Engagement with Art: Interpreting, Describing and Archiving Art for Publication"
   Dr. Susan Jacobowitz, English Department, QCC

Colloquium Event #4: Wednesday, March 4, 2015; 12 p.m.–2 p.m.:

"The Art of Afterward: Documenting Collective Memory"

Mr. Clifford Chanin, Director of Education and Public Programs, National September 11 Memorial and Museum; Founder, The Legacy Project

Dr. Edward Paulino, Department of History, John Jay College of Criminal Justice, CUNY

Colloquium Event #5: Thursday, April 16, 2015, 5 p.m.–7 p.m., KHC Gallery

"Inspired Testimony: QCC Students Respond to Genocide Through Art, Research and Creative Writing"

A Student-Led Exhibition at the KHC

Colloquium Event #6: Thursday, April 16, 2015; 7 p.m.–9 p.m.; QPAC

"Inspired Testimony: QCC Students Respond to Genocide Through Music and Dance"

A Student-Led Performance at QPAC, in Collaboration with the MOTÝL Chamber Ensemble

Note

1. To access this LibGuide, please visit: http://qcc.libguides.com/nehchallenge.

References

Anderson, Lorin W., David R. Krathwohl, and Benjamin Samuel Bloom. 2001. *A Taxonomy for Learning, Teaching, and Assessing: A Revision of Bloom's Taxonomy of Educational Objectives*. Boston: Allyn & Bacon.

Apol, Laura. 2017. Writing Poetry in Rwanda: A Means for Better Listening, Understanding, Processing, and Responding. *Journal of Poetry Therapy* 30 (2): 71–83.

Benson, Philippa J. 1997. Problems in Picturing Text: A Study of Visual/Verbal Problem Solving. *Technical Communication Quarterly* 6 (2): 141–160.

Bishop, Marlon, and Tatiana Fernandez. 2017. 80 Years On, Dominicans and Haitians Revisit Painful Memories of Parsley Massacre. Nation Public Radio. https://www.npr.org/sections/parallels/2017/10/07/555871670/80-years-on-dominicans-and-haitians-revisit-painful-memories-of-parsley-massacre. Accessed 11 Mar 2018.

Carey, S.J. 2012. From the Editor. Peer Review, 14 (3): 3. doi: 1243370533. Accessed 20 April 2017.

Conway, Colleen, and Thomas M. Hodgman. 2008. College and Community Choir Member Experiences in a Collaborative Intergenerational Performance Project. *Journal of Research in Music Education* 56 (3): 220–237.

Damasio, A.R., and Stuart Sutherland. 1994. Descartes' Error: Emotion, Reason and the Human Brain. Nature 372, no. 6503: 287–287. New York: Putnam.

Dewey, John. 1997. Experience and Education. New York: Touchstone. Original work published in 1938 by Kappa Delta Pi.

Elkins, James, ed. 2009. *Visual Literacy*. New York: Routledge.

Freeman, Julie Dawn. 2006. Teaching the Holocaust: The Use of Graphic Imagery. International Journal of Learning, Vol. 12, No. 8, ISSN 14479494.

Gardner, Howard. 1983. *Frames of Mind: The Theory of Multiple Intelligences*. New York: Basic Books.

———. 1999. *Intelligence Reframed: Multiple Intelligences for the 21st Century*. New York: Basic Books.

Goldstein, Thalia R., and Ellen Winner. 2012. Enhancing Empathy and Theory of Mind. *Journal of Cognition and Development* 13 (1): 19–37.

Gorzycki, Meg. 2017. Student-Centered Teaching. The Center for Teaching and Faculty Development, San Francisco State University. https://ctfd.sfsu.edu/content/student-centered-teaching. Accessed 2 May 2017.

Hodges, Donald A. 2010. Can Neuroscience Help Us Do a Better Job Teaching Music? *General Music Today* 23 (2): 3–12.

Howell, J.S. 2011. What Influences Students' Need for Remediation in College? Evidence from California. *Journal of Higher Education* 82 (3): 292–318.

Illeris, Knud. 2002. *Three Dimensions of Learning*. Roskilde, Denmark: Roskilde University.

International Association of Genocide Scholars. 2017. Arts & Culture. http://www.genocidescholars.org/resources/arts-culture. Accessed 20 April 2017.

Jacobs, Tom. 2012. Arts Involvement Narrows Students' Achievement Gap. A New NEA Study Finds Disadvantaged Students Do Better Academically If They Are Intensely Involved in the Arts. Pacific Standard. 2012. https://psmag.com/education/arts-involvement-narrows-student-achievement-gap-40745. Accessed 22 April 2017.

Jarvis, Peter. 1995. *Adult and Continuing Education: Theory and Practice*. New York: Routledge/Psychology Press.

———. 2011. *Adult Learning in the Social Context. Vol. 78*. New York: Routledge.

Johnson, Kelli Lyon. 2003. Both Sides of the Massacre: Collective Memory and Narrative on Hispaniola. *Mosaic: A Journal for the Interdisciplinary Study of Literature* 36 (2): 74–91.

Juslin, Patrik N., and John Sloboda. 2011. *Handbook of Music and Emotion: Theory, Research, Applications*. Oxford: Oxford University Press.

Kearney, Kerri S., Bernita Krumm, Robin Hughes, and James Satterfield. 2013. Organized for Genocide: Student Reactions and Learning From Use of

Emotive Documentaries on the Holocaust. *Journal of Management Education* 37 (3): 342–366.
Knowles, Malcolm S. 1980. *The Modern Practice of Adult Education: From Pedagogy to Andragogy*. New York: Cambridge Books.
Kollontai, Pauline. 2015. Emotional Intelligence in Higher Education: Using Art in a Philosophical Discussion on God, Evil and Suffering. *Research in Education* 93 (1): 66–76.
Kuh, George D. 2008. High-Impact Educational Practices: What They Are, Who Has Access to Them, and Why They Matter. Association of American Colleges and Universities.
Mamiseishvili, Ketevan, and Lynn C. Koch. 2012. Students with Disabilities at 2-year Institutions in the United States: Factors Related to Success. *Community College Review* 40 (4): 320–339.
McNair, Tia Brown, and Susan Albertine. 2012. Seeking High-Quality, High-Impact Learning: The Imperative of Faculty Development and Curricular Intentionality. *Peer Review* 14 (3): 4.
Mezirow, Jack. 1991. *Transformative Dimensions of Adult Learning*. San Francisco: Jossey-Bass.
National Conference of State Legislatures. 2017. Improving College Completion: Reforming Remedial Education. http://www.ncsl.org/issues-research/educ/improving-college-completion-reforming-remedial.aspx. Accessed 29 April 2017.
Newell, William H., and Raymond C. Miller. 1983. The Case for Interdisciplinary Studies: Response to Professor Benson's Five Arguments. Issues in Interdisciplinary Studies.
Perin, Dolores. 2011. Facilitating Student Learning through Contextualization: A Review of Evidence. *Community College Review* 39 (3): 268–295.
Piaget, Jean. 1972. Intellectual Evolution from Adolescence to Adulthood. *Human Development* 15 (1): 1–12.
Reinhart, David. 2012. Teaching with High Impact within a Splintered Culture. *Peer Review* 14 (3): 22.
Sinatra, Richard. 1983. Brain Research Sheds Light on Language Learning. *Educational Leadership* 40 (8): 9–12.
Stokes, Suzanne. 2002. Visual Literacy in Teaching and Learning: A Literature Perspective. *Electronic Journal for the Integration of Technology in Education* 1 (1): 10–19.
Sullivan, Graeme. 2015. *Art Practice as Research: Inquiry in the Visual Arts*. Thousand Oaks, CA: Sage Publications.
Wlodkowski, Raymond J. 2008. *Enhancing Adult Motivation to Learn: A Comprehensive Guide for Teaching All Adults*. 3rd ed. San Francisco: Jossey-Bass.

CHAPTER 3

Textual Approaches to Mass Atrocity Education

Aliza Atik, Kathleen Tamayo Alves, and Mirna Lekić

Our work considers the theoretical and textual approach to Holocaust, genocide, and mass atrocity education, specifically as it relates to the unique status of the refugee, and how this approach informed our design of the 2016–2017 National Endowment for the Humanities (NEH) Colloquium Series, "Fleeing Genocide: Displacement, Exile, and the Refugee," at Queensborough Community College's (QCC) Kupferberg Holocaust Center (KHC). First, we explain how the pedagogical discourse of "difficult knowledge" is instrumental in teaching the diverse fabric of the community college student population. Then, we reposition the narrative of the refugee as a *homo sacer*—a body excluded from the protection of the state—offering this as both the theoretical framework for our series' focus and an example of the textual approach. Next, we outline how the events in our series speak

A. Atik (✉) • K. T. Alves
Department of English, Queensborough Community College, CUNY, Bayside, NY, USA
e-mail: AAtik@qcc.cuny.edu; KAlves@qcc.cuny.edu

M. Lekić
Department of Music, Queensborough Community College, CUNY, Bayside, NY, USA
e-mail: MLekic@qcc.cuny.edu

A. E. Traver, D. Leshem (eds.), *Humanistic Pedagogy Across the Disciplines*, https://doi.org/10.1007/978-3-319-95025-9_3

directly to the specific needs of two-year college students through their engagement with artifacts of genocide. Finally, we provide brief summaries of all the chapters in this volume that offer examples of refugee-related projects and/or employ similar theoretical/textual approaches.

Pedagogy, "Difficult Knowledge," Textual and Transhistorical Learning

Genocide pedagogy is complicated. Some common pitfalls, notes Samuel Totten (2004), include overwhelming students with images of violence and horror so that students resist the information, or, conversely, minimizing the horror of mass atrocity in order to be respectful of students' sensitivities. Developing a clear rationale for a specific pedagogical approach, even for internal use, is one way to negotiate these challenges, with the rationale statement to include, as Totten explains (9), "both cognitive and affective" components, so that a broader spectrum of student needs are addressed. In the urban community college, it is useful to focus, specifically, on the value of diversity and human rights because, as Helen Bond (2008) observes, urban students frequently come from marginalized populations as well, and have often, themselves, been subject to social, political, and legal discrimination. In order to respond to a program focused on genocide, Bond (18) notes, "urban students need to understand their own agency as citizens in a democracy that has sometimes targeted them."

While our 2016–2017 NEH/KHC Colloquium Series, "Fleeing Genocide: Displacement, Exile, and the Refugee," focused on the refugee in a contentious political climate, all discussions of genocide are inherently provocative, so any rationale of such discussion should focus on ways to invite students into the conversation in accessible ways, regardless of political affiliation. One way to approach this complexity is to focus on theoretical and textual engagement with the material at hand in order to successfully improve student learning outcomes. Genocide education requires a complicated relationship between epistemological autobiographies and historical knowledge, in which learners often have to shift their perspective of the moral order of the world (Lubling 2004). Teaching the Holocaust must function in such a way that "engagement with the people, the space, and the ideas of the Holocaust, comes to constitute a real and meaningful experience" (183). It requires a complex relationship with the material that demands a critical pedagogy.

Emerging from the philosophies of Paulo Freire and the Frankfurt School, critical pedagogy is a term that encompasses teaching strategies concerned with "transforming oppressive relations of power in a variety of domains that lead to human oppression" in ways that "directly address the needs of victims of oppression and the suffering they must endure" (Kincheloe 2008, 45; 50). Critical pedagogy involves both how we train teachers to encounter social injustices inherent in the practice of teaching and disseminating standardized knowledge, and the strategies these teachers employ in their classrooms (122). In order to do this, critical pedagogy demands a "theoretical-interpretive" component, so that multiple forms of knowledge as well as underrepresented narratives can shape "critical multiculturalism" in student learning, a process which "combines critical theory with indigenous and subjugated knowledge as well as other forms of knowledge from diverse cultures," in order to decolonize standardized narratives (123; 128; 134). In other words, introducing textual and theoretical practices into pedagogy at every level of learning is an essential practice, one that allows students to challenge traditional hermeneutics of knowledge and to engage with complex material from multiple vantage points.

Practicing a text-based critical pedagogy is especially essential when dealing with what has been described as "difficult knowledge." The concept of "difficult knowledge" is a pedagogical discourse Alice Pitt and Deborah Britzman (2003, 755–756) define as "what learning means when knowledge references incommensurability, historical trauma, and social breakdowns." As Pitt and Britzman note, "For pedagogical theorists, 'difficult knowledge' also signifies the problem of learning from social breakdowns in ways that might open teachers and students to their present ethical obligations" (756). In this model, there is no intuitive way with which to encounter objective facts that is automatically commensurate with learning. For Pitt and Britzman, there is an essential and "intimate" difficulty here, which is that "learning is uncannily organized by repetition of past investments and conflicts—or, in short hand, new editions of old conflicts—projected onto present experiences, people, and events" (761). Phrased differently, as scholars, we bring our own personal histories to the production of knowledge, to the very discourse that we are trying to present, while we simultaneously engage with students who are negotiating their own affective and cognitive matrices.

Exploring this challenge inherent to pedagogy is a concern that Britzman has investigated in much of her work, and it is this challenge that we attempted to address via textual and theoretical approaches to learning. As Britzman (1998, 5) argues, one of the central struggles in framing "difficult knowledge" is "the tensions exercised when the knowledge offered through pedagogy meets the knowledge brought to pedagogy," a reference to the conflicts generated when knowledge and lived experiences intersects with the abstract theories of pedagogy. QCC serves a broad range of students with diverse educational backgrounds, all of whom bring different cultural and personal perspectives to the notion of what it means to be a student, what it means to learn, and how one can participate in a college community. This is further complicated by the fact the topic of our NEH/KHC Colloquium Series was contentious, and also, for many of our students, emotionally taxing—often bringing up personal or cultural traumas that they or their families had experienced. As Britzman (2000, 39) notes, "The paradox is that because learning from another's pain requires noticing what one has not experienced and the capacity to be touched by what one has not noticed, identifying with pain requires a self capable of wounding his or her own ego boundaries, the very boundaries that serve as a defense against pain." How, then, were we to ask for students' powerful reactions—empathy, anger, action—to the series' events when the very act of conveying this knowledge precluded their internalization of these traumatic events?

While appeals to broader, more basic humanitarian goals are tempting, eliding the events that lead to trauma and mass atrocity runs the danger of flattening the discourse into insignificance, rending it into what Britzman (2000) calls a "normotic defense" (46). In his writings on what he terms "critical genocide studies," Alexander Hinton (2012, 9) suggests that genocide studies, as a field, must include "contextualized, as opposed to rigid, pre-existing socio-legal categories." To work in the field of genocide studies, one must understand it as a discipline that has specific challenges that cannot merely rely on abstract representations of trauma (Kincheloe 2008). As Hinton (2012) suggests, the study of genocide as a discourse must historicize lived experience while also conveying that genocidal events are frequently non-linear and that they often defy Western concepts of group identifications. This decentering of the Western narrative of genocidal aggression serves a twofold purpose. First, it allows for the inclusion of diverse groups of people whose borders are porous and often intersectional, such as LGBTQ + people, and, second, it encompasses mass atrocities that may not have been directly state sponsored but were conducted with the implicit consent of the state. It also disrupts the Western telos which insists that acts of genocide are always best understood in the past tense, as an artifact of a savage past, rather than as part of an ongoing phenomenon often ushered in by the institutions of modernity and democracy, such as the permanent scars left by the West's history of slavery and the destruction of indigenous populations (Hinton 2012, 11–12).

To address this in our series, we encouraged theoretical and textual engagement on the topics brought forth by "difficult knowledge" through the framing of the figure of the refugee, the historicizing and spatializing of acts of mass atrocity, and the presentation of genocide as a conceptual, transhistorical phenomenon. We structured our events so that the primary focus was on narrative-based learning, in which students were exposed to a broad range of lived experiences and theoretical perspectives through the use of archives and attending the lectures of invited speakers. This narrative-based learning, however, returned us back to the challenge of listening. There is a psychic wound in listening, particularly listening to "difficult knowledge," something that Dori Laub (1992, xvi, 57) has called the "vicissitudes of listening." For Laub, this involves the demands placed on speaker and listener. The speaker, in relaying the experience, may "reexperience the event," and, more frighteningly, might find an audience that is unreceptive or incredulous to the facts or feelings of the narrative, which is an additional trauma for the speaker that makes possible the "ultimate annihilation of a narrative that, fundamentally, *cannot be heard* and of a story that *cannot be witnessed*" (original italics, 68). Simultaneously, it is incumbent on the listener to witness the story while also being cognizant of the complicated layers of listening. Laub emphasizes that the listener "has to be at the same time a witness to the trauma witness and a witness to himself " (58). By integrating the speaker's trauma, the unique and individual psyche of each listener, and the listener's own experience of response, both as a witness and as someone who is a separate entity, the listener/reader has to challenge his or her own emotional borders and mental resistance to the narrative presented. In developing a series based on listening, we had to consider ways of listening that were productive for both our audience and speakers, and which encompassed the pedagogical goals of the series without retraumatization or, conversely, reducing the content of the series to empty rhetorical gestures.

In their work on teaching with narratives of human rights violations, Bronwen E. Low and Emmanuelle Sonntag (2013, 771) attempt to articulate a "pedagogy of listening" that works to unsettle the passive listening that students are often trained in through the course of their education. They insist that the listener, much like the speaker, needs to be an active participant, so that listening becomes "as an extension of the self toward the other, as a concern and an attention" and a foundation for a "model of dialogue in which students actively make, negotiate, and share meaning from what they have heard" (771). Using this philosophy, we encouraged the incorporation of the "pedagogy of listening" by designing colloquia across multiple spaces so that the students physically had to utilize diverse sites of learning in order to actively engage with the material. To this end, many lectures were held in the KHC to encourage students to conceptually relate the process of "othering" and the act of creating an internal enemy as part of the processes underpinning the Holocaust and other genocides. When learning of genocide in Rwanda, for example, students were able to understand that genocidal events must not be conflated with one another, and yet, in acts of mass atrocity, there is always a concerted effort at dehumanization which makes violence conceivable and justified in the mind of the perpetrator. We also sought to facilitate dialogue between students and speakers, with Question and Answer sessions built into every event. This offered students a proximity to speakers' experiences and a chance to respond to topics narrated, but it also gave the student participants a chance to direct aspects of the conversation. At the end of the series, we had a panel consisting of student poets, writers, and journalists, who reflected on the series' overall theme and its personal resonance to them. These types of practices work with what Michalinos Zembylas (2008, 136) has called a "pedagogy of dangerous memories." By studying genocide and the Holocaust from multiple theoretical perspectives, we hoped to challenge our students by opening up their knowledge of history in ways that resisted standard, monodirectional historical narratives and instead shaped a complex knowledge of the intersectionality of genocide, normative Western institutions, and the acts of exclusion that sit at the foundation of mass atrocity. The creation of these new "dangerous memories," which work to challenge simplistic historical narratives, influenced our pedagogical goals (138). Rooted in Henry Giroux's thinking, Zembylas' work encourages a new "critical understanding" of memory and the group solidarity it inspires. More specifically, it moved us to consider, both transhistorically and critically, how "dangerous memories" can be used to rework "relationality with the Other" (151). These considerations were central to our Colloquium Series, and they informed the approach that many of the series' participating faculty adopted as they aligned their pedagogy with the series events.

Framing the Refugee in the 2016–2017 NEH/KHC Colloquium Series, "Fleeing Genocide: Displacement, Exile, and the Refugee"

In designing the 2016–2017 NEH/KHC Colloquium Series, we worked to implement a program that would allow for a critical textual approach to genocide studies. At QCC, where our students primarily take general education courses, we sought to promote student engagement by incorporating conceptual and theoretical approaches in an interdisciplinary fashion. This was useful as we engaged "difficult knowledge" and "dangerous memories" in our focus on a topic of contemporary urgency and electoral significance: the international refugee crisis. Titled "Fleeing Genocide: Displacement, Exile, and the Refugee," our series was influenced, in part, by the vast and varying discourses surrounding the refugee in the media and the popular imagination. Our challenge, then, was to help our student body, regardless of their political alignment, to productively enter a contentious debate in which the figure of the refugee was read within many divergent narratives. To address this concern, we built our program around the *framing* of the refugee: as a concept, as a lived experience, as a history, and as an imagined future.

In September of 2015, Aylan Kurdi's corpse washed up on the shore of a Turkish beach and entered students' consciousness and subsequent conversations around refugees. He was three years old, and the image of his lifeless, prostrate little body became a symbol of the international refugee crisis. In 2015, the United Nations High Commissioner for Refugees (UNHCR) reported that nearly one million refugees and migrants fled to Europe, escaping violence, genocide, and trauma in their home countries. More globally, the UNHCR (2017) estimates that there are close to 65.3 million forcibly displaced people, including 21 million refugees and 10 million stateless persons. The 2015 UNHCR Global Trends report also estimates that nearly 1 in every 113 people qualifies as an asylum seeker, an internally displaced person, or a refugee (UNHCR 2016). And yet, while the image of Aylan's body—tiny, lifeless, and prone on the beach—gathered public empathy and generated an untold number of media "think-pieces," broader attitudes toward refugees and their resettlement were frequently more negative.[1] As our students were well aware, in the year running up to our series and culminating in November of 2016, a US presidential campaign was successfully built around the proud resistance to accepting refugees, conflating those fleeing mass atrocity with those committing them, and framing refugees as inherent threats to the nation's safety in the guise of potential Trojan horses and "poisonous skittles."[2]

Soon after the 2017 presidential inauguration, an executive mandate came into place arguing for a "Realignment of the US Refugee Admissions Program (SRAP)" in order "to protect the American people from terrorist attacks by foreign nationals admitted to the United States" (The White House 2017). While, as of the writing of this chapter, this order has been stalled in the courts, this mandate would secure "admissions only for nationals of countries for which the Secretary of State, the Secretary of Homeland Security, and the Director of National Intelligence have jointly determined that such additional procedures are adequate to ensure the security and welfare of the United States." Most strikingly, in the context of the empathy generated by Aylan Kurdi's body, this executive order declared: "(c) Pursuant to section 212(f) of the INA, 8 U.S.C. 1182(f), I hereby proclaim that the entry of nationals of Syria as refugees is detrimental to the interests of the United States and thus suspend any such entry until such time as I have determined that sufficient changes have been made to the United States Refugee Admissions Program (USRAP) to ensure that admission of Syrian refugees is consistent with the national interest" (The White House 2017). Abstract compassion, this order suggests, should not outweigh practical concerns for a national security that perceives bodies from these "foreign" spaces as implicitly and explicitly dangerous.

Given that Britzman (2000) urges respondents to atrocities not to fall into the trap of a "normotic defense," we felt it essential that our students and series' speakers critically engage with the international refugee crisis and connect their initial emotional responses to the development of substantive critical stances. One approach that we utilized to historicize students' knowledge of the current international refugee crisis was to connect it to public sentiment toward refugees from the twentieth century. For example, as Ishaan Tharoor (2015) wrote in an article published in *The Washington Post* during the 2016 election season, a 1939 Gallup American Institute of Public Opinion poll indicated that two-thirds of Americans expressed an unwillingness to accept German Jewish refugees, even children, after the events of Kristallnacht. Likewise, in 1939 Britain terminated the visas that had previously been given to refugees, with the argument that "considerations of sympathy with the unfortunate persons cannot be allowed to override consideration of what is best for the security of the country and for the public interest" (Knox and Kushner 1999, 181).

In the post-war years, this tension continued, with refugee movements becoming complicated by anti-Soviet anxiety and other global tensions (Kohcavi 2001). As indicated by these examples, the figure of the refugee is one subject to ever-shifting discursive paradigms that complicate its very meaning.

In building the rationale for our speaker series, we attempted to frame the refugee through multiple vantage points, and to invite speakers who could provide a close textual assessment of the history of the refugee, beginning with the Holocaust. The series began in the fall of 2016 with an event hosted by Dr. Scott Miller from the United States Holocaust Memorial Museum (USHMM), who discussed the American government's refusal of the refugee ship the *St. Louis* on the eve of the Holocaust. In conjunction, and in keeping with our interest in expanding the sites of learning over multiple spaces, we invited students to explore a Holocaust refugee's experiences through "The Jacket from Dachau," an original KHC exhibit curated by Dr. Cary Lane (who enlisted the help of several student interns in the curatorial process). These first two events laid the groundwork for students' understanding of the representation of refugees in the first half of the twentieth century. The next two fall events examined current issues facing refugees, including their resettlement and education, with talks by Sara Rowbottom, Education and Learning Manager at the International Rescue Committee, and Lieutenant General Stefan Feller, Police Adviser to the Department of Peacekeeping Operations at the United Nations.

In the spring 2017 semester, we offered students a local perspective, with visits from New York-based human rights activist and Rwandan Genocide Against the Tutsi survivor Jacqueline Murekatete, and a panel on LGBTQ refugees featuring Daniel Dromm, New York City Councilman and LGBTQ activist; Sebastian Maguire, immigration lawyer and co-founder and director of the Asylum Seeker Assistance Program; and Pamela Denzer, client director from Immigration Equality, the largest LGBTQ immigrant rights organization in the United States. The spring semester drew to a close with events that featured work from members of the QCC community. A pianist and a refugee herself, Dr. Mirna Lekić programmed a public concert, "Echoes of Exile," which showcased various musical testimonies to genocide and exile and was designed to provide an affective complement to the issues presented in the lectures. Likewise, Dr. Kathleen Alves' presentation explored the history of her own family as internally displaced persons during the Japanese Occupation of World War II in Asia. We concluded the series with a reflective workshop, which included the Creative Writing and Journalism programs at QCC, to prompt QCC students to respond personally, politically, and poetically to the questions raised in the final two events.

Taken together, these events sought to explore the complicated figure of the refugee in a way that examined the refugee experience in the past and present; create, shape, and revise multidisciplinary discourses around the question of the refugee; and provide the intertextual material to empower the college community with the means to join these developing global conversations on inclusivity. Central to this theoretical and transhistorical framing was one binding question: What is the power inherent in resisting refugees and reinforcing the physical and psychic borders that frame the nation-state?

Giorgio Agamben (1995) once introduced the biopolitical figure of the *homo sacer*, a term which he drew from ancient Roman law. This figure, Agamben explains, is a subject who in the context of Roman statues can be killed, but not sacrificed for any sacramental services. That is, the *homo sacer* can be killed without penalty, as he is not a legal citizen deserving of the protection of the law, but his body cannot serve any ritual purpose for the law. The *homo sacer* functions as the legal exemption from legality—a body that exists within the state for the function of being an exception to the state. The bodies of *homines sacri* represent more than biological life, since they are defined by their legal opposition to life and the potential violence to which their body is open. The *homo sacer* illustrates that "life exposed to death (bare life or sacred life) is the originary political element" (88). Sacredness, and, by extension, citizenship, is then defined by a body's juxtaposing relation to sacrifice, and its potential to be excluded from any ritual sanctification, whether by religious or state law. Agamben (99) further notes, "the very body of homo sacer is in its capacity to be killed but not sacrificed, a living pledge to his subjection to the power of death. And yet this pledge is, nevertheless absolute and unconditional, and not a fulfillment of consecration." The sacralized body, in other words, is both regulated and protected, and, by contrast, those excluded from sacralization need no protection, since their bodies are invisible and disposable.

The refugee, in many modern figurations, can be read as this *homo sacer*, a body whose exclusion from the protection of the state establishes the boundaries of normativity against which citizens are protected. As Agamben himself notes, "breaking the continuity between man and citizen, citizen, *nativity* and *nationality*" refugees "put the originary fiction of modern sovereignty in crisis" (77). We are humans because we are not the *homo sacer*, and we are citizens because we are *not* refugees. It is a system of supremacy in which all who are given the protection of the state are implicated, and yet it seems an impossible boundary to permeate.

The positioning of one's geopolitics as a citizen-subject and not the *homo sacer*, then, directly impacts the discursive construction of the "other" and the development of internalized feelings of suspicion in regard to the "other," feelings which are dangerously viewed as intuitive. Sara Ahmed (2004, 65) has written extensively about the performative power of negative emotion, and addressing "the affective politics of fear," she points out that fear is temporal—it involves both proximity and the anticipation of proximity so that "the object that we fear is not simply before us, or in front of us, but impresses upon us in the present, as an anticipated pain in the future." Fear also establishes the boundaries of love and hate. As we frame an object—such as a refugee—as that which is to be feared, we automatically invoke the language of love by suggesting that there is an object to protect from the feared entity. The language in refugee discourse often evokes the protection of families and children from the threat of terrorism, a fear or terror that Ahmed points out is "named in the very naming of terrorism" (72). Through the guise of protection, fear and anxiety instruct us to create borders, which, much like the figuration of the *homo sacer*, rely on an instance of what we are not. For the borders to exist, and for them to maintain any power, there must be, at their inception, the potential for transgression, so that "the economy of fear works to contain the bodies of others, *a containment whose success relies on its failure, as it must keep open the very grounds of fear*" (67). A border only has power if breaching its walls is possible. The refugee highlights this potential for rupturing the imagined security of being a citizen in a nation-state.

Moreover, Sianne Ngai (2005, 3) has argued that negative affects, such as fear and hate, are a record of passivity, of "a general state of obstructed agency with respect to other human actors or to the social as such." When another group or person slips out of its subjective boundaries, often the only way to record this transgression is through seeing this body as a site of shame, disgust, fear, or anxiety. Often these affects, like anxiety, Ngai (2005) argues, emerge when the subject recognizes something uncomfortable in himself or herself, and projects it outward toward another. In this paradigm, fear of the refugee can be seen as a fear of personal exclusion from institutions of social normativity. Antagonism toward the refugee, in this model, is an act of public participation through which one can performatively mark oneself as included in the socio-political economy in service to nationalist, geopolitical domination.

This logic echoes many other figurations of personal and national boundary making. Refugees, Nevzat Soguk (1999) argues, are key to understanding the politics of contemporary beliefs about country and community because the presence of refugees often belies and disturbs these carefully formulated concepts. The existence of non-repatriable displaced people is a transgressive disruption of "political, cultural, and socio-economic borders and boundaries, often in the face of loud protests by those who claim control and mastery over those borders and boundaries" (Soguk 1999, 15). With the refugee framed as the agent for penetrating these boundaries and challenging the supremacy of those who police them, resistance to refugees is read as a way in which the nation-state protects its citizens. Ahmed (2004, 74) explains that "the turning away from the object of fear involves a turning towards home, as a 'fellow feeling,'" which anti-refugee sentiment expresses through public performances of wearing flag pins and other overt markers of patriotism. In this way, antagonism toward refugees functions as a deliberate and socially acceptable performance of national pride that marks the performer as one included in the boundaries of the nation-state. The refugee, as Prem Kumar Rajaram and Carl Grundy-Warr (2004, 39) have argued, "is integrally tied into the practices of excluding and including that constitute and maintain the faceted *system* of the nation-state." Thus, and to return to our question—What is the power inherent in resisting refugees and reinforcing the physical and psychic borders that frame the nation-state?—the language framing the refugee presupposes ideological binaries of political identity, in which bodily exclusion from the state establishes the normativity that protects and in turn defines citizens. Also, functioning as interpellated citizen-subjects, we experience the internalized fear and disgust of refugees through acts of patriotism and nationalism.

How then, do we—as global scholars, as social activists, as teachers sensitive to student needs—impart a wider, but also more nuanced, critical lens to our students, enabling them to see bodies, including their own, as discursively constructed? Our series met this challenge through events that engaged different disciplinary perspectives to build on the argument that the condition of the refugee extends across several contradictory spaces of identity—global and local, social and personal. The series also highlighted the critical need for global inclusion, both by demonstrating the deeply multidimensional impact of the refugee experience precipitated by genocide, and by emphasizing the historical and contemporaneous urgency of the topic. Each series event invited students and the broader QCC community into a complex, nuanced conversation about refugees. We wanted students, as a result of their participation in the series, to see the reciprocal relationship between refugee bodies and the reification of the modern nation-state as the binary against which refugees are defined (Soguk 1999), and to generate a broader base of knowledge with which to reflect on the ongoing public discourse regarding refugees.

Media language referencing the growing refugee population is fraught with terms that dehumanize and minimize the horrific reality many refugees have experienced. Rather than exploring the events that have created refugee populations and calling for greater humanitarian aid, many popular descriptions portray refugees as invaders, inhuman floods,[3] burdens for the local populations that house them, and potential criminal agents (Parker 2015). Other descriptive language has also framed refugees as sources of instability—pollutants poised to migrate their home crises into new countries, a motif that works to stoke public anxiety and desensitize readers to the realities faced by diverse groups of refugee populations (Esses et al. 2013). Studies reveal how significant media frames shape public opinion, resulting in different degrees of bias and resistance depending on the shape of the narrative (Bleich et al. 2015). The success of negative frames, in particular, reinforces narratives of dominance and victimization, with "higher social dominance oriented individuals" working to dehumanize refugees and thus "elicit feelings of contempt and lack of admiration" in order to maintain their place in the social and political hierarchy (Esses et al. 2013, 523–524).

To counter these media narratives, some of our series events worked to shift the space of student learning. For example, the series made active use of the KHC exhibit, "The Jacket from Dachau." Central to this exhibit was a jacket belonging to Ben Peres (Benzion Peresetzki). Found in an estate sale after his passing, the jacket was part of Peres' uniform when he was imprisoned in Kaufering (Dachau) during the Holocaust; he had kept it throughout his life, hidden in the back of a closet in his home on Long Island. The exhibit explored Peres' life, the experiences of his family in relation to his incarceration in a displaced persons camp and his survival, the compelling story of how the jacket was found, and more broadly how a single artifact can evoke a sense of connection, engagement, or even responsibility to history. By including this exhibit in our series, we engaged students in a cross-disciplinary, inter-sensory experience of refugee history outside of the classroom model.

Other series events sought to demonstrate that listening can take place outside of the spoken word. "Echoes of Exile," our seventh event and a concert of classical and jazz solo and chamber works, served to highlight the diversity of historical and contemporary experiences of genocide and exile, and to reframe the concept of the refugee in the context of a different medium—musical composition and performance. The concert's selections highlighted the inherent fluidity of all music, which parallels the refugee experience. They also offered a lens different from that of politics and the news media, amplifying the voices of refugee composers whose creative contributions challenge the idea of refugees as "invisible and disposable" pollutants. The concert's commissioned work, a piano trio by faculty member André Brégégère, was inspired by melodies preserved by refugees in the face of cultural genocides. Significantly, while the concert's featured performers included several students, students also filled the concert audience. Enrolled in select music performance courses, these students had previously studied and performed related repertoire in class. After the event, they continued to engage with the concert repertoire via reflective writing assignments that encouraged critical listening. These writings reveal piqued interest (as a response to a medium many found relatable), thoughtful engagement with the topics, and a sense of discovery and challenge. They also reveal how students' "difficult listening" was made more accessible through the medium of music.

Still other series events were designed to promote students' awareness of the intersectionality of politics and history, as well as the various precedents for the current rhetoric. For example, Jewish displaced persons after the Holocaust, even as they subsisted within displaced persons camps, were similarly represented as "troublemakers and extremists" who were burdens on the local populations around the camps and on the soldiers forced to guard them (Kochavi 2001, 96). The end of World War II and related complicated conversations about displaced people and populations eventually led to the 1951 Convention Relating to the Status of Refugees, which determined that a refugee is a person "outside the country of their nationality" as a result of "a well-founded fear of being persecuted on grounds of race, religion, nationality, membership of a particular social group or political opinion" (Gatrell 2013, 108). As Peter Gatrell (2013) argues, this definition continues to be complicated by social and political forces that impact the representation of genocide in public memory and by the ways in which refugee populations are received in new nations. Reception of refugee populations seeking asylum varies, depending on the ethnic and national identity of the group and the source of conflict. For example, in the last 20 years, the United States has primarily taken in refugees from the former Soviet Union, Vietnam, the former Yugoslavia, Iraq, and Myanmar, while other populations have languished (Gorden 2014).

In these ways and more, our Colloquium Series sought to demystify, historicize, and explore the discourse that has, both historically and contemporaneously, shaped the social and political framing of the international refugee crisis. More specifically, it aimed to help students understand both the figuring of the refugee and the history of genocide as processes that rely on acts of "othering" and on reifying constructions of "inside" and "outside." From the model of the *homo sacer* to the discourse of the modern refuge, these narratives intersect in fundamental ways. Understanding this connection is a necessary part of the learning process, an engagement with frames that rely on each other, so that "spaces of inclusion and exclusion become blurred; the boundary between the two is not an empty moment or function of separation that divides two unconnected communities or experiences, but rather is a vibrant space of engagement and intercontamination" (Rajaram and Grundy-Warr 2004, 34). By examining this history, we hope that the series encouraged students' capacity to see these boundaries as porous, constructed, and—with constant engagement—capable of being breached.

Underscoring a Textual Approach: Course-Based Examples

Many chapters in this volume offer additional examples of textual approaches to the study of mass atrocity. Each of these examples makes gestures that help students connect broad, theoretical concepts with subject-specific and interdisciplinary approaches to learning.

In Chap. 12, Dennihy's approach to teaching mass atrocity underscores the polyphonic essence of the experiential narrative. Dennihy taught her students the "curated" quality of history: that a historical event is remembered in different ways for different audiences. Burgers, in Chap. 9, also confronts the problematic issues of history and storytelling in regard to memory. In his upper-level English course centered on Literary Theory, he provided students with the critical language of cultural memory theory to examine the difficulties with Holocaust narratives. The traumatic quality of the cultural memory of the Holocaust is doubly bound in its painful recalling that results in silence, and it is this silencing that gives it more historical urgency. In Chap. 13, Emanuele views the discourse of storytelling in a different way, engaging students in the critical examination of Nazi hate propaganda produced by the Sturmer Publishing House for elementary school-aged children in the 1930s. This project allowed students to witness the discursive constructing of the "other" that, in turn, transforms citizen-subjects to internalize hate.

Many of the contributors' teaching pedagogies draw directly from the decentering spirit of the study of genocide discourse, which opens the inclusion of individuals categorized as "other," historicizes lived experience, and engages students with the "vicissitudes of listening," whether by speaking to people or reading their stories. In Chap. 7, Aikas describes how her criminology course enabled students to witness—through listening to the experiences of the formerly incarcerated women of Hour Children—the complex humanity of individuals who themselves are the survivors of multiple victimizations. Aalai, in Chap. 6, reveals how her class considered the intersections of sex and gender in studies of genocide and mass atrocity, particularly in ways in which female victim survivor narratives have been disenfranchised. Her course's intersectional pedagogy emphasized how multiple marginalized social identities—Jewish and Woman—impacted the experience of victimhood. In Chap. 14, Ferarri-Bridgers disrupts the Western telos of history as past, describing how her Public Speaking course introduced an inclusionary history, informing students of the state-sanctioned genocidal acts against North American Indigenous People that continue to mark their present condition today. In Chap. 8, Atik, Geismar, and Miller outline their cross-disciplinary and collaborative project, which asked students to engage the "difficult knowledge" of others' traumas and, then, to be steeped in their own as subjects of victimization and surveillance.

Other contributors directly address the past and current narratives of the refugee. In Chap. 15, Lekić and Brégégère describe how, along with members of the Music Department, they aligned their courses with the colloquium concert, "Echoes of Exile," a program that engaged students with the refugee's sense of homelessness as a displaced person. Through this unique program, students actively engaged with the "difficult knowledge" of the refugee as a person that embodies the "*homo sacer*," by way of listening in another dimension—through the narrative of music. In

Chap. 17, Wentrack articulates a fresh approach to a "pedagogy of listening" as she describes her efforts to design a course that used another medium of narrative—photography—to invite students to understand the complexities of the social and political environments of refugees. Chapter 16 takes this learning a step further. In it, Sexton outlines how, informed by two fall speakers in the series, his English Composition students worked in teams to create a strategic plan for the global refugee crisis, empowering themselves to be active and responsible members of the global community.

Appendix: 2016–2017 NEH/KHC Colloquium Series, "Fleeing Genocide: Displacement, Exile, and the Refugee"

Program 1. Refuge Denied: St. Louis Passengers and the Holocaust

Wednesday, September 21, 2016
Scott Miller, Author and Director of Curatorial Affairs at the USHMM
Dr. Susan Jacobowitz, Associate Professor of English, QCC

Description: *Scott Miller, Director of Curatorial Affairs at the USHMM, discussed his book, co-authored with Sarah Ogilvie, on the fate of the passengers of the* St. Louis *ship that left Nazi Germany in 1939 only to be turned away by the US and Cuban governments upon arrival.*

Program 2. "The Jacket" Exhibit

Wednesday, October 5, 2016
Dr. Cary Lane, Department of Academic Literacy, QCC

Description: *The exhibit centered around the stories of a very special artifact donated to the KHC: a prisoner's "jacket" from Kaufering (Dachau), discovered to have belonged to Ben Peres, a Lithuanian Jew whose original name was Benzion Peresetzki, who emigrated to Long Island after liberation from a displaced persons camp.*

Program 3. Building a Better Future: Supporting Refugee Youth to Thrive

Wednesday, November 16, 2016
Sara Rowbottom, Education and Learning Manager at the International Rescue Committee
Dr. Kathleen Landy, Director of CETL, QCC

Description: *Sara Rowbottom, Education and Learning Manager at the International Rescue Committee (IRC), highlighted issues relevant to educating refugees, provided information on IRC's educational programs, and discussed the IRC Refugee Youth Summer Academy, a six-week program designed to transition newly arrived refugees into New York schools.*

Program 4. Displacement, Refuge, Migration—The Context of United Nations' Peace Operations

Wednesday, December 7, 2016
Stefan Feller, Director at United Nations
Dr. Beth Counihan, Associate Professor of English, QCC

Description: *Lieutenant General Stefan Feller, the Police Adviser to the United Nations who serves as a Director in the Department of Peacekeeping Operations, discussed crises which cause internal and external displacement, and the challenges of reverting displacement and migration.*

Program 5. A Common Thread of Uncommon Courage, Part I—From Genocide to Human Rights Activist

Wednesday, February 22, 2017
Jacqueline Murekatete, Genocide Prevention and Human Rights Activist
Dr. Trevor Milton, Assistant Professor of Sociology, QCC

Description: *Jacqueline Murekatete, founder of the Genocide Survivors Foundation, spoke about her own experiences as a victim of the Rwandan genocide.*

Program 6. The LGBTQ Refugee Crisis

Friday, March 24, 2017
Daniel Dromm, New York City Councilman
Dr. Amy Traver, Associate Professor of Sociology, QCC
Sebastian Maguire, Esq., Legislative Director & Counsel, The New York City Council
Pamela Denzer, Client Programs Director at Immigration Equality

Description: Through personal stories of LGBTQ refugees and those who advocate for them, this program, led by Councilman Dromm, examined the challenges facing LGBTQ populations as they flee from brutality and oppression, and navigate the complicated world of exile.

Program 7. Echoes of Exile

Thursday, April 20, 2017

Description: *This event featured musical testimonies of resistance, remembrance, and exile by QCC music faculty, Ensemble 365, and the QCC Jazz Ensemble.*

Program 8. A Common Thread of Uncommon Courage, Part II—Girlhood, Displacement, and Resistance During the Japanese Occupation

Wednesday, May 3, 2017
Dr. Kathleen Tamayo Alves, Assistant Professor of English, QCC
Dr. Aliza Atik, Assistant Professor of English, QCC
Dr. Benjamin Miller, Assistant Professor of English, QCC
Prof. Alisa Cercone, Lecturer of English, QCC

Description: *Dr. Kathleen Tamayo Alves addressed displacement, victimhood, survival, and resistance through the girlhood narratives of her family's flight from persecution during the Japanese occupation of the Philippines, supplying the historical and cultural context of World War II in Asia. This program was immediately followed by a student and faculty roundtable discussion.*

Notes

1. See, for example, Pensiero (2015), Laurent (2015), and Kingsley and Timur (2015).
2. See, for example, Haberman (2015).
3. Ahmed (2004, 76), in fact, has discussed how the politics of fear often shapes narratives focused on "floods and swamps" and "of being invaded by inappropriate others, against whom the nation must defend itself."

References

Agamben, Giorgio. 1995. Homo Sacer: Sovereign Power and Bare Life. Trans. Daniel Heller-Roazen. Stanford: Stanford University Press.

Ahmed, Sara. 2004. *The Cultural Politics of Emotion*. New York: Routledge.

Bleich, Erik, Irene Bloemraad, and Els de Graauw. 2015. Migrants, Minorities, and the Media: Information, Representations, and Participation in the Public Sphere. *Journal of Ethnic and Migration Studies* 41 (6): 857–873.

Bond, Helen. 2008. Teaching the Holocaust in the Urban Classroom: The Need to Know. In *Paths to Teaching the Holocaust*, ed. Tibbi Duboys. Rotterdam: Sense Publishers.

Britzman, Deborah P. 1998. *Lost Subjects, Contested Objects: Toward a Psychoanalytic Inquiry of Learning*. Albany: State University of New York Press.

———. 2000. If the Story Cannot End: Deferred Action, Ambivalence, and Difficult Knowledge. In *Between Hope and Despair: Pedagogy and the Remembrance of Historical Trauma*, ed. Roger I. Simon, Sharon Rosenberg, and Claudia Eppert. Boston: Rowman & Littlefield Publishers.

Esses, Victoria M., Stelian Medianu, and Andrea S. Lawson. 2013. Uncertainty, Threat, and the Role of the Media in Promoting the Dehumanization of Immigrants and Refugees. *Journal of Social Issues* 69 (3): 518–536.

Gatrell, Peter. 2013. *The Making of the Modern Refugee*. Oxford: Oxford University Press.

Gorden, Claire. 2014. Coming to America: The 5 Biggest Refugee Groups of the Last 20 Years. *Al Jazeera America*. October 14. http://america.aljazeera.com/watch/shows/america-tonight/america-tonight-blog/2013/10/13/the-5-biggest-refugeegroupsofthelast20years.html

Haberman, Maggie. 2015. Donald Trump Questions Whether Syrian Refugees Are a 'Trojan Horse.' *New York Times*. November 16. https://www.nytimes.com/politics/first-draft/2015/11/16/trump-questions-whether-syrian-refugees-are-trojan-horse/?_r=0

Hinton, Alexander Laban. 2012. Critical Genocide Studies. *Genocide Studies and Prevention: An International Journal* 7 (1): 4–15.

Kincheloe, Joel L. 2008. *Critical Pedagogy*. New York: Peter Lang.
Kingsley, Patrick, and Safak Timur. 2015. Stories of 2015: How Alan Kurdi's Death Changed the World. *The Guardian*. December 31. https://www.theguardian.com/world/2015/dec/31/alan-kurdi-death-canada-refugee-policy-syria-boy-beach-turkey-photo
Knox, Katharine, and Tony Kushner. 1999. *Refugees in an Age of Genocide: Global, National and Local Perspectives During the Twentieth Century*. London: Frank Cass.
Kochavi, Arieh J. 2001. *Post-Holocaust Politics: Britain, The United States & Jewish Refugees, 1945–1948*. Chapel Hill: The University of North Carolina Press.
Laub, Dori. 1992. Bearing Witness or the Vicissitudes of Listening. In *Testimony: Crises Of Witnessing in Literature, Psychoanalysis and History*, ed. Shoshana Felman and Dori Laub, 57–74. New York: Routledge.
Laurent, Olivier. 2015. What the Image of Aylan Kurdi Says About the Power of Photography. *Time*. September 4.
Low, Bronwen E., and Emmanuelle Sonntag. 2013. Towards a Pedagogy of Listening: Teaching and Learning from Life Stories of Human Rights Violations. *Curriculum Studies* 45 (6): 768–789.
Lubling, Yoram. 2004. Teaching the *Shoah*: Philosophy and the Holocaust. In *Teaching the Shoah in the Twenty-First Century: Topics and Topographies*, ed. Simon P. Sibelman, 177–191. Lewsiton: The Edwin Mellen Press.
Ngai, Sianne. 2005. *Ugly Feelings*. Cambridge: Harvard University Press.
Parker, Samuel. 2015. 'Unwanted Invaders': The Representation of Refugees and Asylum Seekers in the UK and Australian Print Media. *eSharp* 23. http://orca.cf.ac.uk/id/eprint/79108
Pensiero, Karen Miller. 2015. Aylan Kurdi and the Photos That Change History. *The Wall Street Journal*. September 11. https://www.wsj.com/articles/aylan-kurdi-and-the-photos-that-change-history-1442002594
Pitt, Alice, and Deborah Britzman. 2003. Speculations on Qualities of Difficult Knowledge in Teaching and Learning: An Experiment in Psychoanalytic Research. *International Journal of Qualitative Studies in Education* 16 (6): 755–756.
Rajaram, Prem Kumar, and Carl Grundy-Warr. 2004. The Irregular Migrant as Homo Sacer: Migration and Detention in Australia, Malaysia, and Thailand. *International Migration* 42 (1): 33–64.
Soguk, Nevzat. 1999. *States and Strangers: Refugees and Displacements of Statecraft*. Minneapolis: U of Minnesota Press.
Tharoor, Ishaan. 2015. What Americans Thought of Jewish Refugees on the Eve of World War II. *The Washington Post*. November 17. https://www.washingtonpost.com/news/worldviews/wp/2015/11/17/what-americans-thought-of-jewish-refugees-on-the-eve-of-world-war-ii/?utm_term=.bda1f8a1399f

The White House. 2017. Executive Order Protecting The Nation From Foreign Terrorist Entry Into The United States. https://www.whitehouse.gov/the-press-office/2017/01/27/executive-order-protecting-nation-foreign-terrorist-entry-united-states. Accessed 20 Mar.

Totten, Samuel. 2004. Issues of Rationale: Teaching About Genocide. In *Teaching About Genocide: Issues, Approaches, and Resources*, ed. Samuel Totten. Greenwich: Information Age Publishing.

The UNHCR. 2016. *Global Trends: Forced Displacement in 2015*. UNHCR. June 20.

The UNHCR. 2017. Global Trends 2015. http://www.unhcr.org/en-us/statistics/unhcrstats/576408cd7/unhcr-global-trends-2015.html. Accessed 25 Mar.

Zembylas, Michalinos. 2008. *The Politics of Trauma in Education*. New York: Palgrave Macmillan.

CHAPTER 4

Outcomes-Based Approaches to Mass Atrocity Education

Amy E. Traver

Despite progress in the development, embrace, and implementation of Holocaust, genocide, and mass atrocity education around the world, scholars point to a significant oversight of this growth: few programs systematically evaluate or assess their outcomes (JESNA 2006; Gallant and Hartman 2001; Totten 2001). According to Lazar et al. (2009), this deficit is most profoundly felt at the university level, where reports on the impacts of Holocaust, genocide, and mass atrocity education are particularly scarce.

Given that the pursuit of evidence permeates all aspects of education in the United States today—including the work of community colleges—this chapter begins with a focus on outcomes assessment in American higher education. It then segues into an exploration of the published research on Holocaust, genocide, and mass atrocity education, using exemplary studies to link that literature back to the outcomes assessment process. It continues with a focus on the 2015–2016 NEH Colloquium Series "Gender, Mass Violence, and Genocide" at Queensborough Community College's (QCC's) Kupferberg Holocaust Center (KHC), attending most specifi-

A. E. Traver (✉)
Department of Social Sciences, Queensborough Community College, CUNY, Bayside, NY, USA
e-mail: ATraver@qcc.cuny.edu

A. E. Traver, D. Leshem (eds.), *Humanistic Pedagogy Across the Disciplines*, https://doi.org/10.1007/978-3-319-95025-9_4

cally to my efforts, as colloquium coordinator, to evaluate and assess the series' impacts. The chapter concludes by connecting outcomes assessment to the aligned work of faculty across the series' years.

Outcomes Assessment in Colleges and Universities in the United States

It can no longer be assumed that Americans understand the value of, or accord value to, higher education (Arum et al. 2016). For example, the media and American policymakers often depict colleges and universities as ill-managed, economically inefficient, and old-fashioned institutions (Middaugh 2010). In tandem, American parents and college students regularly question whether a college education is aligned with the kinds of knowledge and skills required in today's society (Pellegrino et al. 2001).[1] Significantly, these depictions and concerns have not emerged in a vacuum. In many ways, they parallel the standards-based efforts unfolding in American primary and secondary schools, and they follow more general concerns about both the allocation of public funds and increased private responsibility for rising tuition costs (Pellegrino et al. 2001; Middaugh 2010).

Organized efforts to assess (or measure) the value and effectiveness of higher education are both mandated and reasonable responses to this scrutiny—particularly in a socio-historical moment defined by data analytics (Hutchings et al. 2015). For example, the 1998 report from the National Commission on the Cost of Higher Education and the 2006 Spellings Commission defined the collection, analysis, and sharing of data as central to the missions of responsible institutions of higher education. Likewise, American accrediting bodies and voluntary accountability systems (e.g., the Voluntary Framework of Accountability for community colleges) regularly prescribe the measures, processes, and expectations of this data collection and analysis (Middaugh 2010). Rendering these mandates reasonable is the fact that college and university faculty have long been trained to seek out evidence to both support their research claims and understand what/how their students learn (Arum et al. 2016).

Efforts to directly evidence, understand, and document the effectiveness of teaching and learning in American colleges and universities are a kind of *outcomes assessment*, where students' knowledge and abilities are measured and aggregated for the purposes of discovering group strengths/abilities and shifting instruction accordingly (Banta and Palomba 2015).

While outcomes assessment can occur in any and all spaces in which student learning occurs, it most regularly occurs in the context of academic classrooms, departments, and programs (Kinzie and Jancowski 2015; Walvoord 2010).

Walvoord (2010) outlines the three steps of outcomes assessment processes in these contexts. The first step is identifying the goals—or objectives—for students' learning.[2] This is not an easy task, as the identification of learning goals/objectives tends to highlight differences in the ways that students, faculty, institutional leaders, employers, and policymakers define the very purpose(s) of higher education (Arum et al. 2016). The creation/adoption of curricula and the design/clarification of learning activities are key elements of this first step, as well (Banta and Palomba 2015).

Walvoord's (2010) second step is collecting information, that is, selecting the measures and gathering the evidence needed to ascertain and document students' achievement of the aforementioned goals/objectives. In general, this step begs a series of consequential questions, including "What information best demonstrates student learning and the impacts of faculty instruction?" "What methods are most appropriate for the collection of that information?" As many outcomes are attitudinal or affective, and because most involve more than just the mastery of "component skills and discrete bits of knowledge," step two also begs questions about the authenticity and validity of measures, as well as our capacity to isolate the effects of a learning activity (Pellegrino et al. 2001, 102).[3] Additionally, if informed by the desire to remedy or replicate results, step two must also address questions related to the approaches and resources that led to the outcomes of interest (Banta and Palombo 2015).

Walvoord's (2010) third and final step is taking action—using the gathered information to improve student learning. Oftentimes faculty members use outcomes assessment data to adjust their teaching, course sequences, or academic programs. At other moments, this information is used to direct institutional resources to students' general education or "cross-cutting learning" needs (Schneider 2016, 310). Additionally, and of particular significance to community colleges, outcomes assessment data can be used to inform "learning-centered" transfer and articulation agreements (Arum et al. 2016). Also, while primarily focused on student learning, outcomes assessment can yield data of value to communications with stakeholders, as well as institutional-level insight about how to best conduct future outcomes assessment processes (Banta and Palombo 2015).

Outcomes Assessment and the Scholarship of Teaching and Learning in Holocaust, Genocide, and Mass Atrocity Education

Significantly, when outcomes assessment is done well, it can be used to inform contexts and conversations outside of the institution in which it occurs. For example, as Banta and Associates (2002) argue, outcomes assessment experiences and findings can be of value to educational researchers interested in the processes and practices of assessment, that is, *the scholarship of assessment*. Likewise, outcomes assessment can also contribute empirical insight to larger studies of teaching and learning, that is, the *scholarship of teaching and learning (SoTL)* (see, e.g., Traver 2016; Hill et al. 2014; He 2007).

An institution's outcomes assessment process becomes more broadly relevant when it moves from asking/answering questions for the sole benefit of institutionally specific stakeholders to harnessing the principles of scientific inquiry for the production of generalizable knowledge and theory (Erwin 1991). This movement requires three subtle but important shifts in/to the outcomes assessment process. First, faculty introspection/self-consciousness must align with larger theoretical and empirical questions or concerns about teaching and learning (Dickson and Treml 2013). Second, students' rights and welfare must be more formally respected: if faculty plan to publish or pursue grant funding for their assessment-based work, they should consult their college or university's Institutional Review Board (IRB) (Walvoord 2010). Third, and within the parameters set forth by the IRB, outcomes assessment experiences and data must be "publicly shared for critique and use" by communities both within and beyond the institution (Potter and Kustra 2011, 2).

Perhaps because the aforementioned shifts are onerous, there is often a gap between faculty's outcomes assessment efforts and published educational research (Erwin 1991). This is particularly true in the field of Holocaust, genocide, and mass atrocity education, where faculty assessment is limited (JESNA 2006) and the number of studies conducted and published by outside researchers is growing (Eckmann et al. 2016). Presently, the published research in Holocaust, genocide, and mass atrocity education is of two ideal types: (1) *descriptive research*, wherein the researcher's efforts aspire to describe the current state of teaching/learning in the field; and (2) *explanatory research*, wherein the researcher's efforts aim to reveal a causal relationship between specific teaching/

learning practices and outcomes in the field (Fawcett and Downs 1986). Each of these types includes exemplary studies that map on to the three steps of the outcomes assessment process (i.e., identifying goals, collecting information, and taking action); however, within both types, the vast majority of the published research focuses on Holocaust education in secondary school contexts.

Descriptive Research on Holocaust, Genocide, and Mass Atrocity Education

In descriptive research on Holocaust, genocide, and mass atrocity education, researchers eschew a focus on outcomes to instead *describe* the state of teaching/learning in the field. Given this macro-level orientation, such research tends to be quantitative, large-scale, and survey-based, and it is often sponsored by significant organizations with a vested interest in the findings. Researchers engaged in this work often focus on Holocaust educators, a fact illustrated by Donnelly's (2006) survey-based study of 300+ American secondary school teachers. In partnership with the United States Holocaust Memorial Museum (USHMM), Donnelly describes the origins of teachers' knowledge of the Holocaust (personal study or college coursework), their rationales for teaching the Holocaust (personal, educational, and/or historical), and their preferred approach to Holocaust education (through a human rights framework using multiple resources). Similar survey-based studies have followed state mandates to teach the Holocaust in American secondary schools (e.g., Ellison 2002; Ellison and Pisapia 2006) and further described American post-secondary educators' rationales and preferred approaches (Haynes 1998).

While the preponderance of descriptive research on Holocaust educators is survey-based, researchers have also used qualitative methods to understand who teaches what, how, and why. Lindquist's (2002) intensive interviews with six experienced American teachers of the Holocaust evidence the strengths of this approach—uncovering the decision-making processes that lead teachers to adopt specific approaches and materials. Likewise, through her ethnography of four American high school teachers' pedagogical decisions and practices, Schweber (2004) describes how Holocaust curricula is transformed in the classroom, and how teachers' choices have significant consequences for what students learn about the Holocaust. These findings add depth and validity to self-reported, survey-based descriptions of the field.

Researchers often combine quantitative and qualitative methods in their descriptive research on students' Holocaust education experiences. For example, Foster et al. (2014) draw on data from almost 8000 surveys and 244 focus group interviews, as well as support from the Centre for Holocaust Education, to describe British secondary students' knowledge of the Holocaust. Analyzed together, the collated responses paint a dire picture: students know very little about why Jews were the primary victims of the Holocaust; the role ordinary citizens played in the perpetration of the Holocaust; the chronology of the Holocaust; and why and how nations, like Great Britain, entered World War II (Foster et al. 2014).

Researchers' content analyses of major history books also marry the quantitative and qualitative veins of descriptive research in the field.[4] Lindquist's (2009) analysis of the six most frequently used high school history textbooks in America reveals a number of problems with their Holocaust content, in particular: none of the reviewed textbooks provided a comprehensive definition of the Holocaust, contextualized the Holocaust and anti-Semitism, or introduced critical questions about human behavior. Additionally, all of the reviewed textbooks privileged the role of Hitler, used the unqualified language of "race" to describe Jewish people, and contained factual errors. Similar findings have been uncovered through content analyses of textbooks from different historical moments (e.g., Bromley and Russell 2015; Pate 1987), textbooks designed for American college students (e.g., Kanter 1998), textbooks published in different countries (e.g., Carrier et al. 2015), and in state-sanctioned curricula (Dawidowicz 1992).

While lacking an explicit focus on outcomes, descriptive research resembles the outcomes assessment process in that it relies heavily on the second step, collecting information, to guide the third step, taking action. In fact, while descriptive research is often framed as the initial stage of a complex and multi-tiered research protocol, descriptive findings can be put to powerful use. For example, descriptive research studies that identify what, how, and why educators teach the Holocaust help to pinpoint strengths and/or weaknesses of a selected curriculum or instructional program, incentives and opportunities to grow Holocaust education, and openings for professional development (see, e.g., Harbaugh 2015). Snapshots of students' learning are also of value, as they help to unearth the informational deficits, erroneous understandings, and knowledge that students, as a group, possess at a specific moment in time. Finally, strong descriptions of available texts and curricula promote the improved organization and explanation of information in future materials, as well as the creation of standards for accurate coverage of the Holocaust, genocide, and mass atrocity, more generally (see, e.g., Carrier et al. 2015).

Explanatory Research on Holocaust, Genocide, and Mass Atrocity Education

In explanatory research on Holocaust, genocide, and mass atrocity education, researchers aim to reveal a causal relationship between specific teaching/learning practices and cognitive, affective or attitudinal, and action-oriented or behavioral outcomes (Gallant and Hartman 2001). Given this focus on causality (or, at the least, covariation), these studies tend to reflect the tenets of the hard sciences, including the testing of hypotheses/theories, the use of controlled conditions and comparison, and the focus on patterns over multiple cases or periods of time.

Research on the impacts of students' formal educational experiences on their *cognitive outcomes*, specifically their understanding of the Holocaust, exemplifies this positivist perspective. Many of these studies use experimental methods, which attempt to isolate and examine the effect(s) of a treatment. For example, McRoy (1982) uses a classic experimental research design to establish that, at the most basic level, formal Holocaust education matters: American high school students who were exposed to relevant curricula produced more sophisticated essays on the Holocaust than students who were not exposed to those curricula.[5] Other experimental studies make use of pre-/post-test instruments to track students' cognitive gains over the course of an educative exposure. For instance, Davis et al.'s (1999) analysis of American high school students' pre-/post-test content surveys reveals how USHMM online resources improved students' performance on the post-test measure, particularly within low- and middle-achieving student groups. Still other studies integrate pre-/post-testing into a classic experimental design to better understand the factors that lead to students' cognitive gains. For example, Farkas (2003) uses a pre-/post-test control group design to demonstrate the positive impact that multisensory instructional methods had on New York City middle school students' learning about the Holocaust.

Yet, according to Romi and Lev (2007), emotionally laden Holocaust education experiences tend to be more impactful than those aimed solely at developing students' cognition. As a result, *affective or attitudinal outcomes*, as well as outcomes related to students' well-being, are another focus of explanatory research in the field. For example, using multiple psychological and moral testing instruments in a pre-/post-test format, Brabeck (1994) reveals that the Facing History and Ourselves (FHAO) curriculum encouraged American secondary students' development of moral reasoning. Years later, Shultz et al. (2001) built on these findings, administering additional psycho-social testing instruments, in a pre-/post-test control group design, to American eighth-graders. Their results show a link between exposure to FHAO curricula and students' relationship maturity, declining racist attitudes, and declining self-reported fighting behavior, with experimental students evidencing significant gains, relative to control students, in civic attitudes.

Pointedly, Ben-Peretz (2003) rejects students' purely emotional identification with the Holocaust, unless that identification leads to the active pursuit of equality. As a result, *action-oriented or behavioral outcomes* also ground explanatory research in the field. For example, Spalding et al.'s (2003) pre-/post-test observational, interview-based, and student reflection data show that a March of Remembrance and Hope trip fostered American college students' inclination toward social activism. Likewise, Cowan and Maitles (2005) pre-/post-test survey-based research demonstrates that Holocaust education had a positive impact on Scottish students' civic attitudes and disposition (see also Wegner 1998; Carrington and Short 1997). While much of the explanatory research on Holocaust education focuses only on the immediate post-exposure period (Gallant and Hartman 2001), Cowan and Maitles (2007) also examine the longitudinal effects of this learning, revealing, through later and continued research on the same sample of Scottish youth, that Holocaust education had both an immediate and a long-term impact on students' action-oriented or behavioral outcomes (see also Starratt et al. 2017).

With its focus on outcomes and their causes, explanatory research on Holocaust, genocide, and mass atrocity education clearly reflects the first two steps of the outcomes assessment process, identifying goals and collecting information. More implicit, however, is the relationship between explanatory research and the third step of that process, taking action. For example, while explanatory studies demonstrate that Holocaust, genocide, and mass atrocity education can yield cognitive, affective, and behavioral outcomes, they tend to neglect the details—that is, the pedagogical tools, practices, and approaches—that led to these outcomes (JESNA

2006). As a result, while explanatory research goes a long way in promoting Holocaust, genocide, and mass atrocity education, it does so in a manner that, when compared to outcomes assessment (and even published descriptive research), is often of less specific utility.

Outcomes Assessment in the 2015–2016 NEH/KHC Colloquium Series: Gender, Mass Violence, and Genocide[6]

In the 2015–2016 academic year, I coordinated the NEH/KHC Colloquium Series at QCC. As a sociologist, I brought two unique perspectives to the series' organization. First, I was interested in considering the growing body of gender-sensitive research in genocide studies, which argues that gender structures and mediates experiences of mass violence and that attention to gender can lead to a better understanding of the causes, processes, and effects of genocide (von Joeden-Forgey 2012). Thus, the series' eight events featured 15 speakers from a range of humanities and humanities-oriented disciplines—History, Psychology, Philosophy, Women's and Gender Studies, Foreign Languages and Literatures, Comparative Genocide Studies, Linguistics, Political Science, English and Comparative Literature, and Jurisprudence—who offered comparative perspectives and more in-depth reflections on gender and specific processes of genocide across history.[7] Consistent with Fein's (1989) research, the speakers focused on gender-specific and gender-neutral genocides, and they examined both women and men as perpetrators and victims of mass violence and genocide.

Second, and most relevant to this chapter, I was determined to gather and analyze evidence of the series' effects on student learning. As a result, I designed and directed a research protocol that sought to document the series' varied impacts through the use of event evaluation surveys, a faculty-led rubric-based assessment of students' aligned assignments, and an undergraduate research student's content analysis of the same assignments. The details, findings, and implications of those efforts are outlined below.

Survey Evaluation of the Immediate Impacts of the Series' Events

After each of the series' eight events, attendees were asked to complete an anonymous, one-page, IRB-approved event evaluation survey. This survey combined closed, open-ended, and Likert-scale questions to gather descriptive data about the attendees, garner information about attendees' event-based experiences and learning, and ascertain attendees' interest in future opportunities at the KHC. I collected 645 evaluation surveys across the eight events.

While the series' events were open to the general public, my analysis reveals that the vast majority (87 percent) of respondents were QCC students. Faculty buy-in was central to students' participation in the series, with 77 percent of respondents tying their attendance to a class assignment, 79 percent of respondents attributing knowledge of the event to faculty announcements, and 64 percent of respondents reporting that college coursework had primed them for the event. While less than one-third of respondents had attended an event on genocide/mass atrocity before, half of the respondents expressed a desire to attend a future event on the subject. When queried about the preferred format of that future event, most respondents reported a preference for a film screening or museum exhibition. This descriptive data has since helped to inform the design and implementation of events in subsequent series.

Significantly, the event evaluation surveys also produced data that are of broader significance. For example, data from these surveys add nuance to the debate surrounding gender-sensitive analyses of genocide, which seems to be grounded in a fear that, in accounting for differences in experiences of genocide, we compromise our complete understanding of genocide (von Joeden-Forgey 2012).[8] When asked what they had learned at a series' event, most survey respondents reported broad, general takeaways. Some respondents wrote about the sheer number of people impacted by genocide or the terrifying ease with which people engage in destructive group behavior. Other respondents described the central role social institutions play in the genocidal process, or they reflected on issues related to human rights and human rights law. Perhaps paradoxically, then, it was the series' specificity—its gender-sensitive focus—that led to respondents' broad, general learning. In fact, for many respondents and their referring faculty, it was the series' gender-sensitive focus that served as an *invitation*, or an *incentive*, to take up the study of genocide at all.

Rubric Assessment of the Series' Impacts on Students' Achievement of a Specific Learning Outcome

Twelve QCC faculty linked at least one course to an event in the 2015–2106 NEH/KHC Colloquium Series, resulting in a total of 14 aligned courses. These courses reflected the disciplinary diversity of the series' events and the range of humanities perspectives across QCC; Education, English, Sociology, History, Speech Communication and Theatre Arts, Psychology, Art and Design, Political Science, Foreign Languages and Literatures, and Academic Literacy courses were all represented in the alignment. Students in each of the 14 aligned courses were exposed to a curriculum module related to a series event, readings appropriate to the event's content, and a writing assignment that tied together course material and insights from the event. As part of their involvement in the series, the participating 12 faculty agreed to share consenting students' aligned, de-identified, and anonymized papers with a team of four assessment-trained and experienced QCC faculty (including myself). By the end of the academic year, 191 students had consented to participate in the series' assessment, and 75 percent of them—or 144 students—turned in a paper for analysis.

Given that the KHC is a campus cultural resource associated with the Global/Diversity Learning high-impact practice, and that the United Nations Educational, Scientific and Cultural Organization (UNESCO) considers the study of the Holocaust highly compatible with Global Citizenship Education (UNESCO 2017), the team used the Association of American Colleges & Universities (AAC&U) Global Learning VALUE rubric to assess students' efforts to "analyze and explore complex global challenges" (AAC&U n.d.). This rubric consists of six dimensions (or task descriptions) and four performance levels, which combine to give shape to a single outcome: global learning. Before the series began, the assessment team met to discuss the rubric and to reach agreement on the meaning of the rubric's dimensions and performance levels. At that time, we also discussed how to score content missing from, and record exceptional examples of, each dimension.

By the end of June 2016, each of the 144 student papers had been read and assessed by two team members. As there was generally little variability across team members' scores, I calculated an average score for each dimension of each paper. I then calculated a single average for each dimension across the study sample (i.e., the 144 student papers). My analysis of that data indicates that students' aligned learning clustered around the "Global Self-Awareness" dimension of the AAC&U Global Learning VALUE rubric, revealing that the series' events and assignments most profoundly impacted students' development of a "mature, integrated identity with a systematic understanding of the interrelationships among the self, local, and global communities" (AAC&U n.d.). Student learning proved weakest on the "Knowledge Application" dimension of the same rubric, indicating that the series' events and assignments could have done more to encourage students' "ability to apply knowledge and skills gained through higher learning to real-life problem-solving" (AAC&U n.d.).

These findings relate directly to the explanatory research on Holocaust, genocide, and mass atrocity education, particularly those studies that focus on *affective or attitudinal outcomes* and *action-oriented or behavioral outcomes*. For example, the findings indicate that students were affected by their learning at the series' events, but that they were unsure of what to make of that learning and how to act on it in the future. Unfortunately, and consistent with the shortcomings of explanatory research, the assessment team had no information about the pedagogical tools, practices, and approaches that faculty used to facilitate students' development along the "Global Self-Awareness" or "Knowledge Application" dimensions of the rubric. Thankfully, my colleagues Drs. Aliza Atik, Kat Alves, and Mirna Lekić built on these findings in their 2016–2017 NEH/KHC Colloquium Series, "Fleeing Genocide: Displacement, Exile, and the Refugee," offering events that "endeavor(ed) to move our students and community past abstract compassion" and collecting specific evidence of faculty efforts to inspire students' learning (and action) in that regard (Atik et al. 2016).

The four assessment team members' reflections on the scoring process are also valuable, as they add specifically to the scholarship of assessment. For example, we learned that student success on the AAC&U Global Learning VALUE rubric's dimensions was often correlated with the course level and disciplinary skill set through which they did their work. Likewise, we realized that significant areas of student learning fell outside of the rubric's dimensions. For example, while students learned to synthesize multiple types of content—a skill that Gardner (2006) describes as decidedly future-oriented and cosmopolitan—this learning was not captured by the rubric. Finally, and as a result of this assessment experience, we developed interesting questions about the use of baccalaureate instruments of measure, like the AAC&U VALUE rubrics, in the community college context.[9]

Student-Led Content Analysis of Students' Aligned Assignments

During the 2016–2017 academic year, in an effort to better understand those aspects of students' aligned learning that fell outside of the AAC&U

Global Learning VALUE rubric, I mentored Ms. Rolecia Nedd, a QCC undergraduate and CUNY Research Scholar, in her efforts to conduct an IRB-approved content analysis of the same 144 student papers. While aware of the assessment team's work and the rubric's dimensions, Ms. Nedd began her research with a process of open coding, actively identifying emergent themes and commonalities across the 144 papers. After a period of experimentation, my parallel analysis, and conversations about the nature of appropriate evidence, she settled on four broad and inclusive codes: (1) Global Awareness; (2) Emotional Reaction; (3) Planned Action/Response; and (4) Personal Connection. Ms. Nedd then spent the remainder of the fall 2016 semester understanding students' papers through these codes.

During the January 2017 intersession, Ms. Nedd collated her data into Excel. This allowed us to spend the bulk of the spring 2017 semester quantifying and analyzing the patterns that emerged. Two significant findings developed out of that analysis. First, while confirming the assessment team's conclusion that students' aligned learning clustered around their development of a global identity, Ms. Nedd's data exposed differences in *how* students conceive of themselves in relationship to "global communities." In fact, her careful content analysis revealed that students' developing global awareness was generally of two types: *cognitive* or *affective*. Those students who evidenced a *cognitive* global awareness expressed a new, informed approach to the world, marked by a shift in their focus from what's going on in the United States to what's happening around the globe. In contrast, those students who evidenced a more *affective* global awareness expressed an evolving, emotional understanding of human interconnectedness across and despite the bounds of the nation-state.

Second, Ms. Nedd's data also complicated the assessment teams' weak "Knowledge Application" finding: when read closely by a peer, more student papers evidenced the "ability to apply knowledge and skills gained through higher learning to real-life problem-solving." This is because Ms. Nedd recognized that students conceptualized *learning* as a "real-life" solution to the "problem" that was their prior lack of knowledge. In fact, her careful content analysis uncovered the moments in which students framed their acquisition of knowledge, and their efforts to build on and share that newly acquired knowledge, as a distinct form of *action*. For example, when reflecting on a memoir that she read for a series event, one student wrote: "(the event caused me to) pass the book on to my little sister so that she could talk about it to her close friends and eventually pass the book on to others. We even started reading the book together, and she got into it very fast. She's only 12."

The aforementioned findings contribute to the research literature on Holocaust, genocide, and mass atrocity education, encouraging us to consider how students' identities can be impacted both cognitively and affectively by their learning, and forcing us to confront the fact that students may understand their achievement of central learning outcomes in ways that are different from faculty. As these findings result from one student's research into her peers' learning, they also add to the scholarship of assessment. Currently, the research on student-led assessment efforts consists of studies of self and peer assessments of specific assignments and courses (see Falchikov and Boud 1989 and Falchikov and Goldfinch 2000 for reviews of that literature). In contrast, Ms. Nedd's work exemplifies students' participation in and unique contributions to more formal, campus-wide assessment processes—a phenomenon that deserves further consideration and study.

Course-Based Examples

Many chapters in this volume focus on the integration of outcomes assessment in courses aligned with NEH/KHC colloquia at QCC. Some of these chapters focus on the role of outcomes (and objectives) in a faculty member's decision to align with a series event or in their design of an aligned project. For example, in Chap. 11, Dahlke reveals how Backward Course Design—a pedagogical approach to effective teaching that begins with faculty attention to learning outcomes—informed his choral music class' participation in the 2014–2015 Colloquium Series. Likewise, in Chap. 16, Sexton attributes his development of The Refugee Program Project, which ran in concert with the 2016–2017 Colloquium Series, to his evaluation of former English Composition students' weak satisfaction of general education objectives.

Other chapters focus on the seamless integration—and the instructional and learning benefits—of rubrics in series alignment. In Chap. 13, Emanuele, a participant in the faculty working group of the 2013–2014 Colloquium Series, grounds her English 101 students' successful textual analysis of hate propaganda, as well as her quantitative assessment of the project's outcomes, in her development and provision of a clear assignment rubric. In Chap. 9, Burgers describes his rubric-based assessment of literary studies' students' use of three different literary theories, demonstrating how students' active engagement with multiple KHC initiatives underscored their grasp of cultural memory theory, in particular.

Still other chapters reveal the analytic principles and value of assessed alignment, more generally. In Chap. 10, Carroll presents data from her systematic analysis of English language learners' (ELL's) recursive, reflective writings on their participation in the 2015–2016 Colloquium Series to reveal how topics of significance imbue ELL's reading and writing instruction with meaning. In Chap. 15, Lekić and Brégégère present findings from their assessment of those course and series learning outcomes associated with "Echoes of Exile," a program where student performers, listeners, and writers considered issues of cultural genocide and human displacement through music and in alignment with the 2016–2017 Colloquium Series. In Chap. 17, Wentrack's pre-/post-test methodology demonstrates how course and institution-specific outcomes were connected to and satisfied by her History of Photography students' participation in the 2016–2017 Colloquium Series.

Taken together, these chapters demonstrate how the outcomes assessment process can inform teaching and learning in specific classrooms and the larger field of Holocaust, genocide, and mass atrocity education; rationalize and bolster efforts to teach about the Holocaust, genocide, and mass atrocity across the disciplines and to diverse student bodies; and contribute productively to arguments in favor of higher education, more generally. Readers are encouraged to consider these chapters through the lens of the outcomes assessment process (i.e., the three steps of identifying goals, collecting information, and taking action) and the two ideal types of published research in the field (i.e., descriptive research and explanatory research), and to contemplate how such course-based assessments might add to or expand into larger initiatives to understand the impacts of Holocaust, genocide, and mass atrocity education.

Finally, while outside of the outcomes assessment focus of this chapter, the theme of my 2015–2016 NEH/KHC Colloquium Series, "Gender, Mass Violence, and Genocide," begs mention of those chapters that focus on gender. In Chap. 6, Aalai describes her efforts to encourage and complicate social psychology students' exploration of sex/gender in processes of genocide through alignment with the 2015–2016 NEH/KHC Colloquium Series. In Chap. 7, Äikäs connects criminology students' interviews with formerly incarcerated women to restorative justice theory, Holocaust pedagogy, and the 2014–2015

NEH/KHC Colloquium Series. In Chap. 14, Ferrari outlines her public speaking students' understandings of the experiences of indigenous peoples in the United States, demonstrating how gender provided those students with a lens through which to grapple with the conceptual framework and realities of genocide.

Appendix: 2015–2016 NEH/KHC Colloquium Series, "Gender, Mass Violence, and Genocide"

September 30, 2015: Gender and the Future of Genocide Studies

Dr. Elisa von Joeden-Forgey, Assistant Professor of Holocaust and Genocide Studies at the Richard Stockton College of New Jersey

October 28, 2015: Human Rights and Genocidal Rape

Professor Cynthia Soohoo, Director of the International Women's Human Rights Clinic at CUNY Law School

Dr. Natalie Nenadic, Assistant Professor of Philosophy at the University of Kentucky

November 18, 2015: Multiple Girlhoods: Growing up in Bosnia Before and During the Civil War

Ms. Jasmina Dervisevic-Cesic, author of *The River Runs Salt, Runs Sweet*

December 2, 2015: Gendered Experiences in and Memories of the Nazi Holocaust

Dr. Azadeh Aalai, Assistant Professor of Psychology at QCC

Dr. Rochelle Saidel, Founder and Executive Director of the Remember the Women Institute

Dr. Marianne Hirsch, William Peterfield Trent Professor of English and Comparative Literature at Columbia University and Professor in the Institute for Research on Women, Gender, and Sexuality

February 17, 2016: Gendercide: Inclusivity in the Study of Gender, Mass Violence, and Genocide

Dr. Adam Jones, Professor of Political Science at the University of British Columbia

March 23, 2016: Spanish Women and Fascism Under the Francoist Dictatorship

Ms. Luque Delgado, Professor of Phonetics at the Ortega-Marañón Foundation and Middlebury University

Dr. Aránzazu Borrachero, Associate Professor of Foreign Languages and Literatures at QCC

Dr. Aurora G. Morcillo, Professor of History at Florida International University

April 13, 2016: Forgotten Witnesses: Gender-Based Violence in Asia During WWII

Dr. Jimin Kim, Program Director of the Asian Social Justice Internship Program at QCC's KHC

Ms. Chang-Jin Lee, Korean-born visual artist and creator of the documentary film *Comfort Women Wanted*

May 4, 2016: Gender, Genocide, and Justice in Rwanda

Ms. Roxanne Krystalli, Program Manager of the Humanitarian Evidence Program at the Feinstein International Center at Tufts University

Ms. Sara E. Brown, Stern Family Fellow at the Strassler Center for Holocaust and Genocide Studies at Clark University

Ms. Samantha Lakin, Ph.D. student at the Strassler Center for Holocaust and Genocide Studies at Clark University

Notes

1. Significantly, Americans reports more positive perceptions of community colleges than they do any other sector of higher education (Kelderman 2017).
2. Although Walvoord (2010) uses these words interchangeably, Banta and Palomba (2015) distinguish learning goals from learning objectives/outcomes: learning goals are defined as the general articulation of what students are expected to learn (i.e., critical thinking and problem solving), whereas learning objectives are defined as the precise articulation of what students are expected to learn in specific courses or programs (i.e., solve problems using physics principles and facts; apply the sociological imagination to current events; etc.).
3. For an overview of issues of validity in outcomes assessment/evaluation, see Wholey et al. (2010).
4. Glynn et al.'s (1982) early and exceptional example of descriptive research in the field combines each of the reviewed quantitative and qualitative measures: survey and interview-based research with students, telephone and face-to-face interviews with Holocaust educators, and content analysis of four different curricula.
5. Holocaust *educators'* cognitive gains have also been an object of explanatory research. For example, Wolpow et al.'s (2002) pre-/post-test control group

design shows that professional development in Holocaust education increases teachers' confidence and competence in the field.

6. A portion of this text is reprinted with permission from *Liberal Education*, Volume 104, number 1. Copyright 2018 Association of American Colleges & Universities.
7. Videos of and resource lists for each of the 2015–2016 NEH/KHC colloquia can be found at http://qcc.libguides.com/colloquia.
8. Consistent with the historiographical silence that has traditionally surrounded the study of gender and the Holocaust (Mühlhäuser 2014), Haynes' (1998) content analysis of 90 course syllabi reveals how few college-level courses on the Holocaust pay explicit attention to gender. This is despite extensive evidence that gender mattered in/to the Holocaust (see, for example, Mühlhäuser 2014; Hedgepeth and Saidel 2010; Pine 2004; and Grossmann 2002).
9. Since our assessment of the 2015–2016 NEH/KHC Colloquium Series, the AAC&U (2017) has defined community college students' associate-level learning as a step on the way toward the "capstone" measure of baccalaureate-level learning on the AAC&U VALUE rubrics.

References

AAC&U. 2017. *On Solid Ground: VALUE Report 2017*. Washington, DC: AAC&U.

———. n.d.. Global Learning VALUE Rubric. Association of American Colleges & Universities. https://www.aacu.org/value/rubrics/global-learning. Accessed 5 Jan 2016.

Arum, Richard, Josipa Roksa, and Amanda Cook, eds. 2016. *Improving Quality in American Higher Education: Learning Outcomes and Assessment for the 21st Century*. San Francisco: Jossey-Bass.

Atik, Aliza, Kat Alves, and Mirna Lekić. 2016. Introduction. KHRCA Colloquia 2016–2017: Fleeing Genocide: Displacement, Exile, and the Refugee. http://qcc.libguides.com/KHRCA_Fleeing_Genocide2016-17. Accessed 19 June 2017.

Banta, Trudy W., and Associates. 2002. *Building a Scholarship of Assessment*. San Francisco: Jossey-Bass.

Banta, Trudy W., and Catherine A. Palomba. 2015. *Assessment Essentials: Planning, Implementing, and Improving Assessment in Higher Education*. San Francisco: Jossey-Bass.

Ben-Peretz, Miriam. 2003. Identifying with Horror: Teaching about the Holocaust: A Response to Simone Schweber's 'Simulating Survival. *Curriculum Inquiry* 33 (2): 189–198.

Brabeck, Mary, Maureen Kenny, Sonia Stryker, Terry Tollefson, and Margot Stern Strom. 1994. Human Rights Education through the Facing History and Ourselves Program. *Journal of Moral Education* 23: 333–347.

Bromley, Patricia, and Susan Garnett Russell. 2015. The Holocaust as History and Human Rights: A Cross-National Analysis of Holocaust Education in Social Science Textbooks, 1970–2008. In *As the Witnesses Fall Silent: 21st Century Holocaust Education in Curriculum, Policy and Practice*, ed. Gross Zehavit and E. Doyle Stevick, 299–320. Switzerland: Springer International Publishing.

Carrier, Peter, Eckhardt Fuchs, and Torben Messinger. 2015. A Global Mapping of the Holocaust in Textbooks and Curricula. In *As the Witnesses Fall Silent: 21st Century Holocaust Education in Curriculum, Policy and Practice*, ed. Zehavit Gross and E. Doyle Stevick, 245–261. Switzerland: Springer International Publishing.

Carrington, Bruce, and Geoffrey Short. 1997. Holocaust Education, Anti-Racism, and Citizenship. *Educational Review* 49 (3): 271–283.

Cowan, Paula, and Henry Maitles. 2005. Values and Attitudes—Positive and Negative: A Study of the Impact of Teaching the Holocaust on Citizenship Among Scottish 11–12 year Olds. *Scottish Educational Review* 37 (2): 104–115.

———. 2007. Does Addressing Prejudice and Discrimination through Holocaust Education Produce Better Citizens? *Educational Review* 59 (2): 115–130.

Davis, Hilarie B., William R. Fernekes, and Christine R. Hladky. 1999. Using Internet Resources to Study the Holocaust: Reflections from the Field. *The Social Studies* 90 (1): 34–41.

Dawidowicz, Lucy S. 1992. *What is the Use of Jewish History*. New York: Schocken Books.

Dickson, K. Laurie, and Melinda M. Treml. 2013. Using Assessment and SoTL to Enhance Student Learning. *New Direction for Teaching and Learning* 136: 7–16.

Donnelly, Mary Beth. 2006. Educating Students About the Holocaust: A Survey of Teaching Practices. *Social Education* 70 (1): 51–54.

Eckmann, Monique, E. Doyle Stevick, and Jolanta Ambrosewicz-Jacobs. 2016. *Research in Teaching and Learning about the Holocaust: A Dialogue Beyond Borders*. Metropol Verlag, International Holocaust Remembrance Alliance.

Ellison, Jeffrey. 2002. *From One Generation to the Next: A Case Study of Holocaust Education in Illinois*. PhD diss, Atlantic University.

Ellison, Jeffrey, and John Pisapia. 2006. The State of Holocaust Education in Illinois. *Idea: A Journal of Social Issues* 11.1: n.p.

Erwin, T. Dary. 1991. *Assessing Student Learning and Development: A Guide to the Principles, Goals, and Methods of Determining College Outcomes*. San Francisco: Jossey-Bass.

Falchikov, Nancy, and David Boud. 1989. Student Self-Assessment in Higher Education: A Meta-Analysis. *Review of Educational Research* 59: 395–430.

Falchikov, Nancy, and Judy Goldfinch. 2000. Student Peer Assessment in Higher Education: A Meta-Analysis in Comparing Peer and Teacher Marks. *Review of Educational Research* 70: 287–322.

Farkas, Rhonda Dawn. 2003. Effects of Traditional Versus Learning-Styles Instructional Methods on Middle School Students. *Journal of Educational Research* 97 (1): 42–51.

Fawcett, Jacqueline, and Florence S. Downs. 1986. *The Relationship of Theory and Research*. Norwalk, CT: Appleton Century Crofts.

Fein, Helen. 1989. Genocide and Gender: The Uses of Women and Group Destiny. *Journal of Genocide Research* 1 (1): 43–64.

Foster, Stuart, Alice Pettigrew, Andy Pearce, Rebecca Hale, Adrian Burgess, Paul Salmons, and Ruth-Anne Lenga. 2014. *What do Students Know and Understand about the Holocaust? Evidence from English Secondary Schools*. London: Centre for Holocaust Education.

Gallant, Mary J., and Harriet Hartman. 2001. Holocaust Education for the New Millennium: Assessing our Progress. *The Journal of Holocaust Education* 10 (2): 1–28.

Gardner, Howard. 2006. *5 Minds for the Future*. Boston: Harvard Business School Publishing.

Glynn, Mary T., Geoffrey Bock, and Karen C. Cohen. 1982. *American Youth and the Holocaust: A Study of Four Major Holocaust Curricula*. New York: National Jewish Resource Center.

Grossmann, Atina. 2002. Women and the Holocaust: Four Recent Titles. *Holocaust and Genocide Studies* 16 (1): 94–108.

Harbaugh, Corey L. 2015. Informed Pedagogy of the Holocaust: A Survey of Teachers Trained by Leading Holocaust Organisations in the United States. In *As the Witnesses Fall Silent: 21st Century Holocaust Education in Curriculum, Policy and Practice*, ed. Zehavit Gross and E. Doyle Stevick, 375–390. Switzerland: Springer International Publishing.

Haynes, Stephen R. 1998. Holocaust Education at American Colleges and Universities: A Report on the Current Situation. *Holocaust and Genocide Studies* 12 (2): 282–307.

He, Daquing. 2007. Integrating Diversity and Multicultural Education into a Digital Library Course. In *Diversity Across the Curriculum: A Guide for Faculty in Higher Education*, ed. Jerome Branche, John Mullennixs, and Ellen R. Cohn, 298–302. Bolton, MA: Anker Publishing Co., Inc.

Hedgepeth, Sonja M., and Rochelle G. Saidel, eds. 2010. *Sexual Violence Against Jewish Women During the Holocaust*. Waltham, MA: Brandeis University Press.

Hill, Yao Zhang, Tanya Renner, Francisco Acoba, Krista Hiser, and Robert W. Franco. 2014. Service-Learning's Role in Achieving Institutional Outcomes: Engagement, Learning, and Achievement. In *Service-Learning at the American Community College: Theoretical and Empirical Perspectives*, ed. Amy E. Traver and Zivah Perel Katz, 169–182. New York: Palgrave Macmillan.

Hutchings, Pat, Jillian Kinzie, and George Kuh. 2015. "Evidence of Student Learning: What Counts and What Matters for Improvement." In *Using Evidence of Student Learning to Improve Higher Education*, edited by George D. Kuh, Stanley O. Ikenberry, Natasha A. Jankowski, Timothy Reese Cain, Peter T. Ewell, Pat Hutchings, and Jillian Kinzie, 27–50. San Francisco: Jossey-Bass.

JESNA. 2006. *Best Practices in Holocaust Education: Report to The San Francisco Jewish Community Endowment Fund*. New York: The Berman Center for Research and Evaluation in Jewish Education.

von Joeden-Forgey, Elisa. 2012. Gender and the Future of Genocide Studies and Prevention. *Genocide Studies and Prevention: An International Journal* 7 (1): 89–107.

Kanter, Leona. 1998. *Forgetting to Remember: Presenting the Holocaust in American College Social Science and History Textbooks*. Fulbright-Hays Summer Seminars Abroad Program. https://archive.org/stream/ERIC_ED439039#page/n0/mode/2up. Accessed 17 June 2017.

Kelderman, Eric. 2017. People Esteem Community Colleges but Question How Well Higher Ed Serves Students. *The Chronicle of Higher Education*. http://www.chronicle.com/article/People-Esteem-Community/240047. Accessed 26 May 2017.

Kinzie, Jillian, and Natasha A. Jancowski. 2015. Making Assessment Consequential: Organizing to Yield Results. In *Using Evidence of Student Learning to Improve Higher Education*, ed. George D. Kuh, Stanley O. Ikenberry, Natasha A. Jankowski, Timothy Reese Cain, Peter T. Ewell, Pat Hutchings, and Jillian Kinzie, 73–94. San Francisco: Jossey-Bass.

Lazar, Alon, Tal Litvak-Hirsch, Dan Bar-On, and Ruth Beyth-Marom. 2009. Through Psychological Lenses: University Students' Reflections Following the 'Psychology of the Holocaust' Course. *Educational Review* 61 (1): 101–114.

Lindquist, David Hays. 2002. *Towards a Pedagogy of the Holocaust: Perspectives of Exemplary Teachers*. Unpublished diss., Indiana University.

———. 2009. The Coverage of the Holocaust in High School History Textbooks. *Social Education* 73 (6): 298–304.

McRoy, James J. 1982. Content Analysis of Essays from a Cross-National Survey: Implications for Teaching Strategies in Holocaust Studies. Paper Presented at the Annual Convention of the New Jersey Education Association, Atlantic City, NJ, November 11.

Middaugh, Michael F. 2010. *Planning and Assessment in Higher Education: Demonstrating Institutional Effectiveness*. San Francisco: Jossey-Bass.

Mühlhäuser, Regina. 2014. The Historicity of Denial: Sexual Violence against Jewish Women during the War of Annihilation, 1941–1945. In *Lessons and Legacies, Volume XI: Expanding Perspectives on the Holocaust in a Changing World*, ed. Hilary Early and Karl A. Schleunes, 31–58. Evanston, IL: Northwestern University Press.

Pate, Glenn S. 1987. The Holocaust in American Textbooks. In *The Treatment of the Holocaust in Textbooks*, ed. Randolph L. Braham, 231–332. New York: Institute for Holocaust Studies of City University of New York.

Pellegrino, James W., Naomi Chudowsky, and Robert Glaser. 2001. *Knowing What Students Know: The Science and Design of Educational Assessment.* Washington, DC: National Academy Press.

Pine, Lisa. 2004. Gender and the Family. In *Historiography of the Holocaust*, ed. Dan Stone, 364–382. New York: Palgrave Macmillan.

Potter, Michael K., and Erika D.H. Kustra. 2011. The Relationship between Scholarly Teaching and SoTL: Models, Distinctions, and Clarifications. *International Journal for the Scholarship of Teaching and Learning* 5 (1): 1–18.

Romi, Shlomo, and Michal Lev. 2007. Experiential Learning of History Through Youth Journeys to Poland: Israeli Jewish Youth and the Holocaust. *Research in Education* 78: 88–102.

Schneider, Carol Geary. 2016. "A Set of Further Reflections on Improving, Teaching, Learning and Assessment. In *Improving Quality in American Higher Education: Learning Outcomes and Assessment for the 21st Century*, edited by Richard Arum, Josipa Roksa, and Amanda Cook, 299–322. San Francisco: Jossey-Bass.

Schweber, Simone A. 2004. *Making Sense of the Holocaust: Lessons from Classroom Practice.* New York: Teachers College Press.

Shultz, Lynne Hickey, Dennis J. Barr, and Robert L. Selman. 2001. The Value of a Developmental Approach to Evaluating Character Development Programmes: An Outcome Study of Facing History and Ourselves. *Journal of Moral Education* 30 (1): 3–27.

Spalding, Elizabeth, Todd A. Savage, and Jesus Garcia. 2003. The March of Remembrance and Hope: The Effects of a Holocaust Education Experience on Preservice Teachers' Thinking about Diversity. *Multicultural Education* 11 (1): 35–40.

Starratt, Gerene K., Ivana Fredotovic, Sashay Goodletty, and Christopher Starratt. 2017. Holocaust Knowledge and Holocaust Education Experiences Predict Citizenship Values Among US Adults. *Journal of Moral Education* 46 (2): 177–194.

Totten, Samuel. 2001. Holocaust Education in the United States. In *The Holocaust Encyclopedia*, ed. Walter Laquer. New Haven: Yale University Press.

Traver, Amy E. 2016. How Do We Integrate Students' Vocational Goals Into Introduction to Sociology Curricula, and What Are the Effects of Doing So? *Teaching Sociology* 44 (4): 287–295.

UNESCO. 2017. *Education about the Holocaust and Preventing Genocide.* Paris: United Nations Educational, Scientific and Cultural Organization.

Walvoord, Barbara E., ed. 2010. *Assessment Clear and Simple: A Practical Guide for Institutions, Departments, and General Education.* 2nd ed. San Francisco: Jossey-Bass.

Wegner, Gregory. 1998. "What Lessons Are There from the Holocaust for My Generation Today?" Perspectives on Civic Virtue from Middle School Youth. *Journal of Curriculum and Supervision* 13 (2): 167–183.

Wholey, Joseph S., Harry P. Hatry, and Kathryn E. Newcomer, eds. 2010. *Handbook of Practical Program Evaluation*. 3rd ed. San Francisco: Jossey-Bass.

Wolpow, Ray, Natalie N. Johnson, and Kristin N. Wognild. 2002. Designing, Implementing, and Evaluating a Teacher In-Service Program for Enabling 6th–12th Grade Rural Teachers to Integrate Holocaust Studies into their Curricula: A Case Study. *Theory and Research in Social Education* 30 (4): 563–588.

CHAPTER 5

Social Justice Approaches to Mass Atrocity Education

Susan Jacobowitz

For students at a community college or in an introductory course, who may not be familiar with the history of the Holocaust and World War II, a nuanced, comprehensive, and interdisciplinary approach offers the best opportunity for deeper understanding. On the frontispiece of Lawrence Langer's (2006) *Using and Abusing the Holocaust*, he offers the following quote by Giorgio Agamben, an Italian philosopher: "Human beings are human only insofar as they bear witness to the inhuman." As a scholar and the daughter of a Holocaust survivor, I believe that I understand the mission and the urgency of trying our best to bear witness—if such a thing is possible—to the Holocaust. Yet the challenges inherent in both teaching and studying the Holocaust are manifold, and experienced by both student and instructor. They involve the breadth, scope, and depth necessary to study the Holocaust and the emotional toll that the study of the Holocaust can exact. A social justice approach to the teaching of the Holocaust and genocide can provide cohesion and, by offering a path through the quagmire, a kind of opportunity for hope.

S. Jacobowitz (✉)
Department of English, Queensborough Community College, CUNY,
Bayside, NY, USA
e-mail: SJacobowitz@qcc.cuny.edu

A. E. Traver, D. Leshem (eds.), *Humanistic Pedagogy Across the Disciplines*, https://doi.org/10.1007/978-3-319-95025-9_5

This chapter explores my own history and relationship to the teaching of the Holocaust, as well as the establishment of the grant-funded faculty-led yearly colloquium series that has helped to connect the academic departments and disciplines at Queensborough Community College (QCC) to QCC's Kupferberg Holocaust Center (KHC). It explores the need for an interdisciplinary approach to Holocaust humanities education and emphasizes the importance of incorporating social justice approaches to Holocaust and genocide education, providing a strong connection for students to ongoing issues of human rights.

The Interdisciplinary Challenge

The Holocaust is a very difficult subject to teach, as the typical experience of its victims was death. Courses are often built around the testimony of survivors, and often survivors of Auschwitz. But that testimony is by its very nature exceptional: two out of every three European Jews died, and they died quickly. By 1942, Polish Jewry had been destroyed. In contrast, the War Refugee Board wasn't even established in the United States until 1944. What we "know" about the Holocaust—survival at Auschwitz—isn't enough. A recent focus on the mobile killing units that were operating in the East—the *Einsatzgruppen*—and what has been termed "the Holocaust by bullets" has shifted or expanded the emphasis in Holocaust education. Timothy Snyder (2014, 361) writes:

> More Jews were gassed at Auschwitz than at any other site, so its centrality in histories of the Holocaust is fully understandable. But in most respects, Auschwitz was an exception. More Jews were killed with carbon monoxide at other facilities than with hydrogen cyanide (Zyklon B) at Auschwitz. Moreover, in the Holocaust, more Jews were killed by shooting than by either method of gassing. Also, Auschwitz was a large killing facility attached to a large concentration camp. This was unusual … Auschwitz is atypical in another way. It became the major killing site of the Holocaust very late, and so its victims and its survivors do not represent the main Jewish populations that fell victim to extermination. The vast majority of Polish Jews, the largest victim group of the Holocaust, died farther east, in the carbon monoxide facilities or by shooting. The second largest group, the Soviet Jews, was hardly present at Auschwitz at all. Yet, a considerable number of Jews and others survived the concentration camp, which is one reason we are relatively familiar with this death facility.

Real comprehension of the Holocaust lies in understanding how, why, and where people were targeted and put to death. For students, studying the Holocaust from a realistic perspective can feel like the equivalent of watching an action film in which, instead of the protagonist surviving having thousands of bullets shot at him by villains while he runs in a serpentine pattern, he takes a bullet to the head and collapses—dead—within the first five minutes of the film.[1]

As a result, studying the Holocaust must incorporate a strong focus on history even when a course focuses, for example, on the literature of the Holocaust. To teach the Holocaust—whether in a Social Science, English, or History course—an instructor needs to cover a lot of ground. As Michael Berenbaum (2004, 120–121) notes, Raul Hilberg suggested that there were six stages to the destruction of the European Jews: (1) definition, (2) expropriation, (3) concentration, (4) deportation, (5) mobile killing units, and (6) death camps. All of these should be explained and understood. In addition, there is a list of "essential antecedents" that need to be addressed when teaching about this genocide: "the origin of the Jews, the religious roots of antisemitism, the three forms of antisemitism—religious, political, and racial—the Armenian genocide, extreme nationalism, industrialization, social Darwinism, totalitarianism" (120–121). Again, Timothy Snyder offers insight (2014, 368): "First, the history of the Holocaust must include traditional subjects of study as geography, military history, diplomatic history, political economy, and the prewar history of Jewish and non-Jewish Eastern European societies. The study of the Holocaust has veered, following the profession of history generally, toward culture, literature, and memory. These are all valuable approaches from which I have learned. But they can all be enriched and improved upon by a traditional historical grounding."

The challenge, then, is to create an *interdisciplinary* Holocaust education program. The Berman Center (2006, 4) outlines how they "include appropriate content that does justice to historical facts and perspectives; create an atmosphere that is responsive to readiness and emotional sensitivities of the students; create a framework both in history and in the personal connection to historical figures and their perspectives; work across the curriculum and integrates diverse disciplines; [and] use powerful personal artifacts and historical materials." In terms of best practices, the Center suggests that educators use powerful teaching vehicles and materials to engage students using an approach that focuses "not only on historical fact but also poetry, art, music, theology, psychology, literature, and other disciplines" (8).

The need for and strengths of this interdisciplinary approach are evidenced in the relationship between Holocaust literature and the discipline of history. To understand Holocaust literature, students need to understand the complicated chronology and complex history of the Holocaust. Lawrence Langer (2006, 4) writes, "It … require[s] some context because, unlike most other literature, it draws on experiences so foreign to the ordinary reader that one might be inclined to mistake its vision for an alien world of fantasy … Holocaust literature is a literature of the moment, seeking vainly to unite with the stream of time." Yet, and in tandem, literature should also be central to the study of the history of the Holocaust or any genocide, so that the voices and experiences of survivors are present and a strong feature.

This aspect of witnessing is very important. Omer Bartov (2014, 21) focuses on the similarities between genocides and the importance of the testimony of survivors when he writes, "Since the goal of genocide is to destroy groups as such, it behooves the historian to rescue these groups from oblivion, even if only in history and memory. And for that, we must listen to the survivors of genocide, not least because invariably they demand to be heard; we must write down their stories and integrate them into the historical picture. We should never again write the history of genocide with the victims left out." Robert P. Welker (1996, 104) echoes Bartov's argument, addressing the need, when teaching the Holocaust, to present "a richly textured account": "[W]e must provide personal stories behind the overwhelming statistics, stories which in their very narrative sweep can help students make personal connections and discover life courses that indicate how human decisions impact upon the present and the future. Such stories provide moral spaces that allow for a recognition of personal circumstance and the opportunity for student description, reflection, and explanation. Again, it must be said that the collision with horror itself yields neither understanding nor kindness nor even the capacity for outrage." In other words, it isn't enough to shock students with what happened in the past—students have to be provided with approaches that enable them to connect with and process what they are learning.

A richly textured account mandates an interdisciplinary approach. In their essay "Teaching the Holocaust: The Case for an Interdisciplinary Approach," Jacqueline Berke and Ann L. Saltzmann (1996, 131) write:

> By definition, the study of the Holocaust is—and must be—interdisciplinary, for each discipline in and of itself allows us to understand only one

> aspect of the Holocaust: history tells us what happened; psychology probes the psyches of those involved: perpetrators, victims, survivors, rescuers, bystanders (what made them behave as they did?); literature and the arts shape what happened in the Holocaust into an aesthetic form which enables us to enter events imaginatively and vicariously, to feel them 'on the pulse' as Coleridge put it; philosophy and theology raise questions about morality and ethics, the nature of good and evil and the possibilities of leading a meaningful life in the post-Holocaust world … Only in combination do the disciplines provide the many perspectives required for understanding at any depth or breadth. Although the advantages of an interdisciplinary approach seem self-evident, there appear to be relatively few courses built around multiple perspectives.

Elizabeth R. Baer (2004) illustrates how this interdisciplinary approach might unfold in the classroom. Given decades of experience teaching about the Holocaust in an interdisciplinary humanities context, she cites the following objectives in her course syllabus: "acquaint the students with the historical background of the Nazi Holocaust; introduce and discuss the literary and artistic response to the Holocaust; interrogate the issues of memory and memorialization as they relate to the Holocaust; study changing perspectives and attitudes towards the Holocaust; and bring awareness of how the Holocaust bears on contemporary events and thought" (195). This last item—bringing awareness of how the Holocaust bears on contemporary events and thoughts—is at the nexus of interdisciplinary and social justice approaches. The theory behind a social justice focus when teaching the Holocaust and genocide has to do with enabling students to make the strongest and most powerful connections possible by relating what they study and learn to their own societies, communities, families, and lives.

Social Justice Approaches

William R. Fernekes and Samuel Totten (2004, 249–250) address the connection between the Holocaust and social justice in their essay "Human Rights, Genocide and Social Responsibility," writing: "First, genocide (often referred to as 'the crime of crimes') is a human rights violation. Indeed, it is one of the worse violations in the long list of wrongs that governments and others perpetrate. Second, genocide does not develop in a vacuum. Genocide is typically preceded by a host of human rights violations against targeted groups, ranging from deprivation of free speech to discrimination of all types, and from torture to extrajudicial executions."

When teaching the Holocaust, it is important to situate it within the wider context of genocide. Genocide is not a mysterious aberration or one-time event, and there is never the feeling that the threat of genocide has passed. Fernekes and Totten (2004, 250) write: "[D]espite the creation of the Universal Declaration of Human Rights and the United Nations Convention on the Prevention and Punishment of Genocide in 1948, state-sponsored violence of genocidal proportions has remained constant over the years. To more effectively address the prevention of genocide, we believe that scholars, policymakers, and activists need to focus on how the deprivation of human rights often serve as the catalyst for genocide."

This connection to genocide also helps to "establish clear linkages to core human rights concepts and themes" (Fernekes and Totten 2004, 270). In fact, the Holocaust is an ultimate example of widespread deprivation of human rights. To put the focus on connections to ongoing violations of human rights gives students tools to help them to handle the desolation involved in studying the Holocaust. There is the possibility of linking to the present, and to the future. There is hope. Write Fernenkes and Totten (2004, 270–271):

> When all is said and done, the key to education about human rights and genocide is to educate citizens to care about the deprivation of human rights of others and to help them develop the means and methods to act upon their concerns ... To focus, however, solely on human rights violations and not genocide or, conversely, on genocide but not the human rights violations that lead up to and can and often do culminate in genocide, is counterproductive. In order for the world community to combat both phenomena effectively, an effort must be made to prepare individuals—both the average citizen as well as policymakers and activists—to recognize the significance of defending human rights, and how the erosion of human rights' guarantees often serves as a precursor to genocide. An integrated approach to the study of human rights and genocide can promote citizen action to enforce human rights standards and to take proactive steps supporting genocide intervention and prevention.

One of the goals of Holocaust education involves the ideal of enlightened citizenship. These links provide hope for instructors as well, who also plunge into the void when teaching the Holocaust and genocide (Bassman 1996).

In "Education and Crisis, or the Vicissitudes of Teaching," Shoshana Felman (1992, 53) writes: "In the era of the Holocaust, of Hiroshima, of Vietnam—in the age of testimony—teaching, I would venture to suggest, must in turn *testify*, make something *happen*, and not just transmit a passive knowledge, pass on information that is preconceived, substantified, believed to be known in advance, misguidedly believed, that is, to be (exclusively) a *given*." That "something" that needs to happen, I believe, has to do with both making interdisciplinary connections to inform a more complex and nuanced understanding of the Holocaust, genocide, and human rights *and* applying that understanding in and to action. Teaching the Holocaust is different from teaching other subjects. Students are striving not only to learn the content—what happened in the past—but also to connect the past to the present and the present to the future. They need to meet the challenge of confronting themselves and their own societies, and relating what they can of their own experience to what they are learning. The study of the Holocaust involves constant examination and interrogation of the self and society, to engage with the responsibility for a shared future it is our responsibility to work to create.

Personal Reflections on the Need for Interdisciplinary and Social Justice Approaches to Mass Atrocity Education

Before I began my doctoral studies, I earned an M.F.A. degree in English and Creative Writing. My thesis, "Far From Childhood: A Holocaust Memoir," focused on what I had been able to find out about my father's experiences as a child during the Holocaust, and my own recollection of growing up in a survivor family.[2] My father never wanted to speak about his experiences when I was growing up, and so I knew very little—part of "Far from Childhood" is the story of how I struggled to get the story, and what it came to represent and mean to me in terms of my own identity and heritage. My father wanted his children to be burdened as little as possible by the past, and to embrace all of the opportunities and advantages of blending in with other American children.

When I was a doctoral candidate in English and American Literature at Brandeis University in the 1990s, I wanted to continue to learn about the Holocaust and so I spent a year completing coursework in the Department of Near Eastern and Judaic Studies, focusing on Eastern European Jewish history, the Holocaust, and Holocaust and Jewish literature. I had the good fortune to work with Dr. Antony Polonsky, the Albert Abramson Professor of Holocaust Studies—a joint position at Brandeis University and the United States Holocaust Memorial Museum (USHMM)—and the author of many historical works on the Holocaust, and an expert on Polish Jewish history. In 2014, he was named Chief Historian of the new POLIN Museum of the History of Polish Jews in Warsaw, Poland, on the site of the former Warsaw Ghetto.

I remember Dr. Polonsky giving me advice once and saying, "You must, of course, do something other than Holocaust work." I didn't ask questions at the time. I felt I understood what he was saying. I knew that I wouldn't move forward as strictly a Holocaust scholar because of the language challenge. I had studied German, Hebrew, and Yiddish but, as Holocaust scholar Timothy Snyder (2014, 468) points out, the study of multiple foreign languages is key. To specialize in the history of my father's area, I would have needed to also attain proficiency in Polish, Hungarian, Czech, Ukrainian, Russian, and—arguably—Romanian. It is often said that those who have the languages lack the academic training, and those who have the academic training lack the languages.

And I knew that Dr. Polonsky was also referring to the emotional toll it would take to only do Holocaust work. Over the years I have thought about authors such as Terence des Pres and Iris Chang. Terence des Pres was one of the first critics to write about Holocaust literature; Iris Chang was a journalist who published a seminal book about the rape of Nanking. Both died by their own hand. While I am certain that there were multiple factors beyond the focus of their writing that contributed to their suicides, I do feel there is reason to be cautious when one studies and teaches the Holocaust or genocide. As an example, I remember a student coming to class once, early, with a swollen face and red-rimmed eyes. Alarmed, I asked her what was the matter. "It's that book!" she replied. We were working our way through Sara Nomberg-Przytyk's (1985) memoir *Auschwitz: True Tales from a Grotesque Land*. Since that experience, I have tried to always warn students when we begin a Holocaust unit or a Holocaust literature course that they may find themselves feeling very upset, even depressed, or experience nightmares, broken sleep, or bouts of weeping. I think those are some of the reasons why some of us who do Holocaust work within our teaching or research choose not to focus only or exclusively on the Holocaust, and I think that is how I understood the warning that Dr. Polonsky was trying to communicate when I was in graduate school.

The Holocaust work that I would do would be different, coming from an English and humanities background, and so it has been—I have continued with my creative writing and research in Germany and Eastern Europe, to better explore and understand my father's story and what happened to the small community of Carpathian Jews who were almost completely wiped out. My scholarship has focused on the creative work of sons and daughters of Holocaust survivors—second-generation experience—with a focus on issues of trauma and its inheritance across the generations and conflicts/challenges of Jewish identity. I have continued with professional development through multiple opportunities available to faculty, participating in The Jack & Anita Hess Faculty Seminar, "Literature and the Holocaust," led by David Roskies and Sara Horowitz, at the USHMM in Washington, DC, in January 2007; The Holocaust Scholarship Academic Seminar, in association with the Israel Ministry of Foreign Affairs; The United Nations Academic Impact (AI) Programme and the Holocaust and United Nations Outreach Programme, at the International School for Holocaust Studies at Yad Vashem in Jerusalem, in December 2012; and the Curt C. and Else Silberman Seminar for Faculty, "Teaching the Holocaust: Causes, Course, Consequences," with Dr. Peter Hayes, at the Jack, Joseph and Morton Mandel Center for Advanced Holocaust Studies at the USHMM in 2015. I have focused on finding more and better ways to connect the study of the Holocaust to contemporary issues and to integrate it into a strong interdisciplinary, humanities curriculum.

The 2013–2014 NEH/KHC Colloquium Series, "The Holocaust in a Global Context: Connections Across the Community College"

I began teaching at QCC in 2000. QCC is located in the Borough of Queens, the most diverse county in the United States, and is one of seven public, open-admissions two-year colleges in the City University of New York (CUNY) system—the largest urban public college system in the nation. As detailed on QCC's website, our student population comprises nearly equal populations of African Americans, Asians, Caucasians, and Latinos, representing 139 nations of birth and 87 languages. Many of our students are immigrants or the children of immigrants—many are the first in their families to earn college degrees. Very few of my students are Jewish or have any kind of personal connection to the Holocaust. Many have grown up in countries where there is no mandated Holocaust education.

At QCC, I teach a unit on Holocaust literature in my introduction to literature classes for beginning students. Consistent with the research reviewed in this chapter, the challenge has always been to provide the context and connections necessary to make an event that happened so many years ago, on a different continent, involving people who are "other," relevant in the twenty-first century. To accomplish this, I do three things. First, I provide a range of materials; students watch films, view archival footage, review primary source documents and maps, and read letters, diary excerpts, memoirs, poetry, and short stories. They also learn about the lives of the people whose work they are reading and the lives of other survivors. For example, I often share parts of my father's story, or they hear a presentation by a volunteer at the Center. Second, I relate the struggles of that time period to social justice issues and challenges today. There are many connections that my students make—many know what it is like to have to escape war or persecution, to lose citizenship and become a refugee, to deal with discrimination or being targeted because of race, sexual orientation, or religion. Third, I involve them in a research project that makes use of digital archives at two Holocaust museums—the USHMM and Yad Vashem—and oral history interviews with local survivors that are available at the KHC. By working with these archival collections, students interact directly with objects and testimony from the past and do original research and creative writing to generate work that is personal and immediate. As they explore objects that have been excavated or donated only recently to these museums, they realize that survivors are passing away, that all of the stories have not been told, and that they themselves have become a part of this perpetuation.

In addition to teaching introduction to literature courses at QCC, I was able to revive a Holocaust literature course, which hadn't been taught for many years, by working with the curriculum committee of my department and the college to institutionalize the course as a permanent upper-division special topics elective course. I recruited other faculty members who said they were willing to teach the course so that I wouldn't have to teach it every semester. I also began working with the KHC's director at the time, Dr. Arthur Flug, to strengthen the connections between the Center and the academic departments and students at QCC.

In fact, as a result of this work, I was invited to be part of a team that wrote a successful grant application for the KHC that helped to provide more Holocaust programming and educational opportunities at QCC. In 2010, the National Endowment for the Humanities chose six community colleges with a focus on creating national demonstration models of effective incorporation of campus-based cultural resources into the humanities curriculum. With NEH matching support of $500,000, the KHC raised $1,000,000 to endow a program that generates $50,000 each year to support a yearlong series of faculty-coordinated events that are both open to the public and available for incorporation into the syllabi of classes across the campus.

While I was at Yad Vashem, participating in a conference organized by the United Nations that brought together Holocaust scholars and academics from around the world, I realized that there is a huge international focus on Holocaust education even in countries that were not directly involved—there were several scholars from African nations who were hoping to create and promote Holocaust education programs. Through interaction with the representatives of the United Nations education division, I came to understand that there is a conviction that genocide will continue to be a problem going forward, as a result of war and conflict and because of the continuing vulnerability of ethnic and religious minorities. There is an expectation that factors such as climate change will contribute to more scarcity of resources, more struggles, and the creation of more displacement. All of these pressures contribute to the likelihood of ethnic violence and genocide. Historian Yehuda Bauer (2001, 2–3) writes:

> Let me state my biases. I think that the planned total murder of a people was an unprecedented catastrophe in human civilization. It happened because it could happen; if it could not have happened, it would not have done so. And because it happened once, it can happen again. Any historical event is a possibility before it becomes a fact, but when it becomes a fact, it also serves as a possible precedent. And although no event will ever be repeated exactly, it will, if it is followed by similar events, become the first in a line of analogous happenings. The Holocaust can be a precedent, or it can become a warning. My bias is, in a sense, political: I believe we ought to do everything in our power to make sure it is a warning, not a precedent.

Holocaust education involves understanding that it can definitely happen again, and that the goal must always be working toward anything that will prevent it.

It was at Yad Vashem that I began to put together the proposal to be the faculty coordinator of the 2013–2014 NEH/KHC Colloquium Series, "The Holocaust in a Global Context: Connections Across the Community College." I wanted the series to be interdisciplinary—open to anyone and everyone on campus who wished to participate, and utilizing speakers from various disciplines from both our faculty and the outside—and I wanted to encourage faculty and student participation by enlisting faculty within my own department, both adjunct and full-time, to create units that could be part of the required English classes that every student on campus takes: Introduction to Composition and Introduction to Literature. Toward this end, I formed a faculty working group. Instructors were encouraged to be creative and to work with their own strengths, instincts, and interests to create small units that would provide connections to the colloquia, without students having to be in designated Holocaust courses. The faculty working group met during the fall to design their units, and participants taught their units in the spring. Fourteen English faculty participated, receiving funding and support to work on creating these units for their introductory courses. Some are still being taught.

I also wanted the colloquia to reflect a social justice perspective. As in my classes and with my teaching, I wanted students to be able to make connections between the persecution of the past and ongoing struggles in the present. One of the most difficult things about studying the Holocaust is that we are too late. We are too late to save a single person or change the fate of even one victim. I remember attending a conference for survivors and children of survivors in the 1980s. Holocaust memorials and museums were going up everywhere—I believe, at last count, there were 87 in the United States alone. One survivor told me, "I wish they would stop raising money for museums. Take that money and use it to save one mother and one child who are suffering somewhere now."

I have often felt that almost everything bad that is happening in the world today can be traced back to or related to something bad that was happening during the Third Reich: discrimination, prejudice, racism, persecution, occupation, murder. When something is happening during our own time or within our own society, at least we have the possibility of engaging and making a difference. Thus, I planned a special session entitled "Being 'Other' in America Today" and asked one of my colleagues in the English Department, Dr. Trikartikaningsih Byas, to facilitate. This event featured speakers including Dr. Rose-Marie Äikäs, Professor of Criminal Justice at QCC, who discussed the prison population today and issues of legal justice in America; Ms. Jessica Rogers, a lecturer in the English Department at QCC at the time who was knowledgeable about New York's controversial "stop-and-frisk" policy; Mr. Jordan Schneider, a lecturer in the English Department at QCC who discussed class, race, and issues in public higher education; New York City Councilman Daniel Dromm, who spoke on behalf of the challenges facing the Lesbian, Gay, Bisexual, Trans and Queer (LGBTQ) community, particularly in New York City; and Dr. Genny Beemyn, director of the Stonewall Center at the University of Massachusetts at Amherst, who had published and spoken extensively on the experiences and needs of trans people, particularly the lives of gender-nonconforming students. I was hoping that the students attending would make strong connections between prejudice and discrimination then and the struggle against prejudice and discrimination now—an important goal of incorporating a social justice approach to Holocaust education. Relatedly, my students currently are reflecting on comparisons between what is happening in the United States now, during the Trump Administration, and the rise of Adolf Hitler and the Nazi Party in Germany in the 1930s, particularly as it pertains to rhetoric and the targeting of groups and individuals. In reaction to this learning, one of my students made the comment, "I want to figure out how they did it then, so that I can maybe work to keep similar things from happening now."

Course-Based Examples of Interdisciplinary and Social Justice Approaches to Mass Atrocity Education at QCC

To return to the ideas expressed by William R. Fernekes and Samuel Totten (2004), genocide is a human rights violation (the "crime of crimes"), does not develop in a vacuum, and is typically preceded by a host of human rights violations against targeted groups. This makes it all the more urgent to incorporate a focus on human rights in humanities education and to establish clear linkages—across the disciplines—to core human rights concepts and themes when teaching about the Holocaust and other genocides.

Multiple chapters in this volume offer examples of interdisciplinary and social justice approaches to mass atrocity education at QCC. Some of these chapters foreground interdisciplinary perspectives and partnerships in the creation of units and assignments that connected students to the NEH/KHC Colloquium Series. In Chap. 6, Aalai details how the integration of textual perspectives from psychology *and* sociology helped her to counter many of the challenges inherent in teaching the Holocaust. In Chap. 8, Atik, Geismar, and Miller describe their effort to bridge the gap between Holocaust history and students' daily lives by linking an English literature course, a dance choreography course, and an English Composition course. In Chap. 10, Carroll outlines an Academic Service Learning (ASL) project that wove together the goals/needs of Education 101 students and English Language Learners enrolled in an advanced reading class.

Additional chapters reveal how faculty from very different courses within different academic departments engaged a social justice approach in their alignment with the NEH/KHC Colloquium Series. In Chap. 7, Äikäs describes how her criminology students drew on genocide, mass incarceration, and restorative justice frameworks to explore testimonials by formerly incarcerated women in New York City. In Chap. 11, Dahlke discusses his choral music students' ASL partnership with the Corona Youth Music Project (CYMP), a non-profit organization that offers music instruction and performance opportunities to children from an underserved neighborhood in Queens, New York. In Chap. 13, Emanuele details a project that required English students' close reading of some of the vilest hate texts ever written, their assessment of these texts for patterns in language and image composition, and their creative efforts to reframe them to promote tolerance and understanding. In Chap. 14, Ferrari-Bridgers outlines her efforts to engage—and empower—public speaking students through the study of North American Indigenous Peoples' histories and lives. Finally, in Chap. 10, Sexton reveals how efforts to globalize his English Composition course encouraged his students to see themselves as active participants in their local communities and the world. The range illustrated by these chapters and projects is a testament to how far this faculty has come in a relatively short period of time with regard to integrating quality Holocaust and mass atrocity education into the humanities curriculum at QCC.

Appendix: 2013–2014 NEH/KHC Colloquium Series, "The Holocaust in a Global Context: Connections Across the Community College"

Digital Presentation of "The Soap Myth," followed by a Q&A with playwright Jeff Cohen, 09/26/13

The horrific possibility that the Nazis turned Jews into soap is the catalyst for "The Soap Myth," a play by Jeff Cohen. Cohen's lead characters, a survivor and a young investigative journalist, go on a collision course to ascertain how much fact is needed for something not to be fiction. See www.TheSoapMyth.com.

Jeff Cohen is an American theater director, playwright, and producer. His play, "The Soap Myth," was produced by the National Jewish Theater Foundation at the Roundabout Theater Company's Steinberg Theater Center in the Spring of 2012. The production, directed by Arnold Mittelman, featured Andi Potamkin, Greg Mullavey, Dee Pelletier, and Donald Corren. That production caught the attention of prominent Holocaust scholar, Michael Berenbaum, who, in an editorial in the *Jewish Forward* (among other places), has championed the play as authentically capturing the tension between Holocaust survivors and Holocaust historians, and promoting a detente between the two groups.

"Narratives of Belated Experience: Musical Testimony from the Holocaust," Dr. Joseph Toltz, Lecturer and Tutor, Sydney Conservatorium of Music and University of Western Sydney, 11/6/13

Music has featured as a discourse in Holocaust narrative and has served a commemorative function for the Jewish community, a pedagogical tool in performance, a feature of testimony, and a complement of historical narrative. This presentation drew on three unique collections of musical testimony from survivors from distinct periods.

Dr. Joseph Toltz is Research Associate and Lecturer at the Sydney Conservatorium of Music. His specialty is musical memory and recall in Jewish Holocaust survivors. Toltz has published in *Holocaust Studies: A Journal of Culture and History*, as well as book chapters and articles on the electronic group Kraftwerk, the children's opera Brundibar, and the Jewish approach to illness. In 2011, Toltz was a Barbara and Richard Rosenberg Fellow of the Center for Advanced Holocaust Studies of the USHMM, and his presentation was co-funded by the Campus Outreach Lecture Program of the USHMM's Center for Advanced Holocaust Studies, supported by the generosity of the Jerome A. Yavitz Charitable Foundation, Inc., and Arlyn S. and Stephen H. Cypen. Formerly a Cantor for 13 years, Toltz continues to work as a professional musician.

"Disabilities and the Holocaust: A History Revealed," Dr. Simi Linton and Christian von Tippelskirch, coordinated by Dr. Amy Traver, Sociology, QCC, 11/20/13

This one-hour lecture on disability and the Holocaust was followed by a viewing of the documentary *Liebe Perla*, which introduces the history of brutality toward and murder of people with disabilities in Nazi Germany. There was also an audience Q&A with Dr. Linton and Mr. von Tippelskirch.

Simi Linton has been at the forefront of disability studies since its early days. While on the faculty at Hunter College, she wrote the groundbreaking study of this field, *Claiming Disability: Knowledge and Identity* (New York University Press, 1998). Linton was a CUNY faculty member from 1985 to 1998. She was awarded a Mary E. Switzer Distinguished Fellowship by the US Department of Education's National Institute on Disability and Rehabilitation Research, and has been the Co-Director of the University Seminar in Disability Studies at Columbia University since 2003.

Christian von Tippelskirch is a US filmmaker originally from Germany, where he studied Psychology and Sociology in the 1970s. He was an active member of the movement against the institutionalization of people with psychiatric diagnoses that emerged in Germany in response to the treatment of disabled people before, during, and after the Holocaust

Simi and Christian are the Directors and Producers of the documentary film, *Invitation to Dance.*

"The Body, Disabilities and the Holocaust," Dr. Sarah Chinn, coordinated by Dr. Amy Traver, Sociology, QCC, 12/4/13

This lecture by Dr. Sarah Chinn, Associate Professor of English at Hunter College and author of *Technology and the Logic of American Racism: A Cultural History of the Body as Evidence* (Continuum, 2000), focused on the historical intersections of legal, medical, and racial discourses in the United States.

"Being 'Other' in America Today," coordinated by Dr. Trikartikaningsih Byas, English, QCC, 2/19/14

This event featured speakers who discussed the prison population and issues of legal justice in America. These speakers included Dr. Rose-Marie Äikäs, professor of Criminal Justice at QCC; Ms. Jessica Rogers, a lecturer in the English Department at QCC; Mr. Jordan Schneider, a lecturer in the English Department at QCC; New York City Councilman Daniel Dromm; and Dr. Genny Beemyn, director of the Stonewall Center at the University of Massachusetts at Amherst.

"Jewish Community Cookbooks," Dr. Megan Elias, Department of History, QCC, 3/5/14

Although there were a few very well-known cookbooks for Jewish families published before the World War II in America, the postwar period saw a tremendous increase in the numbers of this genre. In particular, Jewish groups all over America published community cookbooks, usually for the purpose of fundraising. These books represent a new pride in identity that was intimately tied to the very public nature of Jewish suffering during the Holocaust. This presentation, which drew on the important collection of Jewish Community Cookbooks at the Dorot Division of the New York Public Library, sought to put these cookbooks into the context of postwar American culture and an emerging sense of global citizenship.

"Mentally Ill People as Unfit for Society," Dr. Christian Perring, Department of Philosophy and Religious Studies, Dowling College, 4/2/14

This lecture examined the concept of unfitness in 1930s Germany that led to the Nazi persecution of people with mental illness and its relation to eugenic movements in other parts of Europe and the United States.

"Developing Cultural Sensitivity and Awareness," Ms. Lorraine Cupelli, Department of Nursing, QCC, 4/23/14

This seminar presentation was aimed at nursing students and those interested in health fields. It focused on developing cultural sensitivity and awareness and bridging cultural gaps to foster improved health outcomes.

Topics included pursuing the impact of the Holocaust on survivors and spotlighting cultural beliefs as they relate to decisions regarding health, prevention of illness, treatment of illness, and end-of-life issues.

Notes

1. I remember my father telling me once that it is impossible to make realistic films about the Holocaust because after five minutes of watching the way it really was, people wouldn't be able to take any more.
2. My father was from a small town in Subcarpathian Ruthenia that was part of Czechoslovakia in 1929 when he was born. The town came under Hungarian control in 1938, when Hitler restored to Hungary lands that had been taken away after World War I. It was liberated by the Red Army in 1944 and became part of the Soviet Union; now it is part of an independent Ukraine. My father and his family were deported to Auschwitz during the Hungarian Deportations of 1944, when he was 15. Only he and his father survived—his mother and four younger siblings were murdered at Auschwitz.

References

Baer, Elizabeth R. 2004. 'The Terribleness Runs Through You:' An Evolving Paradigm of Holocaust Pedogogy. In *Teaching the Shoah in the Twenty-First Century: Topics and Topographies*, Symposium Series, Volume 78, edited by Simon P. Sibelman, 193–206. Lewiston, Queenston, Lampeter: The Edwin Mellen Press.

Bartov, Omer. 2014. Genocide and the Holocaust: Arguments over History and Politics. In *Lessons and Legacies XI: The Place of the Holocaust in a Changing World*, ed. Theodore Zev Weiss and Hilary Earl, 5–30. Evanston, IL: Northwestern University Press.

Bassman, Michael F. 1996/2001. Teaching the Holocaust and Making It Relevant for Non-Jewish Students. In *New Perspectives on the Holocaust: A Guide for Teachers and Scholars*, ed. Rochelle L. Millen, 212–220. New York: New York University Press.

Bauer, Yehuda. 2001. *Rethinking the Holocaust*. New Haven: Yale University Press.

Berenbaum, Michael. 2004. Case Studies of Genocide Perpetrated in the Twentieth Century, Case Study 3: The Holocaust. In *Teaching About Genocide: Issues, Approaches, and Resources*, ed. Samuel Totten, 119–132. Greenwich, CT: Information Age Publishing.

Berke, Jacqueline, and Ann L. Saltzman, eds. 1996. Teaching the Holocaust: The Case for an Interdisciplinary Approach. In *New Perspectives on the Holocaust: A*

Guide for Teachers and Scholars. Rochelle L. Millen (Ed.), 131–140. New York: New York University Press.

Best Practices in Holocaust Education. 2006. Report to The San Francisco Jewish Community Endowment Fund, submitted by The Berman Center for Research & Evaluation in Jewish Education. Leora W. Isaacs, Ph.D., Director.

Felman, Shoshana. 1992. Education and Crisis, Or the Vicissitudes of Teaching. In *Testimony: Crises of Witnessing in Literature, Psychoanalysis, and History*, ed. Shoshana Felman and Dori Laub, 1–56. New York: Routledge.

Fernekes, William R., and Samuel Totten. 2004. Human Rights, Genocide and Social Responsibility. In *Teaching About Genocide: Issues, Approaches, and Resources*, ed. Samuel Totten, 249–274. Greenwich, CT: Information Age Publishing.

Langer, Lawrence. 2006. *Using and Abusing the Holocaust*. Bloomington, IN: Indiana University Press.

Nomberg-Przytyk, Sara. 1985. *Auschwitz: True Tales from a Grotesque Land*. Ed. Eli Pfefferkorn and David H. Hirsch and Trans. Roslyn Hirsch. Chapel Hill: The University of North Carolina Press.

Snyder, Timothy. 2014. Holocaust History: An Agenda for Renewal. In *Lessons and Legacies XI: Expanding Perspectives on the Holocaust in a Changing World*, ed. Theodore Zev Weiss and Hilary Earl, 357–368. Evanston, IL: Northwestern University Press.

Totten, Samuel. 2004. *Teaching About Genocide: Issues, Approaches, and Resources*. Greenwich, CT: Information Age Publishing.

Welker, Robert P. 1996. Searching for the Educational Imperative in Holocaust Curricula. In *New Perspectives on the Holocaust: A Guide for Teachers and Scholars*, ed. Rochelle L. Millen, 99–121. New York: New York University Press.

PART II

Approaches to Mass Atrocity Education in the Community College Context: Course-Based Examples

CHAPTER 6

Students Reflect on the Intersection of Sex, Gender, and Genocide from a Social-Psychological Perspective

Azadeh Aalai

Serving as faculty for Queensborough Community College (QCC), a community college in one of the country's most diverse counties, comes with its challenges. As a minority-serving community college, there is a great range of diversity on our campus. As such, the experiences of our students are wide in scope, and the academic backgrounds they have been exposed to before enrolling in our college are similarly diverse. Thus, students come into class with their own preconceived notions of the Holocaust—or, in many cases, minimal or no knowledge of this atrocity unless there is a specific connection in their family backgrounds.

Perhaps, then, it is not surprising to find that scholars have identified that even at the college level, with few exceptions, textbooks that cover the Holocaust are not adequate in recognizing the full range of issues regarding the genocide (Medoff 1996). Similarly, one of the overarching goals that I have when presenting the Holocaust to students is to identify the

A. Aalai (✉)
Department of Social Sciences, Queensborough Community College, CUNY, Bayside, NY, USA
e-mail: AAalai@qcc.cuny.edu

A. E. Traver, D. Leshem (eds.), *Humanistic Pedagogy Across the Disciplines*, https://doi.org/10.1007/978-3-319-95025-9_6

complexities of this genocide, and to present students with different textual or theoretical perspectives with which to understand and analyze it. One of the benefits of teaching this topic in higher education is that students have the emotional maturity and academic competence to handle the complexity of the topic. Indeed, "as students mature, they can participate in increasingly complex examination of the event, with such examinations necessarily including the consideration of topics that are emotionally and intellectually challenging" (Lindquist 2006, 220).

Understanding the Holocaust from a Social-Psychological Perspective

Despite our students' great potential, it remains, of course, even within higher education, a challenge to get them to engage the full scope and breadth of the Holocaust. In my case, the topic comes up within the context of a social psychology course (200-level), so it is discussed within the larger unit of aggression, mass violence, warfare, and genocide. The psychology of evil is the overarching theme that integrates concepts from earlier in the semester to the specifics of the Holocaust. Fusing the topic with notions of evil is a common tactic for introducing the Holocaust to students. For instance, "studying the Shoah forces students to consider what it means to be human and humane by examining the full continuum of individual behavior, from *ultimate evil* to *ultimate good*" (Lindquist 2011, 26–27). This is consistent with the theoretical framework within social psychology that I use to present the Holocaust to my students.

While students are engaged and participatory at the start of this unit, they oftentimes come into the discussion with a very simplistic notion of the Holocaust—Hitler was the architect, the typical student may state, and thus he was the force of evil behind the genocide. Or they understand the atrocity in the shadows of the Second World War. My goal is to get students to apply concepts from our social psychology course that we have covered earlier in the semester—stereotypes, prejudices, and discrimination; the power of the social situation; group behaviors such as destructive conformity and obedience; media influences; bystander effects; and the basics of aggression and violence—to understanding how an atrocity such as the Holocaust could occur. Of course, one cannot blame students for having a simplistic notion of the atrocity prior to exposure in an academic context. Regarding the challenge of pedagogical approaches to this topic, scholars identify that "(t)he Holocaust's scale … is beyond most people's cognitive or affective ability to comprehend" (Lindquist 2006, 215).

Thus, one of the goals of educators should be to convey to students the vast scope of the atrocities committed during this period while also fusing it with relatable theoretical concepts relevant to the course so that students can begin to digest the topic in a manageable way.

The lectures for this topic happen near the end of the semester, so that students have acquired and are able to apply all of the relevant earlier theories and topics of the semester to the Holocaust. The completion of this unit is bookended by a peace building and conflict resolution discussion (pending time before the end of the semester).

Studying the Holocaust Through a Sex/Gender Lens

In the fall of 2015, as I approached how I would introduce the topic of the Holocaust to my social psychology students, I had the additional variables of sex and gender to consider in regard to their intersection with mass violence and genocide. This was the first time that I introduced the topic of the Holocaust from a gender perspective to my class, and I was hopeful that the addition of this theoretical perspective would add a layer of richness and complexity to student engagement with the Shoah. The catalyst for engaging this theoretical framework was that, in this particular academic year, my class would be participating in a larger National Endowment for the Humanities (NEH) Colloquium Series hosted by QCC's Kupferberg Holocaust Center (KHC). The theme of "Gender, Mass Violence, and Genocide" was explored through eight specific events spanning the 2015–2016 academic school year. I participated in and facilitated a panel discussion, titled "Gendered Experiences in, and Memories of, the Nazi Holocaust," that semester, which students in my course were required to attend. My part of the panel discussion explored how Jewish men and women were often targeted and victimized in distinct ways based on traditional notions of sex and gender within Nazi Germany and occupied territories. Two additional panelists, Dr. Rochelle G. Saidel of the Remember the Women Institute and Dr. Marianne Hirsch of Columbia University, reflected on their specific research regarding the intersection of gender and genocide. After each of us gave our talks, there was a question and answer session where panelists could interact with the audience, which I facilitated.

In addition to being required to attend the event, my students were strongly encouraged to attend at least one other event of the four events being offered that semester, where topics such as gender and the future of genocide studies, human rights and genocidal rape, and gender socialization before and during wartime and genocide were explored. We covered sex, gender, and gender socialization in class before the required event I was facilitating took place so that students would already have a basic theoretical foundation regarding sex and gender before the panel discussion. There was an accompanying paper assignment based on content from my panel event that students were asked to complete. Specifically, in a four-page response paper, students were asked to reflect on the particular ways that gender and genocide intersect, using examples from the Holocaust as applicable. Additionally, students were instructed to explore the role that language played in fusing genocidal policies with notions of masculinity and femininity, and how common tactics used by the Nazi regime (i.e., propaganda, dehumanization posters, etc.) made explicit and implicit references to masculinity and femininity. In other words, students were asked to apply the theoretical concepts of gender socialization specifically to genocidal policies of the Nazi regime during the Holocaust. For example, students reflected on forced sterilization and abortion policies imposed by the regime, as well as other specific and invasive techniques that were used to uproot Jewish families and destroy the core features of Jewish communities.

The inclusion of this program for my course added an additional layer of complexity to the topic of the Holocaust. Thankfully, the perspective being offered also enabled students to interact with other faculty and researchers who were exploring similar themes in their studies. In order to fully explore the ways in which victims of the genocidal regime were targeted differently based on their sex and gender, students had to develop a rudimentary understanding of Nazi policies, in addition to developing a theoretical foundation for understanding sex and gender. Thus, as alluded to earlier, before this topic was introduced we thoroughly covered sex and gender as a unit, identifying the anatomical differences between the sexes, the social and cultural determinants of gender, and the ways in which notions of masculinity and femininity are stereotypically presented within culture and transmitted via powerful institutions such as the media, education, and government. Additionally, students were presented with a lecture introducing them to the idea that hyper-masculinity is associated with the violence seen during warfare and genocide, which would later be fused in an analysis of the ways that women in particular become vulnerable to sexual violence during these times.

Any educator who embarks on the task of introducing the topic of the Holocaust to her students will acknowledge that it is an emotionally challenging process, but one that also holds great potential for insight and transformation among one's students. In reflecting on the "pedagogical emotions" of Holocaust education, Baum (1996, 44) notes that this process for an educator means "beginning with the most fundamental of questions: what is it we want our students to learn?" By identifying a specific theme or set of themes relevant to the Holocaust, it can make the topic more manageable for faculty and the focus clearer for students. Indeed, Lindquist (2011, 27) reflects that this topic has the potential "to be the vehicle by which the central essence of the human condition can be examined." He then concludes that "(s)tudying the Holocaust thus provides a lens through which students can examine their values, giving them an opportunity to ask themselves what they would do in a moment of moral crisis" (Lindquist 2011, 27). By introducing this topic within the larger theme of sex and gender, students were offered the opportunity to explore the way their own lives have been shaped by notions of masculinity and femininity. Given that gender socialization is a common experience all students have and continue to endure, it also enabled them to apply a relatable aspect of their own lives to this event.

In their guidelines for teaching the Holocaust, the United States Holocaust Memorial Museum (USHMM) advises instructors to avoid simple answers to complex questions, a mantra perhaps best reflected in that semester's theme of exploring the intersection of mass violence and genocide with sex and gender. While I was vigilant in identifying for students that not all Jewish women would have the same experiences under the Nazi regime—nor would all Jewish men—gender could become an additional theoretical framework with which to understand the scope of atrocities and discriminatory acts that one *could be* exposed to. For instance, a telling line in the scholarship looking at gender and the Holocaust that was oft repeated during our panel discussion and that appeared to resonate in particular with my students was "different horrors, same hell." Thus, during the panel discussion, and later, as a class, we explored the ways that victims of the Nazi regime were presented with various gender-specific threats. This focus really pushed students to stretch their understanding of how one's life would be altered living under a genocidal regime based on the particulars of demographics, and how gender in particular could mediate the experience for the victims.

In addition to lecture, outside readings, my panel discussion, and the accompanying assignment, students were also exposed to brief clips of footage that showed the liberation of some of the camps near the end of the war, and I read them poignant excerpts from memoirs of survivors, both male (e.g., Primo Levi and Elie Wiesel) and female (e.g., Ruth Kluger). In fact, USHMM has identified the significant role that memoir exposure can play in personalizing stories for students. Wiesel's account, in particular, is identified as a resource in countless guides for teaching the Holocaust (e.g., Russell III 2005). Because this is just one unit in a larger course, students were not explicitly assigned to read any Holocaust memoirs; however, as described, I read passages from notable ones to them during a lecture on the topic. This is consistent with the pedagogical finding that "any consideration of the magnitude [of the Holocaust] must be enhanced by providing students with a lens that allows them to see that 'the individual people—families of grandparents, parents, and children—are behind the statistic'" (Lindquist 2006, 216). Given that the canonical memoirs of Holocaust survivors are generally male, I was sensitive in also selecting a female survivor's story beyond Anne Frank's *The Diary of a Young Girl*, which, though well known, does not fully encapsulate the experience of the Holocaust and, of course, does not reflect a survivor experience.

In fact, the inclusion of memoirs served as a great springboard for discussing how male voices have historically dominated the "Holocaust narrative." The inclusion of Kluger's memoir became critical in that she, herself, reflects in many passages on how her girlhood was shaped by being interned in Auschwitz during her formative years. Moreover, the topic of how women survivor's narratives have been historically marginalized within the field of Holocaust studies was further explored and served as an opportunity to analyze how patriarchy penetrated not only victim experiences but remembrances of the Holocaust to the present day (Davis 2017). In fact, in her presentation on my panel, Dr. Saidel identified how resistant traditional Holocaust scholars were to recognizing that the full scope of Nazi atrocities included sexual violence against Jewish women. The questions of how atrocities are remembered and who is given a voice in the aftermath of genocide became poignant themes during class discussions and in the assignments that students submitted based on the program.

Perhaps it is not surprising, then, that student responses included points like "the female experience is underrepresented" in Holocaust remembrance today and that "the genocide itself was not gender neutral." In looking at how sex roles for women were particularly under siege, one student identified that "the future of [the Jewish human] race and the capabilities the women had were assaulted by sterilization, forced abortions, and sexual humiliation." Another student wrote that "Nazi internment camps separated individuals by sex as a means to sever the unity of the family structure and proceed with the progression of dehumanization." This insight represents a recurring theme of my panel—namely, that in attacking the family unit by separating men and women and targeting them in gender-specific ways, Jews' identities were under assault and their sense of self, family, and community were all similarly and savagely ruptured.

Based on class discussion and what they shared on their papers, this particular link between the family structure and acts of persecution against the Jews appears to have resonated with students. For instance, one student remarked that "when destroying the family unit men were held incapable of saving their loved ones, inherently emasculating them." Similarly, in recognizing rape as an act that threatens the family unit, another student remarked, "the act of rape during genocide always dehumanizes and demoralizes the victims. Therefore, rape is viewed as one of the most powerful weapons used to destroy people." This particular student also made a link between the Holocaust and past genocides to current conflicts across the globe, including the ongoing conflict in Syria and the rise of international terrorist organization (ISIS) across Iraq and other occupied territories in the Middle East. This perhaps best encapsulates why Holocaust education remains relevant—the continued perpetration of genocide and atrocities across the globe in modern times indicates that the lessons that can and should be learned from our past are not being heeded by those in positions of power. In many ways, the theme of this semester enabled students to bridge the experience of the Holocaust to modern-day conflicts that represent similar features and drive warfare and genocide today. This is consistent with Lindquist's (2006, 215) finding that "the Holocaust, if taught with due concern given to content and pedagogy, can civilize and humanize our students and perhaps more effectively than any other subject can sensitize them to the dangers of indifference, intolerance, racism and the dehumanization of others."

Building Empathy and Promoting Civic Engagement Through Personal Connection and Theoretical Inquiry

I have noticed that there is a great opportunity for empathy building in students when they are exposed to Holocaust studies, particularly when they are exposed to personal accounts of survivors. While it was not originally an explicit learning objective for me to present students with this historical event to infuse our course with greater humanistic values, my experiences have taught me that this critical feature is just as important as instilling basic knowledge and a theoretical framework when teaching the Holocaust. Indeed, while many scholars have identified the significance of personalization in Holocaust education, Holocaust survivor Edith Carter poignantly implores of educators: "Help your students become more human" (Lindquist 2011, 26).

In my experience, when students are given the time and space to reflect on the various aspects of the Holocaust from different conceptual and theoretical perspectives, there is an enormous potential for an expansion of their empathy and for a recognition of our shared humanity. In introducing the topic and preparing students emotionally and psychologically for the lecture, I will often tell them to keep in mind a helpful line that I heard myself when I was participating in a USHMM fellowship for faculty teaching the Holocaust—that the event represents the worst of humanity, but that the stories of rescue and sacrifice also represent the best of humanity. It is implicit, perhaps, but worth noting nonetheless that "confronting the Holocaust forces students to address seminal questions that deal with the essence of what it means to be a human being" (Lindquist 2011, 26).

One student, in reflecting on the powerful psychological mechanism of dehumanization, shared that "during the concentration camps, the victims had no clothes, hair shaven, and were referred to as numbers … your name, bodily structure and properties are all key vitals to your survivability. If all that is taken away from you, what sense of identity does that entail?" This response demonstrated the depth to which the student had considered the psychological ramifications of being a target of dehumanization. In fact, virtually all students recognized the role dehumanization plays in inciting genocide. For example, in another paper, a student remarked that "dehumanization is also a big part of genocide" and then continued with specific examples. The same student concluded in the final paragraph of her reflection that, while her initial participation in the

Colloquium Series was "only because it was required," she eventually became "interested and attended more programs because right now the only defense against bigots and genocide is knowledge."

An in-class analysis of dehumanization techniques and exploration of Nazi propaganda was an additional opportunity to get students to develop empathic responses toward the victims of the Nazi regime. For instance, a student wrote that "it was hard for me not to think of my family while listening to the horrors that were happening. I kept imagining what I would do if it were me and my family had to endure what so many people went through during the Holocaust and any other genocide since then and it brought me to tears." This student went on to share that "the Colloquium Series prompted me to have a conversation about the Holocaust with my mother, who never knew it happened since it was not taught in her school in Ecuador." The student concluded her paper by writing that "the Colloquium Series has given me abundant information that I could implement in my paper. Each lecture was extremely insightful not just for my paper, but also for my own personal knowledge. I am glad to say that the series piqued my interest in studying more about sex and gender especially during times of warfare and genocide."

Student responses clearly demonstrate that employing a gender lens and engaging with the larger NEH/KHC Colloquium Series enabled a richer and deeper experience regarding their exposure to the Holocaust. Moreover, students were able to make connections between gender socialization and specific types of persecution during genocide, recognizing that the process of genocide does not occur in a vacuum. Overall, the experience enabled students to cultivate higher-level thought in engaging with Holocaust studies and offered them the opportunity to analyze the historical event from a social-psychological perspective. Educators who have the benefit of other resources promoting Holocaust education within their institution should consider how these programs and events intersect with what is being done in their classrooms. There are, of course, great challenges that come with teaching the topic, and it requires both patience and understanding on the part of educators and students, but, as demonstrated, the payoffs for both faculty and students are profound.

Given the sociocultural environment our students are living in today—particularly within diverse populations of students at community colleges like QCC—and the harsh persistence of systemic racism, sexism, and other forms of discrimination in American culture, I would argue that this kind of exposure is imperative in enabling our students to become more civic minded and considerate of all the ways that civilization is vulnerable. For instance, Lindquist (2011, 28) has identified that "Holocaust education raises issues that are critically important to contemporary American society, leading to classroom discourse that might not occur otherwise." Moreover, he notes, "Studying the Shoah becomes a vehicle that allows students to engage in sophisticated conversations that stretch their understanding of the world and their ability to evaluate the many complex, multilayered moral situations they will encounter as adults" (Lindquist 2011, 27). Indeed, there are so many potential benefits and lessons to be gained for students when exposed to a thorough, multifaceted, and textual approach to the Holocaust in an academic environment. For example, "one of the most important reasons why the Holocaust should be taught in schools is that the lessons from this dark page of modern history hold the potential of teaching civic virtue" (Wegner 1998, 168). Reflecting on the role we can play as educators reminds me of how when queried "How can you bear to teach the Holocaust?" one educator responded, "How can you not?" (Lindquist 2011, 28).

Appendix: Additional Homework Assignment: Gender & Genocide Colloquia, KHC

As part of Dr. Aalai's participation in the Gender & Genocide Colloquia this academic year, in addition to being required to attend the December 2 panel discussion (see Syllabus for details) that she will be on (students will also earn extra credit for attendance), students are STRONGLY ENCOURAGED to attend at least one more event this semester (5 extra credit points will be earned for attendance to each event). In conjunction with attendance at these events and in class lecture, students will be asked to construct a 2–4-page paper that follows the American Psychological Association (APA) format and the regular guidelines of written assignments in answering the following questions:

- Identify AT LEAST THREE specific ways in which sex and gender intersect with genocide
  - Offer examples from specific genocides (e.g., the Holocaust), as applicable
- In reflecting on the notion that men and women experience genocide differently, one scholar famously remarked, "different horrors,

same hell." What does this refrain mean to you, and how can you relate it to at least one of the programs from this semester?
- In what ways does the language used during genocide reflect the fusion of gender with this type of atrocity? Use specific examples as applicable, and consider such genocidal practices as dehumanization, propaganda, and persuasion techniques.
- Open comments
  - This is an opportunity for you to reflect on any facet of this program this semester that has resonated with you, that you would like to relate in the context of this discussion, or that you found to be particular compelling or perhaps had questions about.

Please note that Homework 2 is also related to Warfare & Genocide, and, as such, that assignment can be completed in tandem with this one (see Syllabus for details). This assignment must be submitted by **Monday, December 7**. Please note that Homework 2 is also due during this week, so students who would like to complete this assignment earlier can submit it before this due date. This assignment will be worth 20 reflection points.

References

Baum, Rachel N. 1996. 'What Have I Learned to Feel:' The Pedagogical Emotions of Holocaust Education. *College Literature* 23 (3): 44–58.

Davis, Angela. 2017. Belonging and 'Unbelonging': Jewish Refugee and Survivor Women in 1950s Britain. *Women's History Review* 26 (1): 130–146.

Lindquist, David H. 2006. Guidelines for Teaching the Holocaust: Avoiding Common Pedagogical Errors. *The Social Studies* 97 (5): 215–221.

———. 2011. Meeting a Moral Imperative: A Rationale for Teaching the Holocaust. *The Clearing House* 84: 26–30.

Medoff, Rafael. 1996. Teaching About International Responses to News of the Holocaust: The Columbus Dispatch Project at Ohio State University. In *New Perspectives on the Holocaust: A Guide for Teachers and Learners*, 166–185. New York: NYU.

Russell, William Benedict, III. 2005. Teaching About the Holocaust—A Resource Guide. *The Social Studies* 96: 93.

Wegner, Gregory. 1998. 'What Lessons Are There From the Holocaust for My Generation Today?' Perspectives on Civic Virtue from Middle School Youth. *Journal of Curriculum and Supervision* 13 (2): 167–183.

CHAPTER 7

Incarceration Through the Lens of Genocide and Restorative Justice

Rose Marie Äikäs

In the fall of 2014, I, along with my criminology students, participated in the National Endowment for the Humanities/Kupferberg Holocaust Center (NEH/KHC) Colloquium Series, "Testimony Across the Disciplines: Cultural and Artistic Responses to Genocide," which took place at Queensborough Community College's (QCC) KHC. As part of the series, students in my course drew on genocide, mass incarceration, and restorative justice frameworks to explore testimonials by formerly incarcerated women at Hour Children, a community service organization located in Queens, New York, that helps formerly incarcerated women re-enter their community, reconnect with their families, and begin to build independent and stable lives.[1] Our project was recorded in order to capture students' engagement with the women and that documentary recording was later shown at the capstone event of the colloquium series. This chapter outlines how I integrated a restorative justice perspective, Holocaust programming, and documentary filmmaking into criminal justice coursework. In doing so, it reveals how Holocaust-related content can

R. M. Äikäs (✉)
Department of Social Sciences, Queensborough Community College, CUNY, Bayside, NY, USA
e-mail: RAikas@qcc.cuny.edu

A. E. Traver, D. Leshem (eds.), *Humanistic Pedagogy Across the Disciplines*, https://doi.org/10.1007/978-3-319-95025-9_7

help students better understand incidents of mass violence and restorative justice theory and how students' reflective experiential learning of complex material can help inspire them to social action.

Theoretical Justification for the Focus on Women and Restorative Justice

Of the 2.3 million people incarcerated in the United States in 2014, about 9.7 percent (217,700) were women (Walmsley 2015). To contextualize this data, while the United States contains 5 percent of the world's female population, it holds close to 30 percent of the world's incarcerated women (Kajstura and Immarigeon 2015). Women are entering American prisons at nearly twice the rate of men, and they represent the fastest-growing prison population in the United States. This growth is linked to two macro-level issues: (1) severe federal and state criminal laws regarding drug-related crimes and (2) mandatory minimum sentencing, which eliminates judicial discretion, for various federal and state crimes.

In my fall 2014 criminology course, I focused on the experiences of formerly incarcerated women through a restorative justice lens. I did so for four theoretically grounded reasons. First, most of the introductory criminology textbooks that I have used over the years make only scant mention of restorative justice as a viable method to reduce mass incarceration and foster healing between crime victims, lawbreakers, and communities impacted by crime. As a result, students who are denied information on the restorative justice perspective are potentially deprived of the ability to think about lawbreakers (e.g., the women of Hour Children) beyond a punitive framework.

Second, as few research studies focus on the unique trajectories that lead to women's imprisonment (Messina et al. 2006; Bloom et al. 2004; Hall et al. 2004; and Mauer et al. 1999), criminal justice curricula rarely focus on the fact that incarcerated women are overwhelmingly survivors of multiple victimizations. In fact, the mainstream criminal justice system, which tends to focus on lawbreakers and retribution, regularly overlooks these mediating factors when deciding punishment, thereby fortifying the boundary between offenders and victims (Parent 2010, 286). As many criminal justice students will one day be employed by local- and state-level agencies that implement policies and practices that can add to this victimization, it is imperative that they learn about the restorative justice perspective's victim-centered approach to crime and offenders (Zehr 2015).

Third, according to Stutzman and Mullet (2005, 15), "restorative justice promotes values and principles that use inclusive, collaborative approaches for being in community. These approaches validate the experiences and needs of everyone within the community, particularly those who have been marginalized, oppressed or harmed." While most of my students come from communities that are disproportionately policed and imprisoned, few have experienced prior incarceration or met a previously incarcerated woman. As a result, opportunities for active engagement with the principles of restorative justice also become opportunities for multicultural learning, where students meet and recognize the humanity of persons who are different from themselves (Boyle-Baise 2005, 446–458).

Fourth, the restorative justice framework connects criminology coursework to other topics of significance across the humanities through its focus on the humanity of the "other." Restorative justice models invite perpetrators, victims, and community members to view each other not as symbols of crime, victimization, or evil but as complete and complex human subjects.

Theoretical Justification for the Integration of Holocaust Programming

In the movie *The House I Live In*, David Simon compares the War on Drugs in the United States to a Holocaust in slow motion, as it created a chain of destruction decimating communities of marginalized people. While there is no question that American drug policies differ vastly from the policies of the Third Reich, Simon makes this comparison to illustrate what happens whenever a society excludes and persecutes a particular group of people.

According to Hilberg (1996), the chain of destruction during the Holocaust consists of five stages: identification, ostracism, confiscation, concentration, and, finally, annihilation. Identification posits that a group of people is singled out as a source of problems in society. Ostracism leads to this group losing their homes and other places of habitation: they are forcibly moved into hyper-segregated neighborhoods (e.g., ghettos), underscoring their physical and psychological isolation from mainstream society. Through confiscation people are deprived of their civil rights and property via political and legal discrimination. Concentration incapacitates people, moving them into secure facilities, such as camps and prisons, where their labor is exploited in a systematic fashion. While annihilation can occur through deliberate killings, it can also take place indirectly (e.g., through the withholding of psychiatric or medical care and food). Thus, in the context of my course, we used the unfolding chain of destruction that was the Holocaust as a model through which to explore the systematic, destructive nature of mass incarceration.

Along these stages, the Holocaust and mass incarceration share additional commonalities and techniques. For example, both depend on the willingness of thousands of people to work within a system that is wrong and unjust (Osler and Bennet 2013). For Osler and Bennet (2013), the Holocaust and contemporary sentencing policies evidence a failing moral compass at the societal and individual (i.e., among those who exercise discretion to build and maintain mechanisms of injustice) levels. Bauman (1991, 2) elucidates this idea in his work on the Holocaust, illustrating how moral indifference can be produced through bureaucratic procedures that rely on the ethics of the civil servant, who substitutes "moral responsibility" with "discipline" and "self-denial." As my course is a requirement for future employment in the criminal justice system, students were encouraged to interrogate the systematized and bureaucratized immorality of mass incarceration in light of the ultimate moral failure, that is, the Holocaust.

The Holocaust and American incarceration policies also evidence techniques of "Othering," which include the creation and implementation of ideology, obedience to authority, peer pressure, deindividuation, unity in primary groups, and even career-based motives (Browning 1998). In "Dehumanization, Social Contact and Techniques of Othering," Smith (2015, 11–12) writes that "the techniques of Othering at work in the concentration camps were primarily based on dehumanizing situational factors and Nazi ideology." According to Levi (1986), these techniques began upon arrival in the camps, when individuals were kicked, beaten, undressed, and had their hair cut, among other degradations. For this reason, my course regularly connected our study of the dehumanization of mass incarceration to the centrality of dehumanization in the Holocaust.

Additionally, my course drew on the challenges Holocaust survivors, who were not guilty of any "crime" other than being Jewish, faced in finding willing and capable audiences with whom to share their story as models of the type of alterity and difference the women of Hour Children represent. It also informed students, many of whom plan to work in the American criminal justice system, about the Holocaust's historic impact on the forming of international criminal law, tribunals, and efforts by both international and local communities to address and respond to genocide in the present-day world (Meyer 2011).

Project Description

In light of the aforementioned theoretical justifications, my fall 2014 criminology course was designed with the goals of the 2014–2015 NEH/KHC Colloquium Series in mind. That year the series produced literal and concrete forms of remembrance that culminated in a capstone event at the KHC. The capstone underscored multiple means to understand the roots of mass atrocity, prevent its recurrence, and remember and honor those who perished in or survived the Holocaust. To best align my course with the series, I designed an inquiry-intensive project that engaged students in the rehumanization of a marginalized group of women released from New York State Department of Corrections' custody and control to the borough of Queens. Through structured face-to-face meetings with the women of Hour Children, as well as documentary filmmaking, the project aimed to create an opening for truth-telling to counter narratives that distort or demonize women who have criminal justice histories (Minow 1998). It also sought to introduce students to the idea that "simply telling one's truth can serve as a form of justice" (Tutu 2007, 6). Likewise, by creating "a body of memories, images and messages to embrace, reject, critique and resist," it sought to create a record through which QCC students, staff, and faculty could learn about people who, due to their criminal justice system-designated labels, can provoke feelings of discomfort and fear (Minow 1998, 138).

The project began in class, as my students and I reviewed the concepts, principles, and values of restorative justice and generated lists of questions to be asked of the women at their meeting. At this time, my students were also introduced to how Hour Children incorporates the women's harms, and harm reduction strategies, into their re-entry program. This application of restorative justice content added scope, depth, and additional critical thinking content into the course. It also complemented students' learning of mainstream criminological narratives, which are most often written by white male academics to explain male offending and that tend to ignore the fluid identities of women who have negative contact with criminal justice settings.

We then visited Hour Children in Astoria, Queens. Upon our arrival, we were met by the organization's staff and directed to a conference room, where we were welcomed and given a brief orientation by the employment coordinator, herself a formerly imprisoned woman. This orientation provided an overview of the agency, its mission, and the range of services available to women and their children (e.g., family reunification). After this, we watched a short documentary about Hour Children, which featured personal testimonies of several women assisted by the agency over the years. Multiple staff persons also spoke during the orientation to encourage students to participate in the organization's internship and mentoring programs.

After the orientation, students broke off into small groups, each containing one or two formerly incarcerated women. Thus began their mutual conversations using the basic principles of restorative justice as a guide. First, students were tasked with defining the principles and sharing how they might allow the women to repair something that is damaged. The women then responded with information about their general incarceration trajectories, as well as details about their more personal experiences. After about an hour and a half of conversation, all group members returned to the conference room for a debriefing. At this time, the students and women were encouraged to share what they had learned with the group. One woman stated that it had never occurred to her that the person whose life she took was also a victim. While decades of imprisonment had never prompted this realization, it is notable that one conversation with a student about the principles of restorative justice had had this impact.

Significantly, all of these interactions and conversations were filmed by staff from QCC's Marketing Department, who joined us at Hour Children for the day. This footage was later transformed into a short documentary film, which debuted at the KHC during the 2014–2015 NEH/KHC Colloquium Series' capstone event, "Testimony across the Disciplines: QCC Students Respond to Genocide through Art and Writing." The film was projected onto a video screen, where it played continuously; a nearby binder of students' reflection papers collated what they had learned through the experience.

Student Reflections on the Project

Students' reflection papers were written in response to prompts designed to encourage their consideration of incarceration through a restorative justice perspective. My analysis of these papers reveals the extent of students' learning in the following areas or categories: critical thinking and the multidimensionality of harm; awareness of bias and the humanity of the other; and remembrance as a mechanism of agency. This analysis involved my reading students' papers twice to capture the aforementioned "indigenous categories" and then my careful line-by-line review of the papers to identify meaningful examples of each category (Strauss and Corbin 1990).

Critical Thinking and the Multidimensionality of Harm

According to Hackman (2005, 106), "thinking about an issue is not equivalent to critical thinking, which demands focusing on information from numerous, non-mainstream perspectives" and "seeing those (perspectives) as independently valid and not as an add-on to the dominant, hegemonic one." Evidence from students' reflection papers indicates that the project encouraged their complication of conventional narratives of incarceration, "de-centering (their) analytical frame and opening their minds to a broader range of experiences" (Hackman 2005, 106). For example, one student wrote about the crimes that a woman from Hour Children had committed—crimes that, in the student's opinion, were minor yet punished by the full force of the law. The student then reflected specifically on the woman's children, who were forced to endure the collateral consequences of their mother's choices. The student also described how the woman began to cry as she recounted her story, and how, when the student underscored the importance of moving "toward positivity" with the lessons learned behind bars, the woman had stopped crying to express her appreciation for the student's empathy. This reflection opened the student up to the possibility that, given its emphasis on analyzing and assessing multiple perspectives, critical thought might require us to "'see' through someone else's eyes" (Vilen 2015). This is particularly true if critical thinking is to lead to compassionate social action (Vilen 2015).

Another student's reflection paper revealed how critical thinking led her to consider the ways in which the retributive justice system might also do harm. Illustrating her ability to "(analyze) the effects of power and oppression," she wrote at length about the ways in which experiences of incarceration impact women long after their release, often through discriminatory practices and policies (Hackman 2005, 106). For instance, she described a woman from Hour Children who had recently gone on three job interviews and been turned down at each interview because of her past. Through this example, the student had come to grapple with legal discrimination and to learn about the complex barriers, both legal and regulatory, that family and community re-connectivity entails. In fact, many students wrote that the restorative justice perspective had encouraged them to think critically about the multidimensionality of harm, both self and state inflicted. My students began to recognize that communities may be harmed, materially and morally, by wrongs to their members and to their resources, including their moral resources of trust and hopefulness (Fawcett et al. 2000). For example, one student wrote that harm can take many different forms, and that it is not exclusive to crime victims. Another student described how it is important for a person to account for her actions, learn from her mistakes, and make amends to repair fractured relationships. That student wrote specifically about the role restorative justice could play in a woman's efforts to repair her relationships with her children, immediate family members, and community. She also identified evidence-based programs like Hour Children, which treat offenders as survivors of multiple victimizations, as essential to that repair. Other students reflected on missed opportunities for restorative justice-focused interventions during the women's incarceration experiences, noting how they could have accelerated the women's rehabilitation, skill development, education, and re-entry. In each of these reflective writings there was evidence that students were beginning to question the retributive paradigm and to "(inquire) into what alternatives exist with respect to the current, dominant view of reality of this issue" (Hackman 2005, 106).

Awareness of Bias and the Humanity of the Other

A particularly effective high-impact pedagogical technique involves introducing students to a landscape where they can introspectively examine what makes that landscape distinctive from other landscapes and where "(the) sense of discovery is present all the time" (Medoff 1996, 167). According to Pompa (2002, 69), it is this "interplay of content and context (that) provides a provocative juncture that takes the educational process to a deeper level." Students' presence at Hour Children facilitated such junctures, including recognition of biases and the humanity of the "Other." For example, in her reflection paper, one student described feeling surprised by the appearance of her formerly incarcerated partner, writing that she was struck, in particular, by the woman's youth (they were both twenty-years-old) and her look of "innocence." Two other students reflected on similar assumptions and biases, noting their nervousness about meeting formerly incarcerated women and visiting an unusual landscape. Another student, who denied feeling frightened when meeting her partner, wondered whether her partner felt any fear related to their meeting.

Pompa (2002, 68) writes that when students "are provided direct, unadulterated exposure to the exigencies of a particular context," they experience "the ultimate border-crossing." Thus, in a way, this project also engaged my students in a form of border-crossing, albeit within the borough of Queens. Consistent with the aims of a multicultural education (Howard-Hamilton 2000), this border-crossing encouraged students' awareness and understanding of their positionality in relationship to the women of Hour Children, whose identities are linked and determined by their prior incarceration. Communities and community agencies can also serve as actors or as guarantors of repair and restoration of relationships by opening doors to future criminal justice professionals to meet with persons they will most likely encounter in the future (Fawcett et al. 2000). For example, one student wrote about how society tends to see the women of Hour Children solely as formerly incarcerated people—an identity that limits our recognition of their complete experience and the totality of their humanity. Indeed, these realizations, which, again, unfolded within the specific landscape of Hour Children, encouraged students to revisit and rethink their own biases, prompting them to replace labels like "ex-offender," "crack addict," and "parolee" with those like "mother," "college student," "employee," and "sister," which reflected their shared identities and positions.

Remembrance for Agency

Predota (2010) posits that an essential step to restoring justice is remembrance, and students' reflective writings reveal the extent to which they will remember meeting the women of Hour Children. In fact, students indicated that these memories had already transformed their thinking about mass incarceration, offending, women and children, the notion of retribution, and the power of listening and sharing painful memories. Students also described how these memories inspired them to be change agents, rather than "bystanders," in the world. For example, one student wrote that the project had caused her to consider the many female offenders who have been victimized and to realize how we often fail to create a space for them in society. In line with this realization, she then acknowledged that her own perceptions and actions needed to change in this regard. This realization echoes the work of Osler and Bennet (2013, 120), who write that "beneath it all is something more important than any academic theory or statistical set: the real lives of people who have been over-incarcerated by our hands and the hands of those who will continue this work until the machine is stopped."

Other students described how the aforementioned memories stood to benefit their schoolwork and their future careers in the criminal justice system. For example, one student, in writing about her admiration for Hour Children, described the significance of programs that both encouraged formerly incarcerated women to repair the harms produced by their actions *and* provided them with the skills necessary for work and life. Through such memories and realizations, students emerged as active bridge builders and boundary spanners who, through "the production of new historical narratives and accounts that build bridges between past and present," stand to engage in social justice and peace-building work, as well as criminal justice reform (Minow 1998, 133).

Conclusion

According to Shiman and Fernekes (1999, 55), "human rights education, particularly when informed by study of the Holocaust and other genocides, requires students to grapple with questions related to ethnocentrism, relativism, universalism, responsibility, conflict and justice." In this chapter, I described one effort to connect issues of mass incarceration and restorative justice to the aforementioned topics of "responsibility, conflict and justice" using an inquiry-intensive project that weaved together QCC criminal justice students, formerly incarcerated women from Hour Children, and the 2014–2015 NEH/KHC Colloquium Series. Students' written reflections indicate that the project had a significant impact on their learning, particularly in the following areas: critical thinking and the multidimensionality of harm, awareness of bias and the humanity of the other, and remembrance as a mechanism of agency.

Throughout the semester the students endeavored to incorporate lessons from the Holocaust into their understandings of the struggles of victims of our criminal justice system while also maintaining the crucial and substantial differences between the experiences of formerly incarcerated lawbreakers and the experiences of Holocaust survivors. In spite of these differences, the students found revelatory connections. For example, students' conversations with the women of Hour Children underscored the collateral consequences of women's incarceration, particularly the psychological impacts of that imprisonment on the women's children. This intergeneration trauma is not unlike that experienced by the children of Holocaust survivors, who "have sometimes been raised in a psychological atmosphere poisoned by the scarring that their survivor parents have brought to their childbearing task" (Danieli 1985, 299). Additionally, these conversations also highlighted the women's broader struggles to re-enter society—an experience that parallels themes in Holocaust survivors' testimonies. The women's testimonies underscore abuse and dehumanization during and after incarceration akin to treatment of Jews after the Holocaust. According to Danieli (1985, 298), as they sought to rebuild their lives, most Holocaust survivors experienced feelings of "isolation, loneliness, and mistrust of society" and a sense that "no one who had not undergone the same experience 'could really understand' them." Finally, these conversations identified the extent to which silence mediates formerly incarcerated women's re-entry into society. Danieli (1985) explains how a conspiracy of silence, consisting of pervasive negative societal reactions and attitudes of avoidance, indifference, and repression, also surrounded Holocaust survivors' re-entry into postwar society. The principles of restorative justice, which ground the work of Hour Children and have informed justice and reconciliation processes after genocide, go a long way in countering that silence.

It is also important to note that this project drew on elements of Holocaust pedagogy, as well. Charlesworth (1996, 174) describes how visits to a site of Nazi atrocity and an exhibition on the Minsk Ghetto imbued his course with "an immediacy impossible to acquire in a classroom." In the criminal justice framework, Bryan Stevenson of the Equal Justice Initiative asserts that, if we want to counter mechanisms of moral indifference and injustice, "we must get proximate to the challenges we want to solve." Our visit to Hour Children contributed to the criminology course in these ways: providing students with a sense of place and immediacy in their learning and creating a landscape upon which students could apply the restorative justice perspective. The use of documentary filmmaking only added to this contribution by helping to position the students and women in proximity, break down barriers between and within both groups, and engage the filters of meaning and memory. In a manner similar to the testimonies of Holocaust survivors, the visit and documentary film served as opportunities for truth-telling, healing, and learning.

Appendix: Restorative Justice Assignment

PART I—Choose a formerly incarcerated woman at Hour Children and explain the basic philosophy of Restorative Justice to her. Then ask her about an experience of injustice or harm experienced or directed at her and how restorative justice could and/or could not apply to this particular situation.[2]

1. Who did you choose to explain it to?
2. Why?
3. What comments/questions did the other person have about restorative justice?
4. How was the experience?
5. What did you learn about restorative justice through the process?
6. What did you feel your partner learned about restorative justice through this process?
7. What suggestions would you make to restorative justice advocates as a result of your efforts?

Academic Component (Do students show an increase in academic content acquisition after the Restorative Justice/Hour Children Project?)

1. Describe and illustrate difficulties encountered by women in New York City upon their release from prison.
2. What might help in reducing recidivism rates? What factors may increase them?
3. What types of programs (prison/community) are most helpful? What types are not?

Personal Growth (Are students more aware of how the work of a community partner impacts their personal lives after the Restorative Justice/Hour Children Project?)

1. What did you know about formerly incarcerated individuals before this project?
2. What were some of your perceptions or beliefs about formerly incarcerated individuals before this project?
3. What can you do to improve the situation of formerly incarcerated individuals?

Civic Engagement (Are students more aware of the civic implications of their community partner's work after the Restorative Justice/Hour Children Project?)

1. What do you know about the effects of incarceration on the individual and on society?
2. How do you think our course has had an effect on the women served by Hour Children?
3. What skills from our course do you think you can use to address the particular problems faced by the women at Hour Children?

Notes

1. Hour Children provides comprehensive services that include transitional and permanent supportive housing, licensed childcare, mental health and substance abuse counseling, before and after prison release adult mentoring, workshops on health and nutrition, resume and soft skills building, financial literacy, parenting, educational and employment training, and placement opportunities. According to the organization's website, as of June 20, 2017, 84 percent of the women of Hour Children had been incarcerated for non-violent crimes, while 60 percent had been incarcerated for drug-related offenses, with many drug sentences related to mandatory sentencing guidelines. The majority of the women of Hour Children are women of color: 57 percent are African American, 27 percent are Latina, and 16 percent are Caucasian. Less than 50 percent of the women of Hour Children had ever been employed in any capacity before their arrests and nearly two-thirds (65 percent) had poverty-level incomes. The majority of the women receiving services at Hour Children were parenting children under the age of 18.
2. Adapted from Judah Oudshoorn's "PACS 302 Special Topic: Restorative Justice" Syllabus (Conrad Gebel University College, Waterloo, Ontario ON N2L 3G6, Canada, 2009).

References

Bauman, Zygmunt. 1991. *Modernity and the Holocaust*. Oxford: Polity Press.

Bloom, Barbara, Barbara Owen, and Stephanie Covington. 2004. Women Offenders and the Gendered Effects of Public Policy. *Review of Policy Research* 21 (1): 31–48.

Boyle-Baise, Marilynne. 2005. Preparing Community-Oriented Teachers: Reflections from a Multicultural Service-Learning Project. *Journal of Teacher Education* 56 (5): 446–458.

Browning, Christopher. 1998. Ordinary Men or Ordinary Germans? A Reply to the Critics. In *The Holocaust and History. The Known, the Unknown, the Disputed, the Reexamined*. 252–265.

Charlesworth, Andrew. 1996. Teaching the Holocaust Through Landscape Study. In *New Perspectives on The Holocaust: A Guide for Teachers and Scholars*, ed. L.M. Rochelle, T.A. Bennett, J.D. Mann, J.E. O'Connor, and R.P. Welke, 174–185. New York: New York University Press.

Danieli, Yael. 1985. The Treatment and Prevention of Long-term Effects and Intergenerational Transmission of Victimization: A Lesson from Holocaust survivors and Their Children. *Trauma and Its Wake* 1: 295–313.

Fawcett, Stephen B., Vincent T. Francisco, Jerry A. Schultz, Bill Berkowitz, Thomas J. Wolff, and Genevieve Nagy. 2000. The Community Tool Box: A Web-based Resource for Building Healthier Communities. *Public Health Reports* 115 (2–3): 274.

Hackman, Heather W. 2005. Five Essential Components for Social Justice Education. *Equity & Excellence in Education* 38 (2): 103–109.

Hall, Elizabeth A., Michael L. Prendergast, Jean Wellisch, Meredith Patten, and Yan Cao. 2004. Treating Drug-abusing Women Prisoners: An Outcomes Evaluation of the Forever Free Program. *The Prison Journal* 84 (1): 81–105.

Hilberg, Raul. 1996. *The Politics of Memory: The Journey of a Holocaust Historian*. Chicago: Ivan R. Dee, Inc.

Criminal Justice, Featured, Race & Racism Blog, April 12. http://www.rifuture.org/symposium-on-mass-incarceration-confronts-challenges-unites-system/. Accessed 11 Mar 2018.

Hour Children. "Who We Serve". http://www.hourchildren.org/?page_id+11. Accessed 20 June 2017.

Howard-Hamilton, Mary F. 2000. Creating a Culturally Responsive Learning Environment for African American Students. *New Directions for Teaching and Learning* 82: 45–53.

Kajstura, Aleks, and Russ Immarigeon. 2015. States of Women's Incarceration: The Global context. Prison Policy Initiative. prisonpolicy. org/global/women/. Accessed 1 Dec 2015.

Levi, Primo. 1986 [1989]. *The Drowned and the Saved*. Trans. Raymond Rosenthal. London: Abacus.

Mauer, Marc, Cathy Potler, and Richard Wolf. 1999. *Gender and Justice: Women, Drugs, and Sentencing Policy*. Washington, DC: Sentencing Project.

Medoff, Rafael. 1996. Teaching About International Responses to News of the Holocaust: The Columbus Dispatch Project at Ohio State University. New Perspectives on the Holocaust: A Guide for Teachers and Scholars: 166–173.

Messina, Nena, William Burdon, Garo Hagopian, and Michael Prendergast. 2006. Predictors of Prison-Based Treatment Outcomes: A Comparison of Men and Women Participants. *The American Journal of Drug and Alcohol Abuse* 32 (1): 7–28.

Meyer, Kathrin. 2011. Die Task Force for International Cooperation on Holocaust Education, Remembrance, and Research. Holocaust-Gedenken und Prävention gegen Antisemitismus als staatliche Verpflichtung. [The Task Force for International Cooperation on Holocaust Education, Remembrance, and Research. Commemorating the Holocaust and Prevention of Anti-semitism as an Obligation of the State]. *Jahrbuch für Antisemitismusforschung* 20: 105–112.

Minow, Martha. 1998. *Between Vengeance and Forgiveness: Facing History After Genocide and Mass Violence*. Boston: Beacon Press.

Osler, Mark, and Mark W. Bennett. 2013. A Holocaust in Slow Motion: America's Mass Incarceration and the Role of Discretion. *DePaul Journal for Social Justice* 7: 117.

Parent, Geneviève. 2010. Reconciliation and Justice After Genocide: A Theoretical Exploration. *Genocide Studies and Prevention* 5 (3): 277–292.

Pompa, Lori. 2002. Service-Learning as Crucible: Reflections on Immersion, Context, Power, and Transformation. *Michigan Journal of Community Service Learning* 9 (1): 67–75.

Predota, Alexandria. 2010. Restoring Justice After the Holocaust. https://micupoftea.wordpress.com/restoring-justing-after-the-holocaust/. Accessed 3 April 2017.

Shiman, David A., and William R. Fernekes. 1999. The Holocaust, Human Rights, and Democratic Citizenship Education. *The Social Studies* 90 (2): 53–62.

Smith, Peter Scharff. 2015. Dehumanization, Social Contact and Techniques of Othering 1: Combining the Lessons from Holocaust Studies and Prison Research. In *Punishing the Other*, 11–29. London: Routledge.

Strauss, Anselm, and Juliet M. Corbin. 1990. *Basics of Qualitative Research: Grounded Theory Procedures and Techniques*. Thousand Oaks, CA: Sage Publications.

Stutzman Amstutz, Lorraine, and Judy H. Mullet. 2005. The Little Book of Restorative Discipline for Schools. Intercourse.

Tutu, Desmond M. 2007. Reflections on Moral Accountability. *The International Journal of Transitional Justice* 1 (1): 6–7.

Vilen, Anne. 2015. Empathy + Critical Thinking = Compassionate Action. Education Week's Learning Deeply (blog), September 21. http://blogs.edweek.org/edweek/learning_deeply/2015/09/empathy_critical_thinking_compassionate_action.html

Walmsley, R. 2015. *World Female Imprisonment List*. 3rd ed. London: Institute for Criminal Policy Research.

Zehr, Howard. 2015. *The Little Book of Restorative Justice: Revised and Updated (Justice and Peacebuilding)*. New York, NY: Skyhorse Publishing.

CHAPTER 8

Dancing to Connect: An Interdisciplinary Creative Arts Approach to Holocaust Education Within Liberatory Pedagogy

Aliza Atik, Aviva Geismar, and Benjamin Lawrance Miller

In the fall semester of 2014, we had the opportunity to create an interdisciplinary pedagogical project involving an English literature course, a dance choreography course, and an English composition course at Queensborough Community College (QCC). This was part of Students Working in Interdisciplinary Groups (SWIG), a collaborative project of the sort described by George Kuh (2008) and supported by the QCC's Center for Excellence in Teaching and Learning (CETL).

This chapter is a collective reflection about this collaborative pedagogy, which resulted in student-generated creative responses that were included in "Testimony Across the Disciplines: Cultural and Artistic Responses to

A. Atik (✉) • B. L. Miller
Department of English, Queensborough Community College, CUNY, Bayside, NY, USA
e-mail: AAtik@qcc.cuny.edu; BMiller@qcc.cuny.edu

A. Geismar
Department of Health, Physical Education, and Dance, Queensborough Community College, CUNY, Bayside, NY, USA
e-mail: AGeismar@qcc.cuny.edu

A. E. Traver, D. Leshem (eds.), *Humanistic Pedagogy Across the Disciplines*, https://doi.org/10.1007/978-3-319-95025-9_8

Genocide," the 2014–2015 National Endowment for the Humanities (NEH) Colloquium Series at QCC's Kupferberg Holocaust Center (KHC). We believe our methods could inspire others to undertake interdisciplinary collaborations, and that readers might see the liberatory potential to undertaking such projects at the community college level specifically. At the center of our collaboration was a simple idea that creative investigation could be a meaningful way to learn about ideas related to the Holocaust, such as discrimination, surveillance, and hierarchies of power. Our students explored these subjects through writing, dancing, and filmmaking.

Historicizing Biopower by Spatializing Pedagogy (Aliza Atik)

In working on this project, I wanted to explore the Holocaust and genocide with students by examining the ideological process that takes place before acts of mass violence are carried out. While students may be at least vaguely familiar with the events of the Holocaust, it often, to them, is an experience that happened in the abstract, as part of a "history" wholly disconnected from their own lives. My goal was to move the discussion to the familiar, by exploring the systems of power that foreground my students' own lives and examining their unique, lived experiences. Once they were able to identify the ways in which they themselves were subject to hierarchies of power, we were then able to explore how these same social and political gestures have been utilized in politically sanctioned genocides such as the Holocaust. Our project had the double function, then, of helping students recognize the sociopolitical structures behind genocide, as well as preparing the students for the subsequent unit, in which they would be reading the poetry of Paul Celan, Tadeusz Borowski, and Jerzy Ficowski, as well as Sherman Alexie's poem "Inside Dachau," which discusses the Holocaust and the genocide of Native Americans. When reading these poems and reflecting on the horrific stories they depict, students were able to draw upon their own reflections on the functioning of power.

As this was an introduction to literature class, I began the project by asking students to see poetry as a form of storytelling relevant to their lived experiences, and so, selected poems for reading that I thought would evoke familiar events and themes. Together, we looked at Julia Alvarez's "Queens 1963," which deals with race and immigration in a Queens, NY neighborhood; "Sure You Can Ask Me A Personal Question" by Diane

Burns, which deals with a series of "unhelpful" questions the speaker gets asked as a Native American; and "Immigrants in Our Own Land" by Jimmy Santiago Baca, which deals with life on the border of citizenship and incarceration in the United States. After we did the basic work of understanding the ideas and literary structure of the poems, I decided to introduce a more theoretical component to their project by asking them to read selections from *Discipline and Punish: The Birth of the Prison*, philosopher Michel Foucault's twentieth-century work on modern power structures.

In this work, Foucault traces the history of the modern penal system and explores its interwoven relationship with social hierarchies, power relations, and the understanding of the individual's role in a social body. He explores the transition of a justice system that punished the body of the criminal in the eighteenth century to one that now assesses and punishes the criminal's mind and soul instead. The functions of punishment, for Foucault, demonstrate the fundamental workings of power. Moreover, in a disciplinary society that utilizes timetables in prisons, military spaces, and even schools, power is instituted through constant surveillance, with those on the top of the social hierarchy given the right to observe and demand compliance and regulated behavior from those below. This is the essential notion of biopower.

I expected the students to be overwhelmed by the introduction of these concepts. Surprisingly, this was not the case. Many students, while conceptually familiar with poetry, had little experience reading poetry through an academic lens, so, when I decided to introduce the works of Foucault, most students approached it with the same attitude that they did the poetry—as an unfamiliar discourse that was built into the curriculum, that was neither more or less foreign than the other required texts. We began by exploring the first section of Foucault's book, where he describes the torture of a specular body on a scaffold—a mode of punishment used by kings to demonstrate their inherent power over the body populace and to demand obedience to the king's law. We read this section of the text, and using a basic Google image search, were able to visualize the public torture described. We then followed this up with Foucault's description of the shift to the timetable as a model for imprisonment and asked, as a class, why Foucault cared about this shift. Together, we reviewed Foucault's description of how this created a new system of justice in which, rather than the crime itself being punished, the criminal's soul is now measured, assessed, regulated, and prescribed its "appropriate" place.

Given that this was a basic literature class, I did not ask the students to read *Discipline and Punish* in its entirety, but, in order to guide them toward the concept of the "disciplinary society" that Foucault describes, we read his description of the panopticon—an idealized prison building imagined by Jeremy Bentham, in which prisoners could be kept in a state of "permanent visibility" by the central location of the guard tower in the midst of the prison (Foucault 1977, 201). We then discussed the ways in which this constant visibility "assures the automatic functioning of power" and turned to examples of this in our own lives (201). We transitioned easily into conversations about red light cameras, stop-and-frisk policies, retail workers who follow "suspicious" customers around the store, and stalking and domestic violence. Many students shared the various ways in which, in the private and public spheres, their bodies had been policed by a form of surveillance.

Foucault famously noted that disciplinary power relies on binary logic, so that surveillance can easily codify categories for control. He states that: "Generally speaking, all the authorities exercising individual control function according to a double mode; that of binary division and branding (mad/sane; dangerous/harmless; normal/abnormal); and that of coercive assignment, of differential distribution (who he is; where he must be; how he is to be characterized; how he is to be recognized; how constant surveillance is to be exercised over him in an individual way)" (Foucault 1977, 199). In other words, modern society, based on this disciplinary model, focuses on defining and labeling each individual according to a set of external, socially constituted criteria. Labeled as such, we are expected to conform to these social codes, norms, and spaces. Surveillance—from the state, from juridical authorities, and from social groups and individuals—ensures that we do not violate these sanctioned norms.

To explore this notion, we supplemented our reading with an essay titled "West Bronx as Panopticon" from the book *Overcoming the Magnetism of Street Life* by Trevor Milton (2011). The essay details the life of "Antonio," a resident of the West Bronx who often deals with issues of police surveillance. It also describes how the West Bronx functions as an "enclosure": what Foucault (1977, 141) describes as "a place heterogeneous to all others and closed in upon itself" and what Milton (2011, 85) identifies as a space defined by surveillance that "functions with God-like omnipresence making residents aware that they are being watched without fully being aware of the direction of the gaze." Students understand that the West Bronx works to create a local population, a sense of belonging, but also a sense of exclusion from elsewhere. For many of my students, this also reminds them, to varying degrees, of the neighborhoods and schools in which they were raised. By calling on this more localized experience, students get a better sense of the Foucaultian concept of disciplinary societies that work through "meticulous tactical partitioning" in which "each individual has his place; and each place its individual" (Foucault 1977, 198; 143).

After completing these readings and discussions over the course of three classes, I asked students to compose their own surveillance narratives beginning with a thesis statement that addressed the following two questions: (1) How do unique spaces allow for different acts of surveillance and regulation? (2) How is this reflected in your individual experience? To respond to these questions, students needed to describe their experience as an "other," or a time when they felt "visible" because they were subject to the surveillance and tactical partitioning of a disciplinary society. I was careful to note that the experience they elected to describe did not have to be with a police or juridical authority but any social, personal, academic, or judicial moment where they had to negotiate scrutiny within a hierarchical system. The goal of this assignment was to demonstrate the current spaces of enclosure and the impact of being "outside of place" for students in the demographic of an urban community college.

The student responses I received were as broad ranging as they were intriguing. One student powerfully wrote about how her learning disabilities in school marked her as "abnormal" among her peers as well as her teachers and how this marked identity subjected her to various disciplinary gestures in the educational system. A young man wrote about his experience entering the United States as a new immigrant and described, in detail, the moment he was pulled aside by immigration agents and forced to endure a confusing and somewhat humiliating interview watched and observed by these agents and their peers. Several young men of color wrote about experiences being pulled over by the police while driving in predominantly white neighborhoods. A young female student emotionally described the constant surveillance she was placed under by the gaze of her former partner in an abusive relationship. It was these essays that were then submitted to Professor Geismar's students as the foundational texts from which they would draw their choreography.

My students shared their writing with Professor Geismar's students via the Wiki function in the online platform Blackboard. They corresponded via a series of online Q&As, as Professor Geismar's students put together their choreography over a number of weeks. The two classes then met one afternoon in the dance studio. Many of my students read their writing out loud, and the choreography students performed their dances. Afterwards, we all sat in a circle and discussed our reactions. QCC's technology team documented this day of sharing, and the footage was later passed along to Professor Miller's class. Many of my students had limited or no experience with seeing their work presented to an audience. Seeing their experience read and translated to a new medium generated particularly evocative feedback. One student described how, after seeing his piece set to movement, he was returned to the original moment of experience but layered with nostalgia and emotion. Another explained that this was nearly a dreamlike experience for him, which added new layers of meaning to his story.

This project was designed, in part, to work with Paolo Freire's (1970, 457) concept of "conscientization," which is the notion that learners need to be active subjects in the production of knowledge in order to have any agency in shaping their sociopolitical future rather than a participant in the "culture of silence" who allows hegemony to go unchecked. As Freire (1970, 455) notes, "men's consciousness, although conditioned, can recognize that it is conditioned." By asking students to investigate the multiple gestures through which their bodies were historicized, brought into discourse, and framed within the public sphere, I hoped that they could begin deconstructing some of the social myths surrounding their own bodies. I also hoped to begin a practice of "reparative pedagogy," a term coined by Pauline Sameshima and Dayna Slingerland (2015, 10) to refer to the ways in "which pedagogy rests on the belief that developing skills and knowledge bases are not enough and that transformational learning requires intentional dynamic development of imagination, creativity, flexibility, holistic thinking, interdisciplinary perspectives, and deep mindfulness." In drawing our students through multiple discourses—poetic and aesthetic, the personal and the global, the literal and the danced—I was hoping to help them create new forms of knowledge, simply by the "changing of objective relationships to subjective relationships between learner and content" as we did and by engaging our students with their own lived experiences as texts for academic discourse, asking them to thematically connect fields of learning that they had previously seen as unrelated, and by encouraging them to participate personally and creatively (Sameshima and Slingerland 2015, 19).

This beginning was key to our group project. Once the students could generate a working vocabulary to speak about their own "otherness" in a particular time and place, and to consider how it was enforced via social, educational, or other hierarchical forces, they could then translate it into more specific, historical contexts. After submitting our work to Professor Geismar's class, my students went on to study poetry written in the Holocaust. They did this with the knowledge that the Holocaust, like all mass atrocities, began when those in power had a vested interest in maintaining a clear sense of "otherness" among a portion of the population—a portion that could then be seen as inconvenient or dangerous to a culture more broadly and thus in need of extermination. Professor Geismar's students were able to generate this affect through the dances, and Professor Miller was then able to take this material and guide his students through the process of composing a digital essay that captured the nature of the collaboration.

Liberatory Movements (Aviva Geismar)

For many years I have used movement to explore the Holocaust with groups of students in various settings. As the child of a Holocaust refugee, I have done extensive outreach with my dance company, Drastic Action, exploring this subject. Over this time, I have grappled with different approaches to this overwhelming material. I have looked for ways to help students begin to understand this incomprehensible history, to access their feelings, to relate from their own experience, and to feel empowered through their creative expression.

For many students, movement explorations can provide a safe approach to processing something so frightening. This preverbal mode of expression often allows students to access the uncomfortable feelings that can arise with this kind of investigation in ways that feel manageable. Through physical expression we can often process and release negative emotions more immediately than through language.

Additionally, in introducing Holocaust history to young people, I have found it helpful to start with the personal. For example, when working with a group of German High School students, we began with letters written by Jewish residents of their town during the period before they were deported to concentration camps. We researched the histories and eventual fates of these people and their families. The young people connected personally with these stories, and this empathic response became the foundation of a dance work they created collaboratively under the mentorship of my dance company's teaching artists.

For the collaboration between my choreography class and the English classes, we worked our way in to the subject of the Holocaust and genocide gradually, starting first with experiences my students could relate to via the personal narratives shared with us by Professor Atik's students. Once they were well into their work on the dances that responded to these pieces of writing, we began to address the subject of the Holocaust more directly. My students attended two of the campus-wide colloquia that were part of the 2014–2015 NEH/KHC Colloquium Series. The first, *Culture as Survival: Music and Theater in the Nazi Concentration Camps and Ghettos*, introduced the class to Holocaust history and to artistic practices that were a form of resistance. Some of the students were excited to consider art as a force of political expression or social change for the first time. The second presentation, *Dance, Disability, and the Holocaust*, prompted a heated discussion about the prevailing aesthetics of beauty and how they play out in the dance world. The students identified connections between current standards of beauty and the Nazi idea of a perfect Aryan. As we discussed these presentations, they seemed to make connections between the small acts of surveillance or discrimination that their partners had written about and the more systematic violence carried out against groups of people.

Teaching a creative art is challenging. How do we foster the creative spark—originality, iconoclasm, idiosyncrasy—and still share with students an understanding of craft, the elements of their chosen art, and strategies to communicate with an audience? It is a tricky balance. Although I share with my students an array of choreographic tools and approaches, I try to subvert the traditional power dynamics in which the teacher is the arbiter of what is right and what is wrong. I try to downplay my role as an authority and establish a more liberatory pedagogical approach, where the responses of classmates are as important as the response of the professor. To this end, I establish clear guidelines for students' responses to each other's work. Students are asked to describe what they saw in their classmate's choreography and to try to discern the intention of the work. The viewers are also asked what was effective or not in helping to carry out the creator's intention. We strive to leave out judgments—the "I liked it, I didn't like it" variety of feedback. This demands that students look more closely and dig deeper in analyzing why something was effective or not. Viewing dance, like close reading, is a skill that takes time to develop.

In the three-way collaboration with the English classes, the centrality of the peer audience enhanced the liberatory approach. My students were creating dances based on the writing of fellow students to be seen by those students, as well as a third group of students. There is no question that this sense of student ownership generated a great deal of excitement—and apprehension. Because Professor Atik's English class was more than twice the size of the choreography class, each choreography student was paired with two or three English class partners. Many asked, "Now what? Am I supposed to tell this story in dance?"

Students were asked to first respond in writing to all the authors whose work they had received, thanking them for their writing. I then directed them to choose one image, emotion, word, or phrase from a partner's piece and to explore that in movement. I alerted them that they were not bound to translating the story of the personal narrative into dance—the author had already shared their narrative. Dance communicates with a nonlinear part of our consciousness, where feelings, metaphors, and associations circulate. As such, they were to use the writing of their peers as springboards to create something new.

After having worked on their pieces for two class periods, students showed them to each other and received feedback. At this point the class was also exploring the concept of movement quality. So, as we gave feedback, we paid special attention to how movement quality was used within the works and suggested ways the choreographer could strengthen their work by experimenting with a range of qualities. One particularly striking work that developed during this process featured a gesture of fluttering fingertips surrounding the dancer's head. An airy movement quality gave the gesture a magical sense as it mysteriously materialized and disappeared over and over. This gesture expressed the writer's feeling of being watched, and it was, for me, a resonant physical image, both beautiful and frightening. It was also a striking contribution by a student whose virtuosity as a dancer led him to more often work with full-bodied, high-energy movements than small gestural motifs.

At times, students' creativity was spurred by their connections to their partners' writing. For instance, in one case, both the English student and the choreography student had been watched and pressured by others about their physical appearance and size. In another case, the students shared the experience of being singled out as different because of learning issues. For those young people who had experienced similar histories, this act of sharing was both liberating and empowering.

At other times, however, the writing gave the dance students a glimpse of an unfamiliar experience. This was the case with a dance student whose partner had written about being questioned in a hostile manner by immigration officials. The choreographer used the corner of the dance studio and the small space between the ballet barres and the wall to express the isolation her partner felt. As she struck the walls and struggled behind the wooden barres, she appeared imprisoned, confronting insurmountable obstacles. After showing her piece, she remarked that she never knew about this aspect of being an immigrant. Even though her partner's situation as a new arrival in this country was novel to her, she was able to connect emotionally with his story and to create a resonant physical metaphor reflecting his journey.

Of the nine students who developed short dances in response to the English class writing, two of them further developed those seeds into completed works that were performed in the culminating event of the 2014–2015 NEH/KHC Colloquium Series at QCC's Performing Arts Center. Seeing the project through to this event was a great opportunity for these students' growth. The first participant's dance was inspired by a piece about being under surveillance by an extremely jealous boyfriend. She initially worked with ways to physically explore the feeling of restriction that came from being scrutinized. She started with spatial restriction—being confined to one straight line in space. She then explored a bound movement quality, often choosing to restrain one arm by holding on to it with the other hand. As she continued to work on the piece, I saw her confronting her own restrictions as a performer. The piece became a vehicle for her to deepen her expressive range and her technical abilities.

The second student's dance was based on a piece of writing about being scrutinized for being too thin. Feeling judged for body size is such a common experience in our culture and in the dance world in particular, and this student had grown up feeling self-conscious about her weight. She created a duet in which one figure manipulates and physically attacks the other. Her challenge was to create the interplay between the two bodies, the exchange of energy, and the appearance of violence without the actuality of it. She used a movement vocabulary based in the speed, attack, and body part isolation of hip-hop, which was effective in portraying the violence of the exchange. This piece ended with a sort of revenge fantasy: the victim fights back and leaves her attacker on the floor.

In these two fully developed works students considered multiple Holocaust-related themes, such as institutionalized forms of hate, othering, and violence. They started with their empathic responses to their partner's writing and drew on their own life experiences to create strikingly original dances that expanded both their choreographic and performance skills. The sense of ownership that grounded this exchange went a long way in fostering students' creative investigation. There was a notable sense of trust and pride that marked the exchanges within my class and between my class and Professor Atik's class. I believe it was the openness that Professor Atik's students brought to their writing that inspired a similar kind of honest self-revelation from my students. In the next step of the collaboration, this openness further inspired Professor Miller's students as they worked on their documentary project.

Digital Composition for the Egalitarian Classroom (Benjamin Lawrance Miller)

Ever since I received a Master of Fine Arts (M.F.A.) degree in Writing, I've been drawn to interdisciplinary collaborations. In my graduate program, we were encouraged not only to write creatively but to experiment with art, film, performance, or any other creative discipline that might complicate our writing practice. Now as a composition professor at an urban community college, I often find myself wanting to draw from this interdisciplinary approach to the arts, and I had an excellent opportunity to do so via our SWIG and in collaboration with the NEH/KHC Colloquium Series.

After Professor Atik and Professor Geismar's classes completed their portions of our project, my English 101 class had the daunting task of making a documentary film about the collaboration as a whole. Although this was an English composition class and not a film production class, I thought this project would allow students to practice their composition skills, which thus far had been applied to traditional college essays, in an additional, supplemental creative dimension via technology. Work on the documentary was conducted at the end of the semester in a unit titled "Virtual Places." This was the last of four units that centered on student exploration of various spaces on campus and in their own neighborhoods. Students had been prepared for this work by viewing documentaries, such as *Go Public: A Documentary Film Project*, *The Pruitt Igoe Myth*, and *My Brooklyn*, and by reading essays about encountering the "other," such as *On Compassion* by Barbara Lazear Ascher, *The Joy of Reading and Writing: Superman and Me* by Sherman Alexie, and *Dumpster Diving* by Lars Eighner. Also, students had learned about the Holocaust as part of a class visit to the KHC where they were shown how Jews were stereotyped, surveilled, and signaled out with garment badges—experiences of marked "otherness" that stood to influence students' editing of their own documentary film.

Most digital editing software has a timeline feature at the bottom of the screen where the final film can be viewed during the production. I began the "Virtual Place" unit with the argument that this timeline should be thought about like an essay that students could "compose" by clicking and dragging video clips, photos, and audio to create a coherent story. Most students had almost no experience working with such software, so this would be a challenge to implement, but the hope was that it would be an excellent learning experience for them. By making the film, students could learn about the English and dance collaboration, reflect on the lecture about the Holocaust, improve their technology skills, create a completely original student-made digital film for the campus community to see, and provide a valuable digital artifact that we could use as an assessment tool for the whole interdisciplinary project.

During the course, my students read the personal narratives written by Professor Atik's students, and they watched the footage of when the two classes met to share their work. My students then shared their own responses to these works via the Blackboard Wiki function. Many didn't even know that we offered dance courses at QCC, and most had never viewed a dance performance in its entirety. Once students were introduced to the content that we would be working with, I assigned them into small groups, where each group was responsible for a part of the film. The parts were something that I came up with to give an overall structure to the film: Part 1: Introduction to QCC; Part 2: The Collaboration Explained; Part 3: The Texts; Part 4: The Dances; and Part 5: Student Reflections.

Because there was little time to teach film editing beyond an overview, I suggested that students engage in an *assemblage* process. They would be given clips of dances, clips of dancer reflections, clips of students reading essays, and photos supplied by the students in the other courses. They could click and drag these clips and photos to the timeline and experiment with the Camtasia editing software that we used. An assemblage process, rather than a digital editing focus, allowed me to talk in terms of traditional composition: much like an essay, each segment had to have a logical progression with a beginning, middle, and end.

I would like to say that the semester ended with a coherent digital documentary that movingly brought out the learning experiences of the students, but this didn't happen. Some parts were not coherent, and although every student participated and used their creativity in some way, we didn't have a cohesive final product that could be displayed to the larger campus community. Because it was essential to our student-focused pedagogical design that students created the final product, I did not volunteer to complete the film, but I did approach two of the students who had shown the most enthusiasm for the project. These students stepped forward in a way that demonstrated their leadership potential, and they finished the film over the winter holiday.

The resulting documentary is a nine-minute film that weaves together images and voices of students and professors in all three classes. Viewers are able to see clips from the dances and performed sections from the essays. In what is perhaps the most successful element of the film, students' reflective responses overlay the creative work. For example, one section involves Professor Atik speaking about her hopes for the project; this clip is then interjected with a student reflection split-screened with Holocaust images, a creative pairing decided by the film editors. Another moment in the film involves a literature student's audio reflection about the dream state he experienced when viewing the dances; this clip is positioned next to the dances themselves. The documentary created a space for all the elements of the collaboration to coexist in a singular platform. In fact, I was pleased that my two student editors decided to turn the camera around to film themselves talking about what they were learning and how the project was significant for them personally. One student expresses his happiness that he participated in the project. Another student comments about how working on the film transformed his feelings about the college. In addition, one of my students chose to film himself explaining the connections between surveillance, "otherness," and the Holocaust, which signified his burgeoning capacity to think across and through multiple experiences and texts.

The film is very emotional and inspirational, and I think it is an example of how community college students can produce relevant contemporary art. It is not perfect, however. There are audio production issues that make it hard to hear at points. Also, my student editors gave credit to the authors of certain music that was included, but they did not obtain permissions to do so, which makes the final film unsuitable for distribution to wider audiences beyond the campus. I think the original ambition to create one single, coherent documentary might be too ambitious, and in future versions of this collaboration, I might suggest that the small student groups each create a shorter documentary of their own rather than a segment that they may or may not see fitting into a larger vision. The overall process might be smoother.

The film was shown on campus at the culminating event of the 2014–2015 NEH/KHC Colloquium Series, and I know my students were proud to see their names and faces on screen, honestly expressing their ideas and feelings about the project. I think the completion and success of the film assemblage process demonstrates that community college students, who are often underprepared for the challenging realities of twenty-first-century life and work, can produce meaningful, relevant, even moving art that mirrors our current technologically driven existence. More broadly, I think that this project, as a whole, exemplifies how engaging students and faculty in a complex collaboration and exploration of profound humanistic challenges can help accelerate students' understanding of the world and their active, creative place in it.

Conclusion

Rather than approaching the Holocaust in a traditional historical sense, we used creativity as a way to investigate themes such as discrimination, surveillance, and power hierarchies that make acts of mass atrocity possible. Approaching genocide studies this way allowed students to see daunting historical events as part of processes—of hyper-surveillance, social injustice, inequality, and racism—with which they were already familiar. Although these processes don't necessarily lead to genocide, a focus on the Holocaust promoted vigilance and elevated the seriousness of these problems for young people who may view themselves as disconnected from the history they learned in school. In this way, the project asked students to consider the relationship between personal violence and historical violence.

At the same time, this project worked to advocate for an egalitarian pedagogical practice. Students gave us demonstrations of changed social roles in the classroom and beyond. In fact, they were no longer just students but writers, choreographers, producers, editors, and directors. Because of this, we believe that this interdisciplinary collaboration is an example of Freire's (1996) "problem-posing education," as it asked students to take a critical stance on our hyper-surveillance society while still leaving room for them to harness their creative power.

Learning about the Holocaust through a liberatory framework hopefully allowed students to see that our dark human stories—both personal and historical, although significant and worthy of study—are not inevitable. As student artists, they became leaders and equal collaborators in a transformative project. They contributed to a pedagogy where the "teacher is no longer merely the one who teaches but one who is herself taught in dialogue with the students, who in turn while being taught also teach" (Freire 1996, 61). In this sense, the creative component allowed students to re-territorialize social injustice, to move beyond it, and to teach us something, as we all hope for a more just society.

Appendix 1: Essay on Space, Surveillance, Memory, and Otherness (Aliza Atik)

Overview

As we discussed in class, specific sites have the power to call us into being as subjects—making us aware of the hierarchies and discourses around us, which situate us as social beings. This paper asks you to look at this process with an example from your own personal history, and it directs you to examine the ways in which space and discourse shape how we are viewed in the public sphere.

The Task

A. Your goal for this paper is to come up with an independent thesis statement that answers the following questions:
   1. How do unique spaces allow for different acts of surveillance and regulation?
   2. How is this reflected in your individual experience?

The Process

A. After workshopping in class, compose a thesis statement that sets out your agenda.
B. This thesis should be reflected in the body paragraphs of your paper, wherein you describe your experience as an "other" in a specific time or place (2–3 pages).

1. Describe your own experience as an "other." Using the excerpt "Antonio's Story" from Milton's chapter as a source text, describe an experience where you felt "visible" because you were subject to "correctional surveillance" or caught up in a system of "meticulous tactical partitioning" (Milton 2011, 80).

   *The experience you describe does not have to be with a police system or other judicial authority. You can discuss any social, personal, academic, or judicial moment where you were had to negotiate scrutiny within a hierarchical system.
2. What will make this section strong is if you continue to employ coherent paragraph frames that focus on clear topic sentences, as well as vivid details and dialogue as "evidence" to support each paragraph's claim.

Appendix 2: Choreography Assignment (Aviva Geismar)

You will receive a piece of writing from your partners in the English 102 class. (You may receive more than one piece if you have more than one partner.) The writing is on the topic of surveillance. You are going to select some aspect of this writing to respond to through a choreographic study. You might choose a feeling that the piece brought up for you, an image, the rhythm of the language, a word that struck you, and so on. You do not have to retell the narrative of the piece; telling narratives is hard to do in dance and has already been done by the writer. Look for something essential about the writing and allow yourself to respond to that through movement. You can use music if you like, but you do not have to.

We will have time to work on these studies in class and to receive feedback from each other. We will be showing these studies on October 16 to the English 102 students.

Please also respond to the writing that you have received via the WIKI page. You are required to write a respectful response to all your partners who posted writing for you. You may be using one or multiple pieces as inspiration for your dance, but you must write something for each writing assignment posted for you in order to acknowledge that you have received it.

Guidelines for Giving Choreographic Feedback

Start with what you see. Can you describe it in terms of the elements of dance—space, time, and movement quality? Can you see the choreographer's intention—that is, what he/she wanted the piece to do or the effect he/she wanted the work to have? Try to get inside their mind and figure out their intention. Our objective is to help them fully realize their intention. Did the dance suggest any meaning to you beyond pure movement exploration? If so, relate it back to what was happening in movement terms. If you had an emotional response try to relate it back to what was happening choreographically. One of our goals is to deepen our ability to see and articulate what we see. You are trying to help your classmates fully realize their intention by reflecting back what you see in the work.

Things to be cautious about:

- Try to not state an **unqualified** emotional response. (That means an emotional response by itself without explanation.) Explain the emotional response by relating it back to the choreography. An example would be, "It gave me goose bumps." If it gave you goose bumps try to figure out what the choreographer did that had that effect on you.
- Try not to SIMPLY compare it to another work of art. If it reminded you of another work of art, explain why. For example, "It reminded me of Paul Taylor because you respond to the music in such a spatially complex way," or "It reminded me of Malcolm Low's piece because the groupings of dancers on stage were constantly changing like jump cuts in a movie."
- If you find yourself wanting to make a suggestion to the choreographer, look for the observation behind the direction. In other words, if you want to tell someone that they should end the piece by walking off stage, try to figure out why that is the choice you think is most fitting: "Because you began by walking on stage, I felt that the ending in which you remained center stage broke up the symmetry of your structure. Was that intentional? It felt jarring to me." This is the feedback. Maybe their intention was to be jarring; maybe not.

Other Guidelines

- When you are showing share with the audience your title and nothing more besides instructions about when to start the music, and so on. Let the work speak for itself. This is what we want it to do in the theater. If we explain things before we show, we are not letting the work speak for itself.

- When you are receiving feedback please refrain from discussion. Again, your comments will color our view of what you are doing. If you feel the need to discuss or ask questions, do so after all the feedback has been given.

Appendix 3: In-Class Assemblage Assignment (Benjamin Lawrance Miller)

Each group will be working on creating a digital segment for the documentary film. Students in Group 2 will be responsible for creating a brief description of the collaboration that our class has been part of this semester. The purpose of this part is to explain to the audience what exactly the collaboration involves: Who is doing what? Why are they doing it? What is the subject material? Explain what classes are contributing to the collaboration.

Group 2 "The Collaboration"

1. Preview the images in the folder on your flash drive.
2. Organize these images in the program "PowerPoint."
3. Each member in your group should write a paragraph that explains the collaboration. Remember to write it in a formal way.
4. Record your voice reading the text in the program "Audacity." Save the file in the flash drive folder.
5. Combine the recorded voiceover and the PowerPoint in the program "Camtasia." Save the file in your flash drive folder.

Initial ENGL 101 Film Production Timeline

- Fri 8/22, Blackboard shell that includes all three courses will be created
- Thurs 9/18, Literature students will post text to Blackboard Wiki
- Thurs 9/18 to Thurs 10/9, Dance students will be able to comment, reply, and post images or videos as a response
- Thurs 10/9, Deadline for Dance students' responses via Blackboard

- Thurs 10/9 to Wed 11/26, Composition students will create digital profiles of collaborating students and interview Literature students and Dance students about the texts and dances that were created
- Thurs 10/30, Dance students begin a second assignment based on Literature students' texts
- Wed 11/26 to Mon 12/15, Composition students use collected images, audio files, and video to create a digital documentary of the collaboration
- Thurs 4/16 from 5 to 7 pm in KHC Gallery, Attend "*Inspired Testimony: QCC Students Respond to Genocide through Art, Research and Creative Writing*," a student-led exhibition
- Thurs 4/16 from 7 to 9 pm in QPAC, Attend "*Inspired Testimony: QCC Students Respond to Genocide through Music and Dance*," a student-led performance, in collaboration with the MOTÝL Chamber Ensemble

References

Foucault, Michel. 1977. *Discipline and Punish: The Birth of the Prison*. Trans. Alan Sheridan. New York: Vintage Books.

Freire, Paulo. 1970. Cultural Action and Conscientization. *Harvard Educational Review* 40 (2): 452–477.

———. 1996. *Pedagogy of the Oppressed*, 52–67. New York: Continuum.

Kuh, George. 2008. *High-Impact Educational Practices: What They Are, Who Has Access to Them, and Why They Matter*. Washington, DC: Association of American Colleges and Universities. PDF e-book.

Milton, Trever B. 2011. *Overcoming the Magnetism of Street Life: Crime-Engaged Youth and the Programs that Transform Them*. Lanham: Lexington Books.

Sameshima, Pauline, and Dayna Slingerland. 2015. Reparative Pedagogy: Empathic Aesthetic Learning. *Canadian Review of Art Education* 42 (1): 8–25.

CHAPTER 9

Teaching the Holocaust: Making Literary Theory Memorable

Johannes Burgers

Since the mainstreaming of literary theory across English Departments in the 1980s, literary theory courses have presented a challenge to faculty and students alike (Martin 1982, 186–189). Literary theory is a core course for any English major, yet properly sequencing it in the curriculum is challenging. Recondite and esoteric, learning as well as teaching literary theory represents a complex endeavor, even for precocious students and gifted teachers. At the same time, it is a critical pivot that transforms students from readers into scholars of literature (Prince 1984, 38). Given the challenge that literary theory presents within English curricula, surprisingly little has been written recently in terms of "best practices" or "successful pedagogies," especially at the associate level.[1]

In my experience, what is particularly challenging about teaching literary theory at a community college is that many of the students are not English majors, and the usefulness of learning multiple, complex textual

I would like to thank Amy Traver, Dan Leshem, and Tarushi Sonthalia for their thorough feedback on this piece.

J. Burgers (✉)
Department of English, Ashoka University, New Delhi, India
e-mail: johannes.burgers@ashoka.edu.in

A. E. Traver, D. Leshem (eds.), *Humanistic Pedagogy Across the Disciplines*, https://doi.org/10.1007/978-3-319-95025-9_9

interpretation strategies is not always readily apparent. Indeed, since some students have to take this course to fulfill a curricular requirement, and face economic, familial, and social challenges, there is some understandable resistance. Compounding this resistance is the fact that this course is simultaneously meant to prepare English majors, while also creating an engaging curriculum for future nurses, business majors, computer scientists, and a whole host of other professions that, at first blush, are quite a departure from an English classroom. No doubt, these are the baseline challenges for most community college classrooms.

To make the content relevant for non-English majors, I developed a unit on Holocaust literature as part of the 2013–2014 National Endowment for the Humanities (NEH) Colloquium Series, "The Holocaust in a Global Context: Connections Across the Community College," at Queensborough Community College's (QCC's) Kupferberg Holocaust Center (KHC). Under the tutelage of the faculty coordinator of that colloquium and seasoned Holocaust educator, Susan Jacobowitz, a working group of English faculty met during a series of meetings in the fall 2013 semester to share their ideas about incorporating Holocaust literature in their classrooms. This productive discussion shaped my course on literary theory for the better, and, in fact, when I implemented the course in the spring 2014 semester, the strongest unit in the course was that on the Holocaust.

Inspired by this very positive experience, this chapter suggests that teaching literary theory at the community college level generates the productive confusion necessary for critical thinking and is an important curricular step for majors and non-majors alike. Further, it argues that applying literary theory to something with clear historical stakes enhances student engagement and understanding of the theory. Specifically, a topic like Holocaust literature promotes sustained critical thinking precisely because the texts were produced under extreme duress and theory helps readers do justice to this context. Within this framework, one particular method that proved successful was using cultural memory theory to problematize how students read and interpret Holocaust literature.

This chapter begins with a brief overview of cultural memory theory and an explanation of how that theory can function as a pedagogy. Second, the course content and assignment deployment cycle are explained. This is followed by a student paper assessment using QCC's General Education Objectives. Finally, the chapter closes with some best practices.

Ars Memoria: Literary Theory, Cultural Memory, and the Holocaust

Cultural memory theory is not usually incorporated into the larger canon of literary theory, and a survey of the most popular literary theory anthologies reveals that none of them include works by major cultural memory theorists.[2] No doubt, this can be attributed to the fact that cultural memory theory originated in history departments. Briefly, the birth of cultural memory theory started with Maurice Halbwachs' early twentieth-century observation that a person's individual memories are not exclusively his or her own because they are, to a certain extent, mediated and conditioned by a larger "collective memory" (Halbwachs 1980, 48–49). Building on this premise, cultural memory theorists explore the way in which memory moves between the social, the material, and the psychological. Cultural memory studies is, therefore, by definition, interdisciplinary and really "an umbrella term that comprises '*social* memory' (the starting point for memory research in the social sciences), '*material* or *medial* memory' (the focus of interest in literary and media studies), and '*mental* or *cognitive* memory' (the field of expertise in psychology and the neurosciences)" (Erll 2008, 4). Though in existence in some protean form since the late nineteenth century, the field was powerfully shaped by the work of Pierre Nora and Jan and Aleida Assmann. Their respective concepts of *lieux de mémoire*—the "commemorative consciousness" of a "ritualless society"—and *Kulturelles Gedächtness*—the process by which communicated memories over time become the fabric that hold societies together—provided scholars with the theoretical language to think through the complex relationships between memory, society, material culture, and the individual (Nora 1996, 6–7; Assmann 2007, 21).

The burgeoning academic inquiry into memory and remembrance was intimately related to the aging of the Holocaust generation. With increasingly fewer survivors around to tell their stories, there was an urgency for them to adequately represent their narratives to future generations. Though Nora's and the Assmanns' projects focus on historical periods prior to the Holocaust, their ends are coextensive with the work of Holocaust remembrance. In this regard, the work of Holocaust scholar James Young is particularly indebted to Nora's concept of *lieux des memoires.* Young shows that "the performance of Holocaust memorials depends not on some measured distance between history and its monumental representation, but in the conflation of private and public memory, in the memorial activity by which minds reflecting on the past inevitably precipitate in the present historical moment" (Young 1993, 15).[3] The problematics of active remembering are all the more acute with the Holocaust. After all, despite an overwhelming amount of physical and documentary evidence, the traumatic nature of survivors' memories of the Holocaust poses a challenge to recollection. As Primo Levi points out in *The Drowned and the Saved*, "the memory of a trauma, suffered or inflicted, is itself traumatic because it is disturbing, if not painful to recall" (Levi 2015, 2421). Julia Epstein links the problem of individual traumatic memory with the challenge of public remembrance through her concept of "traumatic cultural memory." In her view, "Concentration camp suffering took place in a world apart, a world that has no analogues in ordinary human life" (Epstein 2001, 191). It is impossible to know the camps without having been there, and yet in order to remember the camps, the memory needs to be told. Thus, telling is itself problematic because "The stories cannot fully be communicated or understood without being relived, and it is too much to ask of anyone that such catastrophes be experienced a second time, even if only discursively" (Epstein 2001, 197). In a sense, Holocaust cultural memory is caught in a double bind—its traumatic quality makes it unknowable and, at the same time, its unknowability endows it with historical urgency.

The issues that Holocaust cultural memory raises are intrinsically connected to the epistemological suppositions of literary theory, which establish texts as fundamentally unstable and contingent on the relationship between the reader, the text, and the discursive context. Cultural memory studies, in turn, asks students to evaluate how memories are produced and reproduced in a particular social and linguistic framework. Students have to consider how and why certain narratives and remembrances are prioritized over others. This is an increasingly fraught problem as the number of survivors decreases every year and the amount of popular, and some would argue trivializing, narratives—like the blockbuster movies *Inglourious Basterds*, *The Boy in the Striped Pajamas*, and *Life is Beautiful*—has grown. This is to say nothing of outright Holocaust denial, which, through the ubiquity of the Internet, has gained a stronger voice than ever. In short, the critical work of Holocaust cultural memory studies is closely intertwined to the intellectual heritage of literary theory. Nonetheless, cultural memory studies has tended to live inside, or next to, history departments and is rarely taught in English departments—despite the fact that much great work has been done on literature using cultural memory theory (see, e.g., Rigney 2012; Neumann 2005; Lachmann 1990).

Even in the field of Holocaust pedagogy, the politics of Holocaust memorialization does not appear to be a central concern.[4] This is not surprising given the curricular and practical constraints Holocaust teachers face, not the least of which is the need for accuracy (Crowe 2001). Problematizing how Holocaust history is represented might, inadvertently, distort the factuality of the history. Nevertheless, teaching the Holocaust is arguably an act of memorialization, with the classroom serving as a *lieu de memoire*—a socially mediated space in which memories of the Holocaust are regulated through boundaries of the discipline and the institution.[5] The prospect of introducing a highly technical, metacognitive dimension to a Holocaust pedagogy in secondary education might seem daunting, but certainly the college classroom should be the site of such discussions. Hence, there is room in both literary studies and Holocaust studies to introduce the critical lens cultural memory studies provides.

The Class

During the faculty working group meetings in fall 2013, it was determined that the most suitable course for implementing a Holocaust unit would be my spring 2014 section of "Introduction to Literary Studies." According to the course catalogue, one of the central aims of this course is to provide "an introduction to some of the theoretical issues currently debated in literary studies and a consideration of how such issues have evolved historically" (Department of English 2017). For all intents and purposes, this course functions as a gateway course for possible English majors, as it links up with the articulation requirements of four-year colleges. Yet, since QCC does not currently offer an English major, there is no way to determine how many students taking this course actually end up pursuing a degree in English at a four-year institution. Anecdotally, the overwhelming majority of students use this course to satisfy some requirement for a future major other than English.

The curriculum for my course covered three units on different sets of literary theories. The assignments aligned with each unit increased in complexity and built toward a capstone paper that required a use of literary theory and outside research. To that end, the first unit was about *The Odyssey* by Homer and used classical narratology and theories of rhetoric to discuss the text. Students had to write a 600-word, close-reading paper on one of several assigned passages from *The Odyssey* that was informed by the themes we discussed in class. Students were not required to use any external references to support their readings, but they did need to explicitly engage with themes discussed in class. The second unit revolved around Mary Shelley's *Frankenstein* and made use of feminist, queer, post-colonial, and critical race theory to analyze the text. For this 3–4 page paper, students had to analyze *Frankenstein* using one of the critical sources we discussed. In essence, this required them to reconstruct the theoretical reading using different quotes from the text. The key critical exercise was to identify those passages that aligned with the stated theory. In many respects, these first two sections followed a fairly standard literary theory course structure. The final unit analyzed Holocaust literature using cultural memory theory and trauma theory, focusing especially on Charlotte Delbo's *Auschwitz and After*. This section also featured other Holocaust readings and a visit to QCC's KHC for an informational tour and, later, to listen to a survivor speak. Students were also encouraged to attend the lectures and exhibitions offered during the 2013–2014 NEH/KHC Colloquium Series for extra credit. The final assignment was a 6–8 page research paper that compared or contrasted two different Holocaust texts using three different theoretical texts. The theories offered as an example of analysis were all variations of cultural memory theory, with either a focus on the writer's trauma in relation to understanding historical events or understanding historical events in relationship to their meaning within a culture.

While QCC has four main campus-wide General Education Outcomes, the central focus of this course was related to critical thinking and is articulated as: "Use analytical reasoning to identify issues or problems and evaluate evidence in order to make informed decisions" (Academic Senate 2017).[6] In order to attain this objective, the overarching pedagogical approach was to destabilize students' reading of texts. This involved establishing a "true" reading of a text using one theory and then undermining that same reading using another theory. For example, in one class we used a feminist reading to establish that Frankenstein's monster was a projection of Shelley's own birth traumas. In the subsequent class, we challenged that interpretation by reading the monster as a subaltern using a post-colonial reading. Students were constantly forced to self-reflexively question their approach to reading literature. The learning objective thereby shifted from learning an individual literary theory toward thinking theoretically—that is, to learn to approach texts from multiple angles, whether they be mutually exclusive or constitutive.

Initial Impressions from Units One and Two

Having taught literary theory to English majors at a four-year institution on multiple occasions, and being intimately familiar with both *The Odyssey* and *Frankenstein*, I felt confident that I could spark engaging discussions and intense critical thinking about these texts; however, this proved to be challenging. While it is hard to measure the intellectual acumen of any class given all of the variables involved, it did appear that this class was particularly bright and motivated. What set them apart from traditional English majors is that literary theory was not unquestioningly assumed to be necessary or useful. In the beginning, students could make the connection between a literary text and a literary theory but could not explain why that connection was important. To be sure, this is generally an issue when teaching English literature at a community college, but it is perhaps more acute in a literary theory class because so few students will ever end up using any of the theories in their future profession.

This skeptical attitude was evidenced in the first two sets of student papers collected. Throughout the course, all of the student essays were evaluated using a rubric that broke down the paper along the dimensions: thesis, analysis, coherence, evidence, and grammar and style. For all the student papers submitted during the semester, proficient analysis was defined as those papers that were able to connect the thesis with evidence and then explain why that connection was important. For the *Odyssey* paper submitted in week seven, only 5 of 22 papers showed proficiency in terms of analysis. This, in contrast to 8 papers that showed proficiency in thesis construction, and, more strikingly, the 11 papers that demonstrated proficiency of finding appropriate evidence to support claims. What this bifurcation suggests is that students were comfortable making an argument and finding evidence for it but had a harder time explaining why that argument was important. More bluntly, they could not explain why their reading of the text mattered.

For the *Frankenstein* critical reading paper submitted in week ten, the analytical dimension was actually somewhat stronger. Eight students were able to show proficiency in analyzing *Frankenstein* using a literary theory. Perhaps the uptick in the score can be attributed to the fact that the importance of discussing gender, sexuality, race, and post-coloniality may have been more readily apparent to some students. Nonetheless, this is also where there was a curious split in the papers, as some students' papers did not even meet the minimum assignment requirements. In fact, in three cases this was directly tied to the analysis in these papers, which was too short and underdeveloped. In class discussions too, the importance of theory as an instrument for broader social critique was not explicitly apparent to the whole class.

Since these are instructor-driven self-assessments, they necessarily lack the objective rigor of an external assessment. Nevertheless, they reflect the struggle that was happening with the content in the classroom. Students managed to understand the text and the theory to some extent, and even make valuable links, but the greater question of why literary theory was necessary, or even useful, in analyzing the text and the world around us remained unanswered.

Unit Three: Low-Stakes Assignments

Since cultural memory studies is a necessarily abstract field, students were prepared for the basic principles of unit three through a series of low-stakes assignments. The first of these was a Socratic discussion establishing the critical terms for discussing Holocaust literature and, more so, why our discussion had to be framed using critical terms.

To help students understand how memories are socially mediated, I opened up the class discussion with my own memory of 9/11. As it happens, I had a much harder time telling it than I anticipated, and my candor backfired in a spectacularly productive fashion. I was expecting students, most of whom were living in New York at the time of the attacks, to have stories to share. None were able to because they actually had no memory of the event, as they were around four or five when it happened. This false start then took a surprising turn. When I asked them how they remembered 9/11, they all described the similarly iconic images of the smoking Twin Towers. Notably, none of them mentioned other possible memories such as the destruction of the Pentagon, the wreckage of Flight 93, the collapsing buildings, the crying newscasters, or any of the other horrific images of that day. Importantly, this memory was not their own. In their initial accounts, there was no recollection of actually having seen that iconic news footage; instead, they acquired that knowledge at a later time. This unsettling tension between their private memory and the larger public remembrance was fertile ground for opening up discussion about the interplay between private psychological experiences and socially mediated versions of events. I subsequently guided them through a series of increasingly complex questions that got at the core of cultural memory theory. They were as follows:

- Why do we have memories?
- What is the difference between memory and knowing?
- Are some memories more important than others?
- How do we know our memories are accurate?
- Are our memories stable or do they change over time?
- Are our memories our own or are they shaped by other people?
- Can we have memories without language?
- If language precedes us, to what extent are memories always already shaped before they happen?

Without a doubt, these questions were quite challenging as they asked students to explore both the social and linguistic nature of memory. They were supposed to conclude that memories are not exclusively our own and are shaped by the language available before the event of the memory takes place. Paradoxically, our future memories are, to a certain extent, predetermined in language. These concepts paved the way for a critical understanding of the traumatic cultural memory of the Holocaust. Our remembrance of the Holocaust is socially mediated and is problematic because there is no language available to explain its true horror, either to the survivors who experienced it or to the subsequent generations learning about it. Holocaust fiction and non-fiction texts are constantly grasping at an inexpressible truth—events that are true in that they happened but mediated by the limits of language and the influence of other accounts.

These problematic tensions in Holocaust cultural memory were productively unpacked using the poetic and incisive epigram of Delbo's first book in her trilogy, *None of Us Will Return*. She opens the text by musing, "Today, I am not sure what I wrote is true. I am certain it is truthful" (Delbo 1995, 1). The subsequent texts were all analyzed from the paradoxical position of the author shaping the cultural memory of the Holocaust, while at the same time trying to speak truthfully in the absence of truth. These texts included primary documents like Abraham Lewin's "Diary of the Great Deportation," poetry by Abraham Sutzkever, non-fiction by Primo Levi, and more narrative accounts like "This Way for the Gas, Ladies and Gentlemen" by Tadeusz Borowski. Students were also shown significantly different documentary accounts of the Holocaust, including Alain Resnais's *Night and Fog* and Claude Lanzmann's *Shoah*.

In these initial discussions, students were generally adept at understanding different perspectives on the Holocaust, but could not yet make critical value judgments. They felt that people should be able to remember the Holocaust in whichever way they want. On the face of it, this seems positive because it speaks to an open-mindedness to other people's views. What is problematic is that, within this highly relativistic framework, students had few problems with popularizations and vulgarizations of Holocaust remembrance. On the one hand, they had a firm grasp of the theoretical issues and how they related to the texts, but, at the same time, they could not quite process why this was important.

Unit Three: Medium-Stakes Assignments

This lack of critical thinking shifted during the most impactful moments of the semester when students visited the KHC for two presentations. The first presentation was a historical overview and tour of the artifacts given by the KHC's assistant director, Marissa Hollywood. During this visit, students were able to get a more tangible, material understanding of the history of the Holocaust. They were also able to listen to recorded accounts by survivors.

A Holocaust survivor gave the second presentation at the KHC. Students were briefed about the kinds of details they might expect to hear, and we discussed what types of questions might be appropriate and what questions might be inappropriate. Students' initial response to the survivor was positive, but they were very hesitant to ask questions in an open forum. Only in the informal chat after the formal presentation did they feel comfortable asking questions.

Just how deep an impression the meeting had made on students only became apparent in the following class session, when we had our debriefing. Students expectedly gravitated toward the horrifying experiences the survivor recounted but also how the survivor overcame those experiences and built a successful life in the United States afterwards. Importantly, the fact that they heard the speaker's complete life made her more than a survivor locked in time but turned her into a real person. Students may not have considered that many Holocaust survivors lived for many years after, and had to confront how society shaped and remembered their most intimate and violating experiences. Another lesson was that in Holocaust memorialization, the voices of actual survivors can be marginalized, even ignored, in favor of uncomplicated representations of good and evil, as is often the case in Hollywood and other popular outlets. In short, Holocaust memorialization suddenly became consequential because they were able to identify the people whom it would affect.

Unit Three: High-Stakes Assignment

These low-stakes assignments and medium-stakes class activities all built toward the final research paper for unit three, which read as follows:

Introduction: The point of this paper is to synthesize different literary sources with critical theory and thereby highlight a relationship between the two texts.

Instructions: The goal of this paper is to write a 6–8 page critical analysis of two literary texts, one of which must be Charlotte Delbo's *Auschwitz and After* and another Holocaust text of your choosing. You must analyze these using at least three literary theoretical texts for support. In essence, this is a compare or contrast paper, but you are using the theory to support your analysis. (See Appendix for the full assignment.)

To help students complete this assignment, I created a curated database through the course content management system, Blackboard. Students were encouraged to search for their own articles, but they could also draw on this annotated bibliography. The research paper was assigned roughly four weeks before the end of the semester, and students had an opportunity to peer review the papers before the final due date. The papers were to be the culmination of everything they had learned throughout the semester, and they were meant to incorporate close reading, critical theoretical reading, and outside research.

Along with the research paper, there was also a course final that asked students to review the information they had learned throughout the course. The second part of the final was a reflection prompt that asked the following:

> The last section of this course was dedicated to studying the literature of the Holocaust. How has this section shaped your views of the Holocaust? What did you already know? What did you learn? What was a really productive moment of insight? What could have been left out? What would you like to have known more about?

There were no wrong answers to this prompt, and the evaluation was based on whether students could successfully articulate what they had actually learned.

The assessment of these high-stakes assignments was quite revealing. In both sets of papers, students had a firmer grasp of the importance of theory for understanding literature and, more broadly, the Holocaust than they did for the papers assigned during the previous two units. Twelve out of the 22 research papers assessed demonstrated proficiency in connecting theory with evidence and then explaining the importance of this connection. This broad assessment is, of course, somewhat impressionistic, and the line between developing and being proficient is necessarily blurry. That being said, the proficient papers had a concrete thesis, used a quote from the text to support the thesis, and then proceeded to show how the quote aligned with the argument and why this was important. Certainly, it would be hard to attribute this progression in proficiency to any one factor, and any teacher would hope that students get more proficient over time. Nevertheless, the link between Holocaust literature and cultural memory theory was more readily apparent in these papers because students could negotiate the different consequences of the theory. In sum, students appeared more dexterous in their theoretical thinking because they were able to intuit how different theories shaped the representation of people's lives.

Further support for the positive effect of using cultural memory theory and Holocaust literature to teach literary theory was found in students' final reflections. Almost all students mentioned that learning about the Holocaust was very important and that cultural memory theories, and in particular Delbo's work, helped deepen their knowledge. What was really interesting is that 13 out of 21 students offered that one of the most important moments in their semester was going to the presentation at the KHC and/or listening to the survivor. There was nothing in the way the question was phrased that would solicit this answer, but clearly for many students meeting a survivor had a memorable impact. I suspect this is because meeting a survivor and seeing the material culture helped contextualize the texts students were reading. There was simply not the same connection with *Frankenstein* or *The Odyssey*, no matter how pervasive their narratives are in contemporary culture.

Yet, the relationship between cultural memory theory and the Holocaust was also reciprocal. Not only did studying the Holocaust underscore the importance of theory, cultural memory theory also opened up a new way to study and think about the Holocaust. Many of the students reflected that they had learned about the Holocaust in either high school or some previous context, but they had gained a much deeper knowledge through this unit. To a certain extent, such responses can be attributed to giving socially desirable answers. Still, many students supported this claim with concrete examples that included topics such as traumatic memory, the life of survivors after the Holocaust, and how movies portray the events. To my mind, students had a better sense of the remembrance of the Holocaust as an active and current debate. Thus, while there are many established facts about the Holocaust, the interpretation and meaning of those facts is still very much disputed. Of critical importance in this debate is making sure that the memories and experiences of those who suffered are accurately and respectfully recognized, without being glossed over through an easily digestible narrative.

Conclusions

As with any course, it is easy to theorize how it could have produced better results and suggest different areas of focus. Similarly, it is challenging to predict how any shift in the curriculum in one area might take away from content and skills in another area. Time in the class is, after all, limited. Yet, I can say with some certainty that using the theoretical framework of cultural memory theory to spark discussion about Holocaust literature was a net positive for students. Furthermore, working with colleagues through the 2013–2014 NEH/KHC Colloquium Series's faculty working group to shape the Holocaust unit in advance was extremely useful because it sparked ideas for content and possible challenges. It is likely that I would never have taught the Holocaust in a literary theory class because it would have seemed an unnatural fit and too overwhelming a task. Subsequently, I have taught courses dedicated entirely to Holocaust Literature and have promoted critical thinking using cultural memory studies. Personally, I always have a fear about debating how to interpret the Holocaust, as it might lead to the type of soft relativism that opens up the Holocaust to all opinions. The way I have allayed this anxiety is by having students listen to the firsthand accounts of survivors, and, when those are not available, watching testimonies on video. By anchoring the discussion to the preservation of the memory of the victims, the boundaries of remembrance are always committed to how to best honor that memory.

Appendix: Spring 2014 Research Paper

Word Count: 6–8 pages (1800–2400 word)
Peer Review Date: Tuesday, May 13
Due Date: Thursday, May 15

Introduction: The point of this paper is to synthesize different literary sources with critical theory and thereby highlight a relationship between the two texts.

Instructions: The goal of this paper is to write a 6–8 page critical analysis of two literary texts, one of which must be Charlotte Delbo's *Auschwitz and After* and another Holocaust text of your choosing. You must analyze these using at least three literary theoretical texts for support. In essence, this is a compare or contrast paper, but you are using the theory to support your analysis.

You may choose three different critical modes of analysis: trauma theory, cultural memory, and the politics of representation.

Introduction Outline

Topic sentence
Introduction Text A
Introduction Text B
Thesis: comparison or contrast between the two texts
Specific thesis: How and why are these texts similar or different?

Thesis Example

Comparison: Although Charlotte Delbo's *Auschwitz and After* and Claude Lanzmann's *Shoah* tell the story of the Holocaust through two different media, text and film, both can be productively analyzed using trauma theory. In particular, both demonstrate the impossibility of the medium to capture the memory.

Contrast: Even though Abraham Sutzkever and Charlotte Delbo both write about their Holocaust experiences from a personal point of view, they are engaging its cultural memory in two different ways. While Sutzkever is trying to bear witness to the events around him through his poetry, Delbo is more concerned with the impossibility of ever capturing the true horror of the Holocaust.

Outline

1. Introduction
2. Section 1: First Author
   a. Theory: An introduction to the theoretical article about the text and how it relates to the thesis.
   b. Text: An application of the theory to the text.
   c. Theory: An introduction to the theoretical article about the text and how it relates to the thesis.
   d. Text: An application of the theory to the text.
   e. Theory: An introduction to the theoretical article about the text and how it relates to the thesis.
   f. Text: An application of the theory to the text
3. Section 2: Second Author
   a. Repeat Section 1 outline above
4. Conclusion

Notes

1. Somewhat dishearteningly, many of the same institutional struggles early pioneers in literary theory pedagogy faced over 30 years ago have not abated. If anything, the institutional strictures that gear students toward professionalization and teaching toward assessment have made the open critical exploration of texts more challenging (see, e.g., Scholes 1985; Nelson 1986; Kecht 1992; Davies 1994). There are some good examples of contemporary guides to teaching theory (see, e.g., Brown 2009).
2. Not surprisingly, most of the major literary theory readers used in classrooms do not cover cultural memory theory or historical theory more broadly (see, e.g., Cuddon 2013; Klages 2012; Eagleton 2008; Castle 2007; Waugh 2006; Rivkin and Ryan 2004; Leitch 2001)
3. Young, in turn, inspired other scholars who work at the intersection of cultural memory and the Holocaust (see, e.g., Hansen-Glucklich 2014; Zelizer 1998). Both Zelizer and Hansen provide great insight into the challenges of representing the Holocaust. Hasian Jr. (2006) provides a good discussion on how Holocaust trials shape the collective memory of the Holocaust.
4. A notable exception is the work done by *Facing History and Ourselves*, which has amassed a very robust set of educational resources related to Holocaust memory (Facing History and Ourselves 2017). Marianne Hirsch and Irene Kacandes (2004) have also assembled an anthology that has a number of really important essays on this topic. The excellent collections on teaching the Holocaust assembled by Samuel Totten are invaluable in their

own right, but the works do not touch on the problematics of how the Holocaust is shaped in cultural memory and the fraught politics of representing the Holocaust (see, e.g., Totten et al. 2002; Totten 2001; Totten and Feinberg 2001). Likewise, other works, like those of Short and Reed (2004), do not engage the problematics of Holocaust remembrance.

5. In fact, one way to view Holocaust education is as a formalized way of remembrance (see, e.g., Stevick and Gross 2014).
6. Though QCC's General Education Outcomes were revised in 2016 after the course was run, this General Education Outcome has been in place since 2007.

References

Academic Senate. 2017. *General Education* [cited June 18 2017]. Available from http://www.qcc.cuny.edu/assessment/geoa.html.

Assmann, Jan. 2007. *Das kulturelle Gedächtnis: Schrift, Erinnerung und politische Identität in frühen Hochkulturen*. München: C.H. Beck. Original edition, 1992.

Brown, Kathleen L. 2009. *Teaching Literary Theory Using Film Adaptations*. London: McFarland & Company, Inc.

Castle, Gregory. 2007. *The Blackwell Guide to Literary Theory*. Oxford: Blackwell Publishers.

Crowe, David M. 2001. The Holocaust, Historiography, and History. In *Teaching and Studying the Holocaust*, ed. Samuel Totten and Stephen Feinberg, 24–61. Boston: Allyn and Bacon.

Cuddon, John Anthony. 2013. *A Dictionary of Literary Terms and Literary Theory*. Chichester: Wiley-Blackwell.

Davies, J.M.Q. 1994. *Bridging the Gap: Literary Theory in the Classroom*. West Cornwall, CT: Locust Hill Press.

Delbo, Charlotte. 1995. *Auschwitz and After*. New Haven: Yale University Press.

Department of English. 2017. *English Department Course Offerings & Descriptions* [cited June 18 2017]. Available from http://www.qcc.cuny.edu/english/course-description.html.

Eagleton, Terry. 2008. *Literary Theory: An Introduction*. Minneapolis, MI: University of Minnesota Press.

Epstein, Julia. 2001. Remember to Forget: The Problem of Traumatic Cultural Memory. In *Shaping Losses: Cultural Memory and the Holocaust*, ed. Julia Epstein and Lori Hope Lefkovitz, 186–204. Chicago: University of Illinois Press.

Erll, Astrid. 2008. Cultural Memory Studies: An Introduction. In *Cultural Memory Studies: An International and Interdisciplinary Handbook*, ed. Astrid Erll, Ansgar Nünning, and Sara B. Young, 1–15. New York: Walter de Gruyter.

Facing History Facing Ourselves. 2017. *Memory and Memorials* [cited June 18 2017]. Available from https://www.facinghistory.org/topics/holocaust/memory-and-memorials.

Halbwachs, Maurice. 1980. *The Collective Memory*. New York: Harper & Row.

Hansen-Glucklich, Jennifer. 2014. *Holocaust Memory Reframed: Museums and the Challenges of Representation*. New Brunswick, NJ: Rutgers University Press.

Hasian, Marouf A., Jr. 2006. *Rhetorical Vectors of Memory in National and International Holocaust Trials*. East Lansing, MI: Michigan State University Press.

Hirsch, Marianne, and Irene Kacandes. 2004. *Teaching the Representation of the Holocaust, Options for Teaching*. New York: Modern Language Association of America.

Kecht, Maria-Regina. 1992. *Pedagogy Is Politics: Literary Theory and Critical Teaching*. Urbana: University of Illinois Press.

Klages, Mary. 2012. *Key Terms in Literary Theory*. London: Continuum.

Lachmann, Renate. 1990. *Gedächtnis und Literatur: Intertextualität in der russischen Moderne*. Frankfurt am Main: Suhrkamp.

Leitch, Vincent B. 2001. *The Norton Anthology of Theory and Criticism*. 1st ed. New York: Norton.

Levi, Primo. 2015. The Drowned and the Saved. In *The Complete Works of Primo Levi*, ed. Ann Goldstein, 2405–2574. New York: Liveright Publishing Corporation.

Martin, Wallace. 1982. Literary Theory in/vs. the Classroom. *College Literature* 9 (3): 174–191.

Nelson, Cary. 1986. *Theory in the Classroom*. Urbana: University of Illinois Press.

Neumann, Birgit. 2005. *Erinnerung, Identität, Narration: Gattungstypologie und Functionen kanadischer Fictions of Memory*. New York: Walter de Gruyter.

Nora, Pierre. 1996. *Realms of Memory: Rethinking the French Past*. Translated by Lawrence D. Kritzman. 3 vols., *European Perspectives*. New York: Columbia University Press.

Prince, Gerald. 1984. Literary Theory and the Undergraduate Curriculum. *Profession* 84: 37–40.

Rigney, Ann. 2012. *The Afterlives of Walter Scott: Memory on the Move*. New York: Oxford University Press.

Rivkin, Julie, and Michael Ryan. 2004. *Literary Theory: An Anthology*. Malden, MA: Blackwell Publishers.

Scholes, Robert E. 1985. *Textual Power: Literary Theory and the Teaching of English*. New Haven: Yale University Press.

Short, Geoffrey, and Carol Ann Reed. 2004. *Issues in Holocaust Education*. Burlington, VT: Ashgate Publishers.

Stevick, Doyle, and Zehavit Gross. 2014. Research in Holocaust Education: Emerging Themes and Directions. In *Holocaust Education in a Global Context*, ed. Karel Fracapane and Matthias Haß, 59–76. Paris: United Nations Educational, Scientific, and Cultural Organization.

Totten, Samuel. 2001. *Teaching Holocaust Literature*. Boston: Allyn and Bacon.

Totten, Samuel, and Stephen Feinberg. 2001. *Teaching and Studying the Holocaust*. Boston: Allyn and Bacon.

Totten, Samuel, Paul R. Bartrop, and Steven L. Jacobs. 2002. *Remembering the Past, Education for the Present and the Future: Personal and Pedagogical Stories of Holocaust Educators*. Westport, CT: Praeger.

Waugh, Patricia. 2006. *Literary Theory and Criticism: An Oxford Guide*. New York: Oxford University Press.

Young, James Edward. 1993. *The Texture of Memory: Holocaust Memorials and Meaning*. New Haven: Yale University Press.

Zelizer, Barbie. 1998. *Remembering to Forget: Holocaust Memory Through the Camera's Eye*. Chicago: University of Chicago Press.

CHAPTER 10

Outcomes of an Academic Service-Learning Project on Mass Atrocity with an ELL Population

Julia B. Carroll

Today's community colleges, which are exploding in diversity across the nation, serve as the gateway to a postsecondary education for a wide array of people, including low-income, minority, and first-generation postsecondary education students. Within this broad range of student classifications fall English language learners (ELLs), who will be the primary focus of this chapter.

Hateful rhetoric, mass violence, and genocide remain as persistent challenges worldwide, and community college educators are uniquely positioned to develop the critical thinking skills of ELLs on these topics before they transition to four-year colleges or the workforce. In fact, because it cannot be taken for granted that ELLs were exposed to information about genocide, the Holocaust, or multiculturalism in their native countries or in some type of educational setting in the United States after immigration, these essential skills might *best* be developed in relationship to this content learning.

J. B. Carroll (✉)
Department of English, Queensborough Community College, CUNY, Bayside, NY, USA
e-mail: JCarroll@qcc.cuny.edu

A. E. Traver, D. Leshem (eds.), *Humanistic Pedagogy Across the Disciplines*, https://doi.org/10.1007/978-3-319-95025-9_10

This chapter makes that argument by presenting the outcomes of a recursive reflection-based assessment of a peer-to-peer collaborative project that paired ELLs with EDUC-101 (Contemporary Education: Principles and Practices) students at Queensborough Community College (QCC). This project was designed as an intensive English learning opportunity organized to grow ELLs' knowledge of genocide and multiculturalism within the context of the 2015–2016 NEH-funded Colloquium Series, "Gender, Mass Violence, and Genocide," at QCC's Kupferberg Holocaust Center (KHC). I begin the chapter by providing the backdrop and an initial rationale for my development of the project. I then offer a general description of the project's design and curricular focus. As the chapter unfolds further, I focus on the project from an outcomes perspective, highlighting some of the most pertinent themes of my recursive and formative assessment of students' learning and participation.

A Snapshot of ELL Education Within the Developmental Framework

In order to fully appreciate the aforementioned project, it may be helpful to gain some historical background knowledge on ELL programs in higher education. At both community colleges and four-year colleges in the United States, the first programs designed for ELLs were created in the 1970s by educators who had backgrounds and degrees in Teaching English to Students of Other Languages (TESOL) or Applied Linguistics. These programs provided English instruction in reading, writing, speaking, and listening. For example, in the early 1970s and 1980s, in New York State, extensive financial support was provided to community colleges and four-year colleges to develop multilevel English language instructional programs, primarily in developmental or remedial departments (Cochran and Grujicic-Alatriste 2016). These developmental or remedial programs often comprised two different tracks: one for ELLs and one for native-speaking remedial students. In line with this trend, at QCC, a community college in the City University of New York (CUNY), our developmental program consisted of a subdivision of reading and writing classes for both native and non-native speakers: there were two levels of reading courses and three levels of writing courses designated for ELLs, and two levels of reading courses and two levels of writing courses for native speakers. Upon applying to CUNY, students who were not deemed exempt by their high school averages were required to pass a standardized reading and a standardized writing exam in order to avoid remediation. Students who did not pass one or both of these exams were placed into the appropriate developmental or remedial classes and levels.

Over the years, however, a myriad of political and educational reforms have brought a tremendous change to how ELLs and developmental students are educated. One of the most significant trends in higher education has been the desire to reduce or even eradicate remediation. For instance, in 1999, in New York City, Mayor Rudolph Giuliani and the CUNY Board of Trustees were successful in passing legislation that banned remediation from all of the four-year CUNY colleges. Students who did not pass two of the three placement exams were required to attend one of CUNY's community colleges (Carroll 1998). As ELLs tended to fail these exams at rates higher than native speakers, this contributed to a decline in their overall enrollment in CUNY's four-year colleges. Another programmatic change that occurred in the late 1990s was the introduction of Pre-College Programs, like CUNY Language Immersion Program (CLIP) and other free or low-cost intensive English programs for ELLs at community colleges (O'Riordan 2016).

The most current trend in English language education is mainstreaming ELLs directly into freshmen composition classes, which is seen as an alternative to what many deem as expensive, time consuming, and ineffective remediation (O'Riordan 2016). Support for mainstreaming can be found in the work of researchers who study the process by which students have historically been placed into English language or developmental classes. Concerned primarily with the growing number of Generation 1.5 students (i.e., students who may have received most of their education in the United States but were born elsewhere), these researchers question whether placement in English language classes hinders students' sense of identity or their ability to improve fluency in the target language (Maloy 2016).

Curiously, despite the current trend toward mainstreaming, very little attention has been paid to the content of ELL programs. Traditionally, ELL instructors have shied away from teaching sensitive topics like the Holocaust, genocide, and mass violence, preferring instead to teach more neutral and possibly easily accepted topics like contemporary music, technology, and fashion. In fact, anecdotal evidence points to instructors feeling "safer" avoiding sensitive topics due to worries about students' immigration histories/experiences and concerns regarding how these topics might impact students' perceptions of the class. I, on the other hand, have always felt compelled to research and teach topics that promote social justice, help my students become better readers and writers in the English language, encourage students' critical thinking and moral decision-making, and prepare students to engage in the intensive study of similarly significant content in credit-bearing courses at QCC and beyond.

My Pedagogical and Scholarly Background and Experiences in English Language Learner

For the past 26 years, I have been teaching ELLs in a variety of settings, such as Yale University, Columbia University, Hunter College (CUNY), and Pace University. However, for the past ten years, I have been teaching at CUNY's QCC, where I have found the population to be surprisingly unique from all of my previous teaching experiences. The students who enter my classroom each semester represent different countries, are enthusiastic and highly motivated learners, and have limited proficiency in the English language. During the semester in which this project took place (fall 2015), for example, QCC enrolled students from 132 different countries, who spoke up to 78 different languages (QCC Fact Book 2015–2016). The vast majority of these students came from lower socioeconomic backgrounds and received some form of financial aid. Additionally, a large percentage of these students were also the very first members of their families to attend college. Recently, there has been an uptick in the percentage of ELLs from Asian backgrounds; many of my students are from China, in particular. Large numbers of these students reside in Flushing, Queens, where they mainly speak Mandarin, their native language, for the vast portion of their day. Hence, it is common that QCC's ELLs have limited contact with native speakers and profess to feeling most comfortable speaking their native language with family and friends.

Also at the time in which this project was conducted, fall 2015, ELL was housed in QCC's Department of Academic Literacy, which served both remedial students and ELLs in reading and writing.[1] The Academic Literacy Department offered three levels of writing and two levels of reading, which were all noncredit courses, to ELLs. The last level of reading, BE226 College Reading and Study Skills for ESL Students, was the class that participated in this project. In order for students in this course to advance to EN101, the College's introductory English composition course, they had to pass the class and a standardized reading test—the American College Testing (ACT) (Compass) test—scoring a minimum of 70 percent. Hence, one of my most important objectives in teaching this course has always been to ensure that students pass this exam.

As I have never subscribed to the type of pedagogy that includes formulaic test prep, I have long developed creative teaching activities that spark my students' interests and strengthen their skills through a dynamic thematic curriculum. One pedagogical methodology that I have found to be particularly successful in this regard is Academic Service-Learning (ASL). ASL has provided me with the opportunity to teach ELLs academic reading and writing skills through a content-based thematic curriculum inside the classroom and then supplement this instruction with highly interactive and engaging related activities outside the classroom. In fact, much of my ASL experience has been directly related to teaching students about the history of the Holocaust, the existence of genocide in various parts of the world today, and contemporary hate crimes that occur both locally and nationally. For example, in past semesters, I have asked my students to read and write about the Holocaust and then interview survivors about their life experiences: in the fall 2013 and spring 2014 semesters, my advanced reading students wrote summaries of Holocaust survivors' lives, and this work was displayed alongside the survivors' portraits as a major part of the 2014–2015 NEH/KHC Colloquium Series, "Testimony across the Disciplines: Cultural and Artistic Responses to Genocide."

My most recent scholarship in this area is showcased in several articles that were published in 2014. In a two-part article, "Rethinking Critical Service-Learning in Developmental Reading and Writing Courses at a Two-Year College" (Part One) and "From Obscurity to Valuable Contributor: A Description of A Critical Service-Learning Project at a Two-Year College" (Part Two) in the *Basic Writing e-journal*, I along with two other colleagues, Dr. Jennifer Maloy, who taught writing to native speakers, and Ms. Marisa Berman-Hollywood, the Assistant Director of the KHC, describe our collaborative experiences utilizing an ASL curriculum that incorporated the theme of combating hatred through the study of the Holocaust (Berman et al. 2014a, b). In the same year, I published another article, also with Dr. Maloy, entitled, "Critical Reflection on the Road to Understanding the Holocaust: A Unique Service-Learning Project at the Two-Year College" in *Teaching in the Two-Year College*. In this article, we discuss the implementation of a critical reflective approach to learning, more specifically how the Describe, Examine, Articulate, and Learning (DEAL) Model of Reflective Assessment was utilized to ascertain student-learning outcomes over the course of a semester-long ASL project (Maloy and Carroll 2014).

NEH Collaborative Project with ELLs and EDUC-101 Students

The pedagogical and scholarly experiences depicted earlier served as the backdrop for my involvement in the 2015–2016 NEH/KHC Colloquium Series, "Gender, Mass Violence, and Genocide." Witnessing how engrossed my students had become in their own learning processes when they studied the history of the Holocaust and interviewed survivors, I was motivated to find a way to align my course, an advanced reading class for ELLs, with the theme of the new series. I noticed that one of the eight speakers, Ms. Jasmina Dervisevic-Cesic, had been invited to headline an event about her memoir, *The River Runs Salt, Runs Sweet: A Young Woman's Story of Love, Loss, and Survival.* Originally from the former Yugoslavia, Ms. Dervisevic-Cesic describes how she had escaped the genocide during the war and successfully immigrated to the United States. Immediately, her story appealed to me, as many of my students are also immigrants who have been forced to abandon their countries due to extremely harsh circumstances. I felt that my students would relate to the emotional turmoil that she described, in addition to her struggle to learn English. As I was drawn to the theme of her story, I contemplated how I could create a stimulating and creative project that would incorporate her memoir and ASL.

Fortuitously, I learned that Dr. Amy Traver, the coordinator of the 2015–2016 Colloquium Series, was also intending on assigning the memoir to her EDUC-101 students. This would be Dr. Traver's first experience teaching an introductory education class, and she was looking for a way to enliven her course focus on multicultural education. Dr. Traver's focus on multicultural education also resonated with me, as I was equally concerned that the ELLs in the course increase their fluency in English through knowledge and exposure to a diverse array of cultures. At the time of this writing, fall 2015, the United States had just weathered two significant terrorist attacks, one in San Bernadino, California, and the other in Miami, Florida, which had increased the racial rhetoric leading up to the 2016 presidential election. Thus, teaching my students about diversity and the need for a multicultural education became a top priority in developing my curriculum, as well.

After conversing with Dr. Traver, it occurred to me that we could arrange for our classes to collaborate on various projects that relayed the importance of a multicultural education as they read Ms. Dervisevic-Cesic's memoir simultaneously. In the end, we chose to implement a peer-to-peer collaborative ASL project, as students' design and delivery of lessons for peers has proven effective in encouraging them to think more critically (Owens 2011). In particular, peer-to-peer collaborative projects benefit students by sharpening their "cognitive skills as they practice learning, organizing, and synthesizing material for the purposes of teaching rather than for the purposes of pure rote memorization" (56). In addition, such projects have also proven effective in increasing students' self-esteem, awareness of others, and motivation to learn (57).

The activities in our project counted as ASL because both the ELL students and the EDUC-101 students simultaneously instructed one another or provided "service" to each other as they acquired new academic knowledge of genocide and mass atrocity.

Logically, we framed our peer-to-peer collaborative ASL project around two objectives: first, teaching our students the importance of providing and receiving a multicultural education and, second, in recognition of the ELLs' ACT (Compass) exam and the centrality of assessment to EDUC-101 students' learning, teaching our students how to successfully create and take various types of assessment tasks. Significantly, assessment was also central to *our* administration of the project. Yet, instead of designing a traditional pre-/post-outcomes model of assessment, Dr. Traver and I elected to design a more recursive and reflexive model to assess our students' learning as it unfolded. Our intent was to evaluate students' learning repeatedly after each activity in order to ascertain the project's impacts over the course of the semester.

As one of the three mandatory components of ASL is reflection, which, if used correctly, can also improve students' higher-order reasoning abilities and critical thinking skills, we opted to distribute lists of open-ended reflection questions to our students after each class meeting or learning activity (Ash and Clayton 2004). This approach enabled us to critically assess what was working and what wasn't, thereby providing us with the opportunity to tweak our curricula and pedagogical approaches as necessary. This strategy is particularly important in community college settings, where the needs of one's student population can be in constant flux: what may work in one semester may be a catastrophe in the next semester depending upon who is sitting in the room. Additionally, this strategy might also be warranted when teaching sensitive subjects like genocide, the Holocaust, and multiculturalism to a population of students who may have immigrated from countries due to harsh circumstances and who may continue to experience direct discrimination as members of minority groups in the United States.

Project Details

Over the course of the semester, the ELLs and EDUC-101 students met a total of six times. Both classes commenced the semester by reading Dervisevic-Cesic's memoir. Before meeting Dr. Traver's students, ELLs in my class worked together in pairs to create open-ended reading comprehension questions. These questions were then asked of Dr. Traver's students at our first combined class meeting. Toward the end of that meeting, we administered a general reflection assessment to both groups of students to gauge their prior knowledge of the meaning of a multicultural education and to inquire about their learning that day.

In the second meeting, my students, who were preparing for the multiple-choice ACT (Compass) reading test, provided the education students with a PowerPoint presentation on the various types of multiple-choice questions, as well as specific strategies for how to approach each type of question. They also created sample multiple-choice questions, which were based on the content of Dervisevic-Cesic's memoir, and they posed these questions to Dr. Traver's education students. The class concluded with students completing their second reflection assessment.

Dr. Traver's education students took the lead in the next peer-to-peer component of the project. They were instructed to utilize the information that they had garnered from the ELLs' presentation to create their own multiple-choice test based on a sophisticated essay about multiculturalism and then to administer that test to the ELLs. In the third class meeting, they distributed the essay, as well as an aligned homework assignment, for my students to complete at home. This class also ended with a reflection assessment.

The ELLs took the EDUC-101 students' multiple-choice test at the fourth class meeting. This activity provided Dr. Traver's students with their first opportunity to administer an exam to "real students." Once the

ELLs had completed the test, Dr. Traver's students corrected the exam and homework questions and went over the answers with each of the ELLs. Toward the end of the class, the students worked in small groups to prepare questions for Ms. Dervisevic-Cesic, who would be coming to QCC to discuss her experiences as a Bosnian refugee and a new immigrant to the United States. Our students also completed their fourth reflection assessment.

The fifth time that the students met was when Ms. Dervisevic-Cesic came to speak. The ELLs sat together with the EDUC-101 students in pre-arranged pairs to listen to the presentation. It was clear that the students were ecstatic to meet the author of a text that was of newly personal, academic, and professional significance. In their sixth and final meeting, students discussed their reactions to Ms. Dervisevic-Cesic's talk, as well as the differences and similarities between her memoir and her presentation. They also completed a concluding, final reflection assessment.

Project Curriculum

In the past, when I taught the Shoah, the vast majority of my ELL students knew little of Jewish history or the Holocaust. In those semesters, I did my best to fill that void with relevant films, presentations at the KHC, appropriate books and articles, as well as reading guides and vocabulary glossaries. As a result, I knew that my fall 2015 students would need an expanded curriculum to contextualize and understand Dervisevic-Cesic's memoir, as well as their work with the EDUC-101 students. In particular, they needed a historical understanding of the ethnic cleansing campaign that occurred as a result of the war in Bosnia. They also needed to comprehend the need for policies and curricula that centered multiculturalism as a means to prevent this type of disaster from occurring again.

To this end, I asked students to read another memoir that was co-written by a survivor of the Bosnian War. In *The Bosnia List: A Memoir of War, Exile, and Return*, Kenan Trebincevic describes how, at age 11, he survived genocide and ethnic cleansing and escaped to the United States. He also writes of his desire to gain a stronger sense of identity and his need to deal with grief, both of which prompt him to return to Bosnia years later with a list of things that he wants to accomplish (Trebincevic and Susan 2014).

I also screened films about former Yugoslavia and Tito's plan to create a country where a multitude of people from many different ethnic religions and cultural backgrounds could live side by side, attend the same schools, and play on the same sports teams. These films were supplemented with brief articles that summarized this information, as well as short video clips about the beginning of the war. In addition, students were introduced to terms like "ethnic cleansing," "genocide," "stereotype," "cultural bias," and "discrimination."

As students read both memoirs with the aforementioned information in mind, they were able to experience how two separate individuals—one female and the other male, both Muslims but from different areas of Bosnia-Herzegovina—dealt with the rejection and emotional assault brought on by previous friends, neighbors, teammates, coaches, and teachers from a Serbian background. Students were particularly shocked by this feature of the Civil War, expressing dismay at how individuals who had been described by both authors as "close childhood friends" and "loving teachers" could come to express such deep hatred on the basis of cultural differences. This learning led my students to reveal personal stories about themselves as immigrants—stories that included their experiences being ridiculed, excluded, and harassed because of their ethnic backgrounds. We then discussed the dangerous things that can occur when people begin to hate one another simply because they speak a different language, follow a different religious tradition, or look different from others.

These discussions led to our consideration of a multicultural education grounded in curricula that promote tolerance and appreciation for all cultures. My students were fortunate to be introduced to relevant articles on this topic by their service-learning partners, the EDUC-101 students, who had been separately studying it in their course.

Project Reflections: Emergent Themes

As the project unfolded, Dr. Traver and I met regularly to discuss students' experiences and learning. Guided by the themes that emerged across the reflection assessments, we aimed to measure the impact of the projects' various components and to make adjustments accordingly. For the purposes of this chapter, I offer a summary of those emergent themes that relate to the benefits that ELLs reaped as a result of participating in this peer-to-peer collaborative ASL project aligned with the 2015–2016 NEH/KHC Colloquium Series.

Theme One: Increased Second-Language Acquisition

Oral Fluency Development. One of the most common themes to repeatedly emerge from the reflections was how much the ELLs felt that their oral fluency was enhanced as a result of completing this project. Almost all of the project activities required that the students work in small groups or be paired with a native-speaking counterpart. In these groups/dyads, students engaged in in-depth conversations on complex topics, such as the causes and effects of genocide and the need for multicultural education. According to the reflections, these conversations provided students with ample opportunities to practice speaking English, which was especially enticing as they were speaking about topics of importance with "native speakers." Many also mentioned the impact of preparing and delivering a formal PowerPoint presentation to their ASL partners.

Vocabulary Acquisition. Another benefit that emerged as a major theme in the ongoing reflective assessment was an increase in academic vocabulary, an area of language development that is extremely important to ELLs. The students were proud to have learned many new terms related to topics of importance, like multiculturalism, racism, and genocide. They also mentioned how, once our class had ended, they would be able to use these new words in future essays and assignments for credit-bearing courses.

Reading Comprehension. As the course was an upper-level reading course, one of my main objectives was increasing students' reading comprehension. Based on the themes that emerged from students' reflections, as well as their high overall passing score on the ACT (Compass) reading test, I believe the course succeeded in accomplishing this task. In their reflections, students cited activities like creating a reading comprehension exam based on Dervisevic-Cesic's memoir, designing a lesson about multiple-choice reading questions, and reading complex essays and articles on important topics as reasons why their overall reading comprehension increased.

Theme Two: Increased Self-Esteem

As mentioned earlier, the ELLs in my courses have consistently expressed feelings of inadequacy due to their poor English vocabulary and language skills. They have also acknowledged that they rarely have the opportunity to converse with native speakers or practice their English skills because they often reside in insolated enclaves where they tend to speak in their native languages with family and friends. At the onset of this project, many of my students' reflections conveyed how anxious they were to partner with native speakers, who they perceived as possessing far more sophisticated language skills. They commented on feeling worried that they would be mocked for mispronouncing words or not properly articulating their main ideas while conversing with their ASL partners. What is more, they mentioned feeling utterly petrified to present a formal PowerPoint presentation to native speakers.

However, once they mustered up the courage to create their questions, teach their lessons, and engage in actual conversations with their partners, the ELLs surprised even themselves. In their reflections, they described their EDUC-101 partners as nurturing, pensive, curious, and equally interested in learning from them—all of which inspired them to work even more diligently on their next activity. By the end of the project, the ELLs consistently described feeling an increase in self-esteem and feeling less nervous when speaking to native speakers and more confident in using the English language.

Theme Three: Increased Knowledge of Genocide and Multiculturalism

Before this project, the ELLs in my course admitted to having almost no background exposure to concepts such as genocide, mass rape, or extreme atrocity. Most had never heard about Bosnia or the dreadful events that had occurred there. However, after reading two books on the Bosnian War and many essays and articles on the topic of multicultural education, and after engaging in multiple extended conversations with their native-speaking counterparts, they were able to describe, in detail, the importance of educating young people about these topics in order to prevent similar occurrences from transpiring in the future.

Conclusion

As our college campuses and individual classrooms have grown more diverse, effective cutting-edge pedagogical strategies designed to promote the success of ELLs have become increasingly necessary. As I reflect back on this project, I feel that it serves as a model for both community college and four-year college instructors who desire to facilitate ELLs' deep and critical thought about crucial topics such as hatred, hate crimes, the

Holocaust, and genocide. We, as educators, cannot presume that these students have been exposed to such topics in their prior educational experiences. Hence, it is incumbent upon us to expose our students to curriculum that touches upon these horrors and to seek and engineer creative pedagogical strategies that captivate their interests and empower them to implement the principles of tolerance and multiculturalism. If more and more educators can commit to adopting similar approaches, ELL students—in fact, *all* students—will be better prepared to engage in both complex material and complex realities.

Appendix: Reflection Questions on Multicultural Education for Academic Service-Learning Project with an English Language Learner Population

These questions can be administered at various points throughout the semester.

1. Describe what it means to provide students with a *multicultural education*. Please be specific. You can refer to your personal experience and/or any reading that you have completed.
2. To what extent do you believe that you have received *a multicultural* education and how has it played a role in your overall education? This may include all previous schooling. Please explain with specific examples.
3. How important do you believe it is for students to receive a *multicultural education* and why? Please explain with specific examples.
4. In what ways, if any, will you use your knowledge of a *multicultural education* in the future, either in your career and/or in your personal life?
5. What is the social purpose of a multicultural education? Why might a multicultural education be of value to society?

Note

1. The Academic Literacy Department has since merged with the English Department.

References

Ash, H. Sarah, and Patti H. Clayton. 2004. The Articulated Learning: An Approach to Guided Reflection and Assessment. *Innovative Higher Education* 29 (Winter): 137–154.

Berman, Marisa, Julia Carroll, and Jennifer Maloy. 2014a. Rethinking Critical Service-Learning in Developmental Reading and Writing Courses at a Two-Year College. *Basic Writing eJournal* 13 (1): 1–25.

———. 2014b. From Obscurity to Valuable Contributor: A Description of a Critical Service Learning Project and the Behind the Scenes Collaboration. *Basic Writing eJournal* 13 (1): 1–16.

Carroll, Julia. 1998. Where Are All the Students? *Idiom* 29 (1): 14–16.

Cochran, Papatzikou Effie, and Lubie Grujicic-Alatriste. 2016. Taking Stock of CUNY ESL: What a Survey of ESL Faculty and Administrators Says About the Past, the Present, and the Future: A Collaborative Report. *NYS TESOL Journal* 3 (1): 14–22.

Dervisevic-Cesic, Jasmina. 2014. *The River Runs Salt, Runs Sweet.* Charlottesville, VA: NSPYR.

Maloy, Jennifer. 2016. A Tale of Two Placements: Influences of ESL Designation on the Identities of Two Linguistic Minority College Students. *NYS TESOL Journal* 3 (1): 23–34.

Maloy, Jennifer, and Julia Carroll. 2014. Critical Reflection on the Road to Understanding the Holocaust: A Unique Service-Learning Project at the Two-Year College. *Teaching English at the Two-Year College* 41 (1): 369–383.

O'Riordan, Mary. 2016. Where Are All of the Students? An Update. *NYS TESOL Journal* 3 (1): 2–13.

Owens, E. Julie. 2011. Peer Educators in Classroom Settings: Effective Academic Partners. *New Directions for Student Services* 133 (Spring): 55–64.

Trebincevic, Kenan, and Shapiro Susan. 2014. *The Bosnia List: A Memoir of War, Exile, and Return.* New York: Penguin.

CHAPTER 11

Connecting the Dots: Backward Course Design, Arts Education, and Teaching the Holocaust

Steven Dahlke

In an era of quantitative, "value-for-money" analysis, institutions of higher learning must regularly assess their efficiency and report detailed results to governing bodies. Performance evaluations are particularly important to community colleges, which struggle with relatively low retention and graduation rates (Aud et al. 2010) and which must demonstrate their ongoing effectiveness to retain legislative and financial support. This backdrop has motivated the development of pedagogies that are designed backward, with learning outcomes envisioned and decided upon first, and activities that will lead students to such outcomes designed accordingly (Reynolds and Kearns 2017). The Scholarship of Teaching and Learning has recently been devoted to discovering, testing, and implementing learning activities that will deliver desired learning outcomes that can be documented through student-produced artifacts (Burns 2017). When students demonstrate thorough comprehension of course content, display ability to apply their knowledge to other disciplines, show that they can carry the value of

S. Dahlke (✉)
Department of Music, Queensborough Community College, CUNY,
Bayside, NY, USA
e-mail: SDahlke@qcc.cuny.edu

A. E. Traver, D. Leshem (eds.), *Humanistic Pedagogy Across the Disciplines*, https://doi.org/10.1007/978-3-319-95025-9_11

this knowledge to later stages of their lives, and exhibit initiative to engage meaningfully with a broader community, it is widely understood that valuable and summative learning outcomes have been met (Schober et al. 2016). Such cumulative learning outcomes may be summarized as displaying life-long learner skills and productive citizenship. These aptitudes are some of the most important character traits that any course could instill. Indeed, documentation of these significant outcomes to any accrediting or assessing body should be ample justification of a learning institution's value as an engine for practical, economic, and positive societal growth.

Supporting the earlier meta-outcomes are the learning outcomes of both the choral music courses I teach and of my home institution, Queensborough Community College (QCC). The course learning outcomes may be stated generally as follows:

1. Choral music study will advance intellectual, kinesthetic, and emotional consciousness through the study and performance of choral works from a broad range of backgrounds.
2. Empathy will be expanded in the shared kinesthetic experience of a collective sung expression.
3. Such expression, arrayed actively in the broader community, may promote societal well-being.

Though my choral music courses primarily attract music majors who need to fulfill performing ensemble participation requirements, approximately 20 percent of enrollees come from other departments, citing their desire to learn more about self-expression through singing. Because of my aspiration to make musical expression a more central part of the QCC experience, I have endeavored to design choral music learning outcomes to support those of QCC, which demand primarily that students receive an education of "academic excellence and rigor" (QCC 2017). Specific college outcomes that I seek to bolster in choral music classes are "holistic development of students in a diverse environment"; "cultural and artistic appreciation"; and the charge to aid students to be "successful in a dynamic workforce [through a sense of] global awareness and civic responsibility."

To tackle these outcomes and to meet the learning needs of community college students in general, community college instructors must play multiple roles, and I have striven to develop skills that rise to that challenge. Instructors must teach effectively as generalists and demonstrate competencies in the totality of their discipline, they must become experts in effective and innovative pedagogy, and they must support and/or develop rigorous programs of discipline- or pedagogy-based research. When community college instructors satisfy these job requirements, they can more effectively guide their students through their journey of advancing their empathic and motivational skills (Kisker et al. 2016) and strengthening their interpersonal communicative ability (Morreale and Staley 2016).

Thankfully, understanding the realities of community college education, embracing QCC's learning outcomes, and designing my courses to satisfy them are by-products of my scholarly interests and career trajectory. From early adulthood I have taken great interest in discovering healthful modes of interpersonal communication in an effort to overcome the poor adult modeling I encountered throughout my formative years. This interest has led me to the informal study of Acting, Sociology, Psychology, and Kinesthetic Expression and to formal study of Music Education, Choral Conducting, and Vocal Performance. In the area of acting, I have been most influenced by the empathy-based pedagogy of Sanford Meisner (1987) and the kinesthesia-infused teaching of Wesley Balk (1985, 1991). In studying Classical Vocal Performance, I experienced the varied musical and literary perspectives of several cultures, embedded in exploration of the emotions-based physical awareness and control required for healthful vocal production. The study of Choral Conducting advanced my understanding of purely kinesthetic communication, and experience in the pedagogical approaches of Carl Orff (Frazee and Kreuter 1987) and Emile Dalcroze (Caldwell 1995) taught me the value in Music Education of experiential, kinesthetic-based learning. This path of study has reinforced my interest in providing student-based, emotionally driven learning experiences. My career arc has moreover ignited my desire to craft learning experiences that build empathic and cultural awareness, promote a robust interest in civic engagement, and advance students' abilities to apply curriculum-specific concepts and skills to broad areas of life experience. Though it has taken years of work and discovery to realize it, it is clear to me now that this journey has been preparing me to be a professor of music who teaches the discipline not only for the sake of the discipline itself but also for the sake of advancing the cause of individual and collective wellness.

Backward Course Design in a Multidisciplinary Project

To meet these outcomes, I envisioned a learning project for QCC Choral Music students. The project was called "Musical Responses to the Holocaust" and yielded pertinent general learning outcomes by deploying powerful and varied teaching approaches. “Musical Responses” was part of QCC’s 2014–2015 National Endowment for the Humanities (NEH)/ Kupferberg Holocaust Center (KHC) Colloquium Series entitled “Testimony across the Disciplines: Cultural and Artistic Responses to Genocide.” The series was designed to lend immediacy and depth to QCC students’ grasp of the Holocaust and genocide studies through varied symposia, presentations, and student-based learning activities. “Musical Responses” taught QCC choral students about the Holocaust from the perspective of its victims, deepened their understanding through applying learned concepts to a pertinent piece of choral music, and asked QCC students to then teach the piece and the related human rights concepts to children from an Academic Service Learning (ASL) community partner organization. That organization, the Corona Youth Music Project (CYMP), provides after-school choral and instrumental instruction and performance opportunities to children aged 8–11 in an underserved neighborhood in Queens, New York. The culmination of “Musical Responses” saw QCC students and CYMP children performing the music they learned together at a major concert on the QCC campus. The concert was the capstone of the year’s entire NEH/KHC Colloquium Series, and it included student presentations of performance-based projects from departments across campus.

Learning Activities in “Musical Responses to the Holocaust”

I conceived of “Musical Responses” in four parts. In the first part QCC students learned about the Holocaust through brief in-class lectures, directed class discussions, assigned readings and guided visits to the KHC website, and a short visit to the KHC itself. The second part included learning a piece of choral music entitled “Inscription of Hope,” which expresses the perspective of victims of the Holocaust. In learning the piece, the students were taught to use the meaning in the music and text to actively embody that point of view. In the third part, QCC students taught the CYMP children “Inscription” and modeled for them how to embody the meaning (taught in an age-appropriate manner) of the piece in their singing. The fourth and final part of “Musical Responses” was the CYMP children and QCC students singing “Inscription” side by side at the capstone concert and demonstrating to the audience their understanding of the Holocaust through the expressivity and immediacy of their performance.

The heart of "Musical Responses" lay in Parts 2 and 3, in which historical and emotional meaning was expressed through music, and in which QCC students taught this meaning to the children of CYMP. In Parts 2 and 3, learning activities were designed to focus primarily on advancing emotional and kinesthetic consciousness and expanding empathy. To reinforce students' interpersonal connections, I asked them to participate in several emotional and kinesthetic awareness exercises. An initial improvisational exercise asked students to react facially and physically to music played by our pianist. During the improvisation, the students also noted and responded to each other's reactions.

Afterward, the students performed an improvisatory, emotional awareness exercise. In the exercise, the students spoke in a pseudo chant using a soothing, repetitive rhythmic pattern. The students chanted two sentences. The first sentence was, "What do I want?" and the second sentence was a response, impulsively and definitively given, from the student's emotional core, that answered the question. For example, a pair of sentences chanted by a student might be, "What do I want? I want to feel safe wherever I go." After intoning the first pair of sentences, the student would then continue to improvise, creating different answers each time to the question, "What do I want?" This exercise was also performed while the pianist improvised, with the students all chanting together their individual questions and answers. As the exercise progressed, I called on individual students to continue alone, encouraging them to take a leap into emotional vulnerability. As students revealed their own personal desires and heard those of others, interpersonal and empathic connections were intensified (see chapter's online resources at http://qcc.libguides.com/neh).

Another exercise encouraged students to use full and spontaneous vocalization to demonstrate awareness of one's own emotional state and the emotional state of another. In a call and response format, I would improvise vocally to the pianist's improvisation, then ask the singers to respond to my sounds with their own group improvisation; following this, I would respond to the group's improvised "call." As these physical and vocal improvisation exercises progressed, I asked the pianist to incorporate passages from the piece inspired by the Holocaust, "Inscription," into his improvisation. As a result, these exercises became imbued with the musical meaning in "Inscription." In this way, the students became emotionally connected to the music before being introduced to it formally. This connection was deepened by the students' improvised empathic response to the music (see chapter's online resources at http://qcc.libguides.com/neh).

The group nature of these exercises made it easy for students to participate with full kinesthetic and emotional involvement, without the self-conscious hesitancy that often arises in solo performance. As with the "What Do I Want?" exercise, I called out students' names randomly during group exercises, instructing students to continue alone briefly in their movement and singing when they heard their name called and before the next name was called. Students consistently performed more bravely when they did not know in advance that they would be performing alone and when they discovered that their solo time would be brief and that everyone would have to do it during one session.

After the students were acclimated to the physical, vocal, and expressive flexibility the improvisation exercises required, I looped class activities back to Part 1 of "Musical Responses": consideration of the Holocaust. By linking the empathy-based expressive exercises to discussion of the Holocaust, I sought to increase their comprehension of course content and of issues of the Holocaust and to strengthen their skills in applying knowledge to other disciplines. One example of this linkage was having the QCC students consider photographic evidence of the Holocaust. In class, the students viewed photos of prisoners at the Buchenwald Concentration Camp, discussed their significance, and then utilized their empathic and expressive skills in demonstrating their understanding of that significance. One of the photographs studied showed thousands of newly arrived prisoners massed in the camp's center square for roll call. I asked the students to imagine how those prisoners at Buchenwald felt: forced to stand long hours at attention, uncertain of whether they would live or die, but certain of the organized hatred that had imprisoned them. Together and individually, the students expressed through spontaneous movement and improvised vocalization their embodiment of the perceived emotional and physical state of the prisoners. During the exercise, our pianist played the music from "Inscription of Hope," supporting the students' improvisation.

"Musical Responses" then returned to Part 2 of the learning process, using the study of pertinent choral literature to address the learning outcome of increasing cultural and artistic expression, and to further personalize issues of the Holocaust. The students explored how choral music texts and musical content can illuminate issues of the Holocaust and further discussed how musical expression might serve to help solve humanitarian problems at the root of genocide. At this time, the students formally learned their specific vocal parts in "Inscription of Hope" by Z. Randall

Stroope, which uses a Russian folk melody as its musical foundation. It is set to words by the composer, which include an inscription found on a wall of a cellar in Cologne, Germany, where a family was hiding from the Nazis. The inscription expressed faith in peace and love from God, even when God seems absent (see chapter's online resources at http://qcc.libguides.com/neh).

During the entire process of learning the song, students used concepts of the kinesthetic and vocal improvisatory exercises that they had already learned. At first, students moved spontaneously to the piano accompaniment, as if their movements were embodying the emotional state of the composer and of those persons the song portrays. Then, the students improvised vocally to the accompaniment, continuing to empathize with the song's meaning (see chapter's online resources at http://qcc.libguides.com/neh). The students then undertook a crucial step in "Musical Responses'" process of empathic expression, which was to learn, perform, and ultimately teach (the CYMP children) the precise musical and textual content of "Inscription" as if that content were the spontaneously felt and revealed feelings of others. That is to say, the QCC students strove to perform the piece as if they were composing it spontaneously, and to remove, through musical expression, barriers that exist among groups, cultures, or experiential perspectives. In this activity, "Musical Responses'" goal was to target the learning outcomes of broadening student perspectives and strengthening their communication skills.

To experience empathically the meaning of "Inscription's" text, students chanted the text together, in small groups and individually. By turns, individual students "conducted" the group, indicating with hand and arm gestures which individual or small group should continue the chanting. After a period of "conducting," the conducting student would pass the duty on to another student. This act of shared leadership was an important part of "Musical Responses" in that it sought to strengthen the students' understanding of collective citizenship and mutual responsibility and how individual initiative is a crucial component of aggregate success. All the learning activities in "Musical Responses," therefore, were conceived with shared leadership as a driver. QCC students then applied their empathic improvisation skills to learning the text, performing their "What Do I Want" improvisation from the standpoint of the subjects of "Inscription's" lyrics.

To teach the music of "Inscription," I asked the students to learn and sing their parts as if motivated physically by improvised empathic movements based on the music. In this, the students explored and demonstrated how physical movement can expose and seem to initiate melodic, rhythmic, harmonic, and structural musical meaning. Students experienced the musical elements separately at first and then combined them. In this exploration, leadership was shared and transferred, expression was kinesthetic based, and feedback was immediate and mutual through physical, facial, and vocal expression. Students came to understand that this experimentation was a legitimate performance of the piece, and that it constituted an embodiment of an experience felt by others, separated from us by time and circumstance. Further movement-based exercises included having individual students conduct the rest of the choir in singing the song, using conducting gestures to elicit desired expressive responses in the singers, and using the feedback from these responses to motivate further physical expression.

Throughout these exercises and the learning of "Inscription," students were reminded to sing as if they were creating the music from their own kinesthetic-based emotional responses to the music's meaning, and they were encouraged to reflect orally and in writing upon their individual and collective emotional discoveries. Students' reflections, which included such insights as, "Arts inspire you" and "Learning about something as significant [as this] changes your singing because you sing your heart," suggest that the students encountered a significant learning experience.

In Part 3 of "Musical Responses," QCC students took their experiences and knowledge outside of the classroom, and the following learning outcomes were addressed: application of knowledge to later stages in life; meaningful engagement with the community; and an increased understanding of meaningful career options, based in a global environment. Prepared by their experiences of a shared emotional and physical response to "Inscription," QCC students went to CYMP rehearsals to teach concepts of the Holocaust through choral music. With minimal interference from me, the QCC students led the CYMP children in rehearsals in teams of two. Working in teams helped lessen any anxiety a student might have had about forgetting a learning exercise or about whether his or her leadership would be effective. While the QCC students had learned the full four-part choral piece (soprano, alto, tenor, bass), the CYMP children learned only the melody part, which made the technical aspects of this learning exercise manageable for all. The QCC students first led the CYMP children in the physical, vocal, and emotional bonding exercises outlined earlier, and then they tackled teaching the music and the text, remembering to base all learning on the kinesthetic basis of the musical and textual elements. I encouraged the QCC students to remember the methods we used in class to embody poetic and musical meaning, advised them to transfer leadership roles between themselves and the CYMP children, and then stepped back and watched the QCC students interact with the CYMP children and with the themes of suffering and hope that "Inscription" portrays. The QCC students enthusiastically embraced their leadership roles and remembered course concepts and processes well. I saw evidence of this in the feedback QCC students gave to the CYMP children: "I love how your voice is showing us the hope in this music! Can you let me hear it in your voice, and see it in your face, too?" I was also glad to see the QCC students leading CYMP children in age-appropriate discussions of Holocaust concepts: "Have you ever seen someone treated unfairly because they were different? What would you say to someone who was mean to someone else because of their differences? Show with your bodies and voices what that conversation would look and sound like." I was also encouraged to see QCC students using class concepts to create their own effective learning activities: "Pretend I don't know the melody, and I am not able to hear. Show me with your body and face what the melody sounds like and let me see what it means to you."

CYMP is modeled on the state-sponsored Venezuelan program entitled "El Sistema," which provides immediate substantive performance experiences even as students are first learning to sing or to play their instruments. This "learn by doing" philosophy is noted for having produced internationally recognized conductor and Los Angeles Philharmonic Music Director Gustavo Dudamel. In many ways, "Musical Responses" was also inspired by this perspective and philosophy, as it placed QCC students almost immediately in leadership and mentorship roles and gave them insight into the rewards of teaching and community engagement.

Part 4 of "Musical Responses" was the final performance of the music QCC and CYMP students learned together, and it was a chance for all the learners to demonstrate in a high-stakes situation how they had internalized what they had learned. At the capstone concert of the 2014–2015 NEH/KHC Colloquium Series, the CYMP children and QCC students joined together in singing "Inscription of Hope" and the Stephen Schwartz piece from the movie version of *Godspell*, "Beautiful City." At the end of our final rehearsal together, I had told the QCC students and CYMP children that now all our learning and feelings were in our own hands—the time of practice and reminding was over. Before we went onstage, a QCC student reminded me of this and asked if he could speak to all the singers before we went out to perform. He said to everyone, "Let's pretend we all just met and everything we have learned is a secret inside. Let's go onstage together and then when the music starts, let's suddenly let it all out!" During the performance, the joy emanating from the stage was palpable; the singers' deep awareness of the meaning of the music was unmistakable; and a clear message of community engagement and an emotional connection to learning was sent and, according to the audience reaction, received.

Evidence of Student Learning

QCC students primarily demonstrated how they met prescribed learning outcomes in their reflective writings. The following student reflections encapsulate one of "Musical Responses'" principal pedagogical philosophies, which is to motivate student learning through the power of emotional connection: "I saw how the kids just jumped in. It helped me to not be too shy and made me feel positive"; "I saw the smiles on the children's faces and felt it was going to mean something"; "It felt good for everybody to just 'let it out' by singing"; "Chorus helped me stay positive"; "This helped me be more outgoing"; and "I didn't realize how shy I was. Working with them helped me with that."

The CYMP children gave freely of their joy in singing, learning, and participating, which stimulated QCC students to demonstrate and hone their leadership skills and display their understanding of the value of community engagement: "We showed them how we worked as a group—they mirrored our togetherness"; "I know that I want to help people"; "[We] need to incorporate arts into kids' futures … incorporate peace"; "We were examples for the youth"; "Working with the kids made me proud of my background and made me see myself in them"; and "I can help make future leaders by being a leader myself."

Students also showed appreciation of kinesthetic learning: "I understand that moving around randomly helps. The Students GET that" and "It's intense to move. I am a work in progress." The following reflections indicate that students also learned to transfer knowledge from one area of inquiry to another: "We need to be united instead of segregated because of race" and "People from different ethnic backgrounds have suffered as well and we should focus on their problems as well."

Additionally, student reflections demonstrated that the project deepened their understanding of the Holocaust: "Combining something that grasps your attention makes something boring easier to learn"; "The power attached to the music helped me learn"; "Combining artistic disciplines with other disciplines makes you learn the historical subjects better ... makes it more interesting"; and "It opened my eyes to [the] topic." Advancement of empathy is also evident in their responses: "[You can] understand values of people different from you"; "We were transported to the Jewish folks' place"; and "[The class] made these concepts engrave in me."

Throughout the "Musical Responses" project, I observed QCC students' comments, class performance, and interactions with other students to informally assess their success in reaching class-learning outcomes. Even actions and remarks from students that may have initially seemed inconsequential could illuminate students' grasp of course material and concepts. I witnessed several examples of student behavior that seemed to provide evidence of student learning related to the prescribed outcomes. Recurring and regular student questions and comments indicated advanced comprehension of kinesthesia and empathy in learning and a heightened grasp of issues of the Holocaust: "We should sing 'Remember When It Rained' by Josh Groban! I think that song fits this message perfectly"; "Shouldn't we be singing softer here? That's what the words are saying"; and, directed to a student who was conducting at the time, "How can we sing the way you want when your face isn't showing it?" were all moments when I saw learning outcomes being met.

QCC students' post-project survey responses further indicated that learning outcomes were met. Of 22 students surveyed, 82 percent agreed or strongly agreed with the statement that they would "probably volunteer in the future," and 73 percent agreed or strongly agreed that the project helped them to "understand the needs and problems facing society," suggesting success in meeting the learning outcome of increased civic engagement. Moreover, before and after the project, students rated their understanding of the Holocaust on a scale of 1–10; after the project, the students' assessment of their knowledge rose by almost 3 points on the scale, and 77 percent of students agreed or strongly agreed with the statement that the project had helped them to "learn course material more effectively."

Students' class activities also seemed to reveal that they were meeting the learning outcome of developing skills useful in a global workforce. Particularly notable to me was how enthusiastically and effectively students embraced their roles as mentors and teachers to the CYMP children. One student remarked that she felt motivated professionally: "I loved being with the kids. I know that I want to be a teacher." Another student wrote, "I never would have thought of being a teacher before." There were always several volunteers ready to practice their teaching during our QCC sessions before traveling to CYMP, and students remembered pedagogical approaches we had learned without being prompted. At CYMP, QCC students were eager to work with the children, jumping in if a fellow student briefly faltered while leading the group, providing in-the-moment encouraging feedback as the children sang, and displaying open and inviting body language as they directed the children. One student provided a decent summation of the experience when she asked, "Can we do this again next year?"

The classroom culture that evolved over the semester showed me that "Musical Responses'" function in encouraging emotional connection was working, as well. Students were quick to joke with each other and to laugh at funny moments during sessions. Just as easily, they were able to speak frankly and personally about their emotional reaction to class material or activities, with every other student listening attentively. Often these interactions spontaneously blossomed into lively discussions about course concepts. I would allow a discussion to continue for two to three minutes before putting the class back "on track" and participated only to ask for one student to clarify what another had said or to ask what solutions the class could offer to any problems under consideration. The emotional connection I saw among students and between the students and the material and activities were, to me, signs of success. As one student wrote in an end-of-semester teacher evaluation, "Our class became a family."

Conclusions

Implementing "Musical Responses to the Holocaust" has renewed my commitment to learning-outcomes-based pedagogy that keeps "What will they get out of it?" as an overriding goal. Guided by this question, "Musical Responses" produced an experience that seems to have motivated students to broaden their perspectives of the Holocaust through movement-based emotional engagement, to expand their ability to empathize, to deepen their connection to the community around them, and to ignite their consideration of meaningful career choices. As my list of learning outcomes during the project was always on my mind, I constantly assessed the performance of my students. This created a feedback loop, which kept me alert, active, and motivated, and importantly, kept the learning outcomes in my students' minds as well. This dynamic learning took place in a choral music class that steadfastly targeted learning outcomes from that specific curriculum, as well as related learning outcomes from the college's General Education Objectives. This type of far-reaching, emotional learning seems to be a worthy avenue of inquiry as we strive to effectively reach twenty-first-century students. Incorporating arts study or emotion-based empathic learning into varied curricula may be a viable method of generating, in students, deeper interest in learning, which could last for a lifetime and produce engaged members of society.

Appendix 1: Suggested Supplemental Learning Activities

1. To advance development in students of empathy and its relationship to musical performance and kinesthesia, ask students to view videos of performers from various genres, including genres and artists of their own choosing. Lead a discussion of what the students perceive about the emotional state of the performers. Guide students to observe body language, facial expression, and vocal inflection; in short, ask students to make their observations based on nonverbal cues. When viewing genres with which students are less familiar, such as opera, lead students in discussion about what they feel they have in common with those performers.
2. In any class discussion, ask individual students to paraphrase a question or comment just delivered by another student. Ask students to point out times they either disagree or agree with another student, while acknowledging why a differing point of view may be held.

Appendix 2: Prompts for Written Reflection

Following are prompts given to QCC students for written reflection. These prompts aim to elicit specific examples of students' comprehension of issues of the Holocaust and genocide with regard to Arts Education and continued community involvement.

1. Describe several course concepts we learned in class that relate to this project's study of the Holocaust and genocide. Explain how they relate.
2. Describe possible solutions to any community needs revealed by our study of the Holocaust and genocide. Are there any course activities or concepts that may open avenues to solutions? Please explain.

3. Describe an instance when you saw a course concept come to life during a learning activity shared with the CYMP children.
4. What do you see yourself doing in the future related to finding solutions to these issues?

References

Balk, H. Wesley. 1985. *Performing Power: A New Approach for the Singer-Actor.* Minneapolis: University of Minnesota Press.

———. 1991. *The Radiant Performer: The Spiral Path to Performing Power.* Minneapolis: University of Minnesota Press.

Burns, Kimberly. 2017. Community College Faculty as Pedagogical Innovators: How the Scholarship of Teaching and Learning (SoTL) Stimulates Innovation in the Classroom. *Community College Journal of Research and Practice* 55 (3): 153–167.

Caldwell, Timothy. 1995. *Expressive Singing: Dalcroze Eurhythmics for Voice.* Englewood Cliffs: Prentice Hall.

Frazee, Jane, and Kent Kreuter. 1987. *Discovering Orff: A Curriculum for Music Teachers.* Mainz, NY: Schott.

Kisker, Carrie, Dayna Weintraub, and Mallory A. Newell. 2016. The Community Colleges' Role in Developing Students' Civic Outcomes. *Community College Review* 44 (4): 315–336.

Meisner, Sanford. 1987. *On Acting.* New York: Vintage Books.

Morreale, Sherwyn P., and Constance M. Staley. 2016. Millennials, Teaching and Learning, and the Elephant in the College Classroom. *Communication Education* 65 (3): 370–373.

National Center for Education Statistics. 2010. In *The Condition of Education,* edited by Susan Aud, William Hussar, Michael Planty, Thomas Snyder, Kevin Bianco, Mary Ann Fox, Lauren Frohlich, Jana Kemp, Lauren Drake, n.p. Washington, DC: U.S. Department of Education.

QCC. 2017. Mission. http://www.qcc.cuny.edu/about/mission.html. Accessed June 12.

Reynolds, Heather L., and Katherine D. Kearns. 2017. A Planning Tool for Incorporating Backward Design, Active Learning, and Authentic Assessment in the College Classroom. *College Teaching* 65 (1): 17–27.

Schober, Barbara, Laura Brandt, Marlene Kollmayer, and Christiane Spiel. 2016. Overcoming the Ivory Tower: Transfer and Societal Responsibility as Crucial Aspects of the Bildung-Psychology Approach. *European Journal of Developmental Psychology* 13 (6): 636–651.

CHAPTER 12

Where History Meets Literature: Teaching the Holocaust, Genocide, and Mass Atrocity Through a Creative Approach in the Community College English Classroom

Melissa Dennihy

During my first year as a new tenure-track faculty member at Queensborough Community College (QCC), a colleague asked if I was interested in joining a faculty working group where I would learn how to use campus resources and programming to teach a unit on the Holocaust in one of my English courses. This group was part of a larger initiative aimed at integrating faculty from across disciplines in a campus-wide effort to foster student learning about "The Holocaust in a Global Context," sponsored in part by a National Endowment for the Humanities (NEH) grant through QCC's Kupferberg Holocaust Center (KHC) during the 2013–2014 Academic Year. Although I was interested in the opportunity, I was also hesitant: I had no prior experience in teaching the Holocaust or

M. Dennihy (✉)
Department of English, Queensborough Community College, CUNY,
Bayside, NY, USA
e-mail: MDennihy@qcc.cuny.edu

A. E. Traver, D. Leshem (eds.), *Humanistic Pedagogy Across the Disciplines*, https://doi.org/10.1007/978-3-319-95025-9_12

Holocaust literature—I typically teach courses in American literature. My courses also focus on multiethnic and immigrant US literature, in part because QCC's students, many of whom are immigrants, children of immigrants, and people of color, often find this literature relatable to their own experiences. I wondered, "Would the Holocaust be a topic that students could connect to other social and political issues, including those that have shaped their own lives? Would I be able to help students learn about the Holocaust while maintaining the objectives of a literature course?" After considering these questions, I decided to incorporate a unit into my Introduction to Literature course that would help students learn about the Holocaust while also studying genocide and mass atrocity in global contexts. This unit merged the study of history and literature by focusing on what I and others have called "(hi)stories": the varied stories found in different types of sources—oral and written, literary and historical—that offer different perspectives on the same event. Students studied the Holocaust, genocide, and mass atrocity through a range of texts, including fiction, poetry, and first-person narratives. Because students at QCC come from 139 different countries, including many nations where genocide or mass atrocity has occurred or is currently occurring, the unit also gave students the opportunity to conduct research on a historical or political topic of their own choosing.

This chapter discusses the activities, texts, and assignments that comprised this five-week unit on "The Holocaust in a Global Context: (Hi) Stories of Genocide and Mass Atrocity." In it, I focus on how the study of the Holocaust, genocide, and mass atrocity was made relevant to both the objectives of a literature course and the interests and identities of a diverse group of community college students, through a creative approach. I also argue that, by contextualizing our study of the Holocaust within different global contexts, students learned why Holocaust history remains significant today. Finally, I demonstrate how the unit's interdisciplinary nature, which allowed students to explore historical and political issues through literary works and first-person narratives, also helped students to understand why we study literature and how it—and other creative forms—plays a role in representing history and preserving historical memory.

Scaffolded Steps for Teaching the Holocaust, Genocide, and Mass Atrocity

The creative assignment that I developed for this unit, called the "Multimedia Museum Curating Project," asked students to curate collections of literary, artistic, and historical sources on a topic related to the Holocaust, genocide, or mass atrocity. Students presented their sources to the class in multimodal forms as if their classmates were the audience at a museum exhibit on the topic. The freedom to choose their own topics allowed students to research and learn more about events or issues of interest to them, while the sources that they included in their "museums" allowed them to merge literary and historical study to offer complementary or conflicting points of view. To help students consider how they might approach their projects, we took advantage of programming and resources at our campus Holocaust center, which helped students understand some of the different (hi)stories of the Holocaust itself. We were fortunate to attend a talk by a Holocaust survivor and to have a guided tour of the center's art, artifacts, and resources. After learning about the Holocaust in class and at these events, students began their projects—carried out in the scaffolded steps described later—and presented their "museums" to the class at the culmination of the unit (see Appendix 1 for a week-by-week breakdown of this unit).

To introduce our focus on "(hi)stories," we began the unit by discussing how diverse frameworks, genres, and narrative practices can be used to represent different perspectives and points of view on a topic. I explained that our study of the Holocaust, genocide, and mass atrocity over the next few weeks would focus on how different kinds of texts, sources, and voices—different "(hi)stories"—can offer different perspectives on the same event. As a segue from previous course readings, we discussed how some literary works we had read use multiple narrators and points of view to tell a story from varied perspectives. In Toni Morrison's novel *The Bluest Eye*, for example, various first- and third-person narrators tell the story of Pecola Breedlove, a girl who is raped by her father. We talked about how each narrator tells a different side of the story, and students were able to point out how the novel would be different if certain narrators or points of view were excluded. We also discussed how fictional works, though not "true stories," can offer useful perspectives on events or experiences that might be eclipsed within larger historical narratives. This was a concept we had seen in Jhumpa Lahiri's "The Third and Final

Continent," a short story which juxtaposes the (hi)story of an immigrant's journey to America in 1969 with the celebrated history of Neil Armstrong's moon landing that same year. In telling his story, the unnamed narrator insists that ordinary (hi)stories deserve to be heard alongside historical narratives about immortalized figures like Armstrong. These texts provided a framework for thinking about how literature helps us study history through multiple points of view, a concept we then applied to study of the Holocaust, genocide, and mass atrocity.

After this conversation, students spent time in class writing and talking about their prior knowledge of the Holocaust: what (hi)stories had students encountered in past learning experiences? Their reflections indicated that most students' knowledge wasn't very extensive or multifaceted. Many had seen photographs of Hitler and of Jews in concentration camps, and some had read Anne Frank's diary, but most had no detailed knowledge of the Holocaust. As one student wrote, "I have heard Hitler's name and seen his face many times. The Nazi symbol is immediately recognizable to me. But learning only names and symbols almost desensitizes me to it, especially because I don't know the specifics—like who was involved and what their lives were like during that period." Many students similarly acknowledged that they knew some basic Holocaust history but did not have any understanding of its (hi)stories—of "who was involved and what their lives were like."

However, a few students did have a wider range of knowledge about the Holocaust and could speak in class discussion about the different perspectives and (hi)stories they had encountered. One student had visited the Dachau Concentration Camp and described that memorial site as much more somber than the United States Holocaust Memorial Museum, which he considered a more celebratory site emphasizing American soldiers' roles in liberating the camps. This led us to a discussion of how history itself is curated in different ways for different audiences: how one memorial site represents an historical event might be quite different from how another museum represents it, and how, in any given portrayal, certain accounts or perspectives may be unrepresented. Given that a number of students had read Anne Frank's *The Diary of a Young Girl* in previous high school or college courses, I asked them to consider what kind of perspective that text offers and what other perspectives or accounts of Holocaust history might exist in other texts. One student noted that, while Anne Frank's diary offers the first-person perspective of a victim, Hitler's *Mein Kampf* offers the first-person perspective of the oppressor.

Another said that she had read poetry by Holocaust survivors, who offer perspectives on life after the Holocaust. But many students had trouble imagining more nuanced perspectives beyond the dichotomy of victim and oppressor, and many did not seem aware that such perspectives have also been recorded and historicized.

For example, students were startled by an excerpt that we read from Christopher Browning's *Ordinary Men*, which examines how societal pressures and deference to authority turned "ordinary men" into perpetrators of genocide. They were also surprised to learn that the KHC had featured an exhibit on German-American Nazis in New York, where Nazi summer camps were run on Long Island and rallies were held at Madison Square Garden in New York City. When we looked at anti-Semitic postcards from another past KHC exhibit, students were shocked to see how everyday forms of correspondence played a role in spreading anti-Semitism. After we discussed these different sources and perspectives, I gave a brief lecture to provide necessary context and information about Nazism and the Holocaust, while encouraging students to contrast the objectivity of historical facts cited in my lecture with the subjectivity of some of the sources we had examined. We talked about why all of these types of sources and knowledge are important: we need to know the facts and historical context, but we can better understand both by examining the (hi)stories and perspectives of different groups and individuals.

Following these in-class activities, we attended the talk by a Holocaust survivor at the KHC. In written reflections on this experience, students noted how the intimacy, emotion, and ordinary details of the speaker's (hi)story were very different from textbook accounts of historical events. Students described feeling "outraged," "stunned," "inspired," and "moved in a way I would not have thought possible" after hearing the survivor's testimony. As one student wrote in a reflection, "sometimes you don't understand history the way you should, but when someone who has been through it tells you their story, you *feel* the history, which is something deeper than just knowing the facts." We also discussed how the speaker's personal (hi)story differed from the Holocaust representations that students had encountered in photographs and films. One student pointed out that, while photographs often portray Jews in the camps as weak and passive, the speaker had survived because she snuck from a line of people to be put to death to a line of people to be put to work while an SS soldier had his back turned during a moment of chaos. After hearing this (hi)story, students wondered why we do not hear more stories about resistance or defiance in the camps—as one student asked in her reflection, "why do we only see [photographs] of emaciated victims, or of piles of dead bodies?" Students also pointed out the ways in which the speaker inverted or challenged the narrative of victimization through the act of storytelling itself. One student noted in her reflection that she was quite surprised by how the speaker used humor to tell parts of her story. She described the speaker as "clever and even comic at times" and acknowledged that she had not expected the speaker to laugh at certain points throughout her talk. The student's preconceived notions of what a Holocaust survivor's story would sound like were productively challenged by how this woman told her own (hi)story.

Our attendance at this talk was followed by a guided tour of the KHC's resources and archives, as well as its (then) current exhibit, *Unwelcomed Words: Nazi Anti-Jewish Street Signs.* Exploring the KHC gave students a lot of ideas about possible topics for their own creative projects, as well as the types of sources and points of view that they might include. The KHC, which is described on its webpage as "neither a museum nor a library" but a "learning laboratory," represents Holocaust history using many different sources, mediums, and (hi)stories. During our tour, students viewed paintings, listened to audio recordings, examined propaganda, and saw shoes and clothes worn by people in the camps, and these texts and artifacts—as well as the different visual, audial, and tactile experiences students had engaging with them—gave students a sense of how to curate multimedia "exhibits" of their own. Students also gained a better understanding of what it means to examine the same historical event from different perspectives. For example, one student noted in a written reflection that he was most surprised by the propaganda he saw in the KHC, which showed how Nazis used "cartoons, posters, and even children's books" to portray Jews as the enemy of the German people. As the KHC also connects the Holocaust and genocide study to other processes of mass atrocity, like global sex trafficking and the history of Korean comfort women, students were provided with further ideas for their projects.

Both the survivor's talk and the KHC tour also helped students recognize how lack of knowledge about historical atrocities makes it possible for similar atrocities to keep occurring. One student wrote in a reflection that, "learning about Holocaust survivors reminded me of the Nanking Massacre in China, in which more than three hundred thousand Chinese people were killed. … I now realize these cruel behaviors happen all over the globe, and humans have yet to learn how to live peacefully as part of a shared world." Another student's reflection stated that, "learning about the Holocaust is a reminder to an audience like us that discrimination isn't only in America and against African Americans, but has been against many different racial and ethnic groups throughout history." Again, and in many cases, these connections inspired students' decision-making in their own projects.

The Multimedia Museum Curating Assignment

After the KHC events, students began working in class on the Multimedia Museum Curating Project, the high-stakes student-directed assignment for this unit (see Appendix 2). For this project, students selected an historical or current event relevant to the study of genocide and mass atrocity, which they researched in order to curate and present a collection of sources on the topic, resembling a museum exhibit. They were encouraged to choose topics of interest to them and to give consideration to topics or events they thought may have been underrepresented or misrepresented, allowing them to raise awareness or share new perspectives through their work. To initiate the project, we discussed the *Dictionary.com* definition of "curate": "to pull together, sift through, and select for presentation" and noted that although curation typically refers to curating museums, galleries, or exhibits, it also suggests how history itself can be curated and presented. I noted that curation can also apply to conducting research, as the researcher "pull[s] together, sift[s] through, and select[s]" sources while researching a topic. In fact, this would be their task as researchers and curators: to "sift through" different sources and materials and "select for presentation" a multimedia and multi-genre set of sources on their topic.

Students were expected to decide on a project topic by the class session following the survivor's talk and our tour of the KHC. During this session, students completed a worksheet intended to prepare them to begin their research. They were asked to consider what they already knew about their topics, what (hi)stories they hoped to learn more about while researching, and what kinds of sources they might look for in order to explore a range of perspectives. Students were also asked to consider what sorts of perspectives or points of view might be difficult to account for in traditional sources and where else they might look to find these perspectives. From there, students began their research, much of which was conducted during class time with assistance from myself and a library faculty member (this class had an embedded librarian who was familiar with the assignment and available to work individually with students). Students had about three weeks, including in-class time and at-home work, to conduct research, curate sources, and prepare to showcase their "museums" to the class in the final week of the unit.

In conducting research and curating their museums, students worked with non-fiction, historical, and journalistic sources as well as literary, creative, and artistic works. They were required to have at least five different sources: two *literary works* (poetry, short stories, novels, plays, memoirs, autobiography, creative non-fiction, or similar); two sources of *informative non-fiction writing* (newspaper or magazine articles, peer-reviewed journal articles, historical monographs, primary source documents, or similar); and one *audio/visual source* (a photograph, cartoon, video, speech, interview, musical selection, or similar). In addition to finding and curating sources for presentation, each student wrote a five-page essay consisting of a project rationale and an explanation of their museum exhibit, its sources, and the curation process. I emphasized that the goal of this essay was *not* to write a traditional research paper on the topic but to analyze and explain how this topic is represented in different ways from different perspectives and within different sources. Students were required to provide a written analysis of each source, with quotations from sources when appropriate, to help us understand the perspective or information offered by that source.

Student "curators" were asked to pay particular attention to how sources present different perspectives or interpretations of the same history. They were also expected to explain how different *types* of sources—novels and news articles, poetry and interviews—as well as the different *mediums* used—audio, visual, oral, and print—presented their topic in different ways. In addition, students were asked to analyze how their own choices as curators might impact our understanding of their topics, to explain how their projects might have changed if they had made different creative decisions and/or used other sources, and to consider what points of view might be missing from their projects and why. As an addendum to their five-page essays, students also wrote and submitted one-page reflections on the unit's two main activities, our attendance at a talk by a Holocaust survivor and our class tour of the KHC. In these reflections, students discussed what they learned from these activities, what they noticed about how the KHC's exhibit was curated, and how the experience of hearing a survivor speak compared to seeing and interacting with sources during the KHC tour.

Outcomes: Students' Museums on the Holocaust, Genocide, and Mass Atrocity

Students explored a diverse range of topics on genocide and mass atrocity and made use of a variety of texts in curating their museum projects. A number of students focused on the Holocaust either because they had a personal connection to that history or because their interest was piqued by the KHC events. Other students chose topics that demonstrated their new awareness of the relationship between the Holocaust and other genocides and forms of mass atrocity. Some of the titles of students' projects included: "Museum of Holocaust Survivors in America"; "Museum of Japanese American Internment"; "After 9/11: A Museum of Muslim Americans in the United States"; "Violence Against African Americans Throughout U.S. History"; "Museum of Global Sex Trafficking"; "The Sikh Genocide"; "The Rwandan Genocide"; "The Bosnian Genocide"; "The Untold History of the Nanking Massacre"; "Oppressed Tibet"; "North Korean Concentration Camps"; and "Perspectives On and Of Korean Comfort Women." As these projects suggest, by the unit's end, students saw the Holocaust as related to many other events. In fact, meeting the goals of the 2013–2014 NEH/KHC Colloquium Series, they understood the Holocaust "in a global context." Studying genocide and mass atrocity in global contexts also allowed students to choose topics that they wanted to learn more about because their families or ancestors had been impacted by these events. Some students even picked their topics specifically because they had not had the opportunity to learn about them in academic contexts—as one student wrote in her essay, "I know about [my topic] from my own family history, but I chose it for this project because I was never taught about it in school." In project rationales included in their essays, students expressed the passion, anger, and urgency that motivated their topic choices, offering rationales such as "I want people to know there are human beings in my home country suffering under an oppressive government and denied their basic human rights" and "though my topic cannot be missed by anyone who lives or has family in this country, as I do, it never gets any attention in U.S. news." The significance and personal relevance of the work they were doing led students to become particularly invested in their projects, resulting in some of the best work students produced throughout the semester.

I was particularly impressed by students' work on an aspect of the assignment that I expected to be challenging for them: the use of literature as a means of exploring and understanding history. With guidance from myself and our class librarian, students were able to find texts that made impactful arguments for why literature is valuable in/to the study of genocide and mass atrocity. For example, a student who curated a project on the internment of Japanese Americans during World War II used excerpts from John Okada's *No-No Boy*, the first novel published by a Japanese American writer. *No-No Boy* tells the story of a young Japanese American man struggling with the long-term psychological impacts of spending two years in an internment camp. For the project, the student created slides pairing passages from the novel with photographs of interned Japanese Americans, explaining that while the photographs allow viewers to imagine life in the camps, the novel helps readers to empathize with the lasting psychological trauma of such an experience. Likewise, in a project on Muslims in post-9/11 America, another student used the literary nonfiction essay "Rasha" from Moustafa Bayoumi's *How Does It Feel to Be a Problem? Being Young and Arab in America*, which tells the story of a Syrian American teenager who was pulled from her home in Brooklyn in the middle of the night and imprisoned without trial for months in the aftermath of 9/11. The student noted in her essay that Rasha's story was not found in historical sources; it was told through a "different kind of text, one dedicated to sharing personal stories like hers." Finally, another student, who researched the 1994 Rwandan genocide, used Tierno Monénembo's novel *The Oldest Orphan*, about a teenager in Kigali grappling with his family's death. Monénembo's novel was part of a larger project on writing African genocide into memory, called "Writing So as Not to Forget." The student's essay emphasized the significance not only of the novel's story but also of the project the author was part of and how that project speaks to literature's role in preserving historical memory.

Students also found creative and resourceful ways to include literary works in their projects even when their topics were too recent or obscure to easily find published sources. One student found a spoken word performance on *YouTube*, while another used a blog by an individual who had lived through the experience the student was researching. Both students emphasized the first-person perspective of these sources, as well as the platforms used for storytelling. As the student who used the blog wrote, "my topic is very recent and has not been written about in literary works yet, so I used self-published literature, which is how people tell their own life stories." The process of searching for first-person perspectives or (hi)stories, and often finding them in unexpected places, helped to reinforce the concept that certain (hi)stories get lost or forgotten rather than recorded and memorialized. It also helped students to recognize the importance of the work they were doing: to consider how scholars and researchers uncover forgotten (hi)stories and make those perspectives heard and how academic and cultural institutions like the KHC help to make visible, archive, and honor those stories.

In addition to using literature in interesting and insightful ways, students also made creative use of multimedia sources and presented their topics to the class using multiple modes. Many students played music, showed clips from documentaries or news footage, and shared photographs, artwork, or cartoons. Some acted as storytellers, reading a poem aloud or performing a scene from a play as part of their presentation. One student choreographed and performed an interpretive dance based off of a poem she had used. Many students also took seriously the curator's task to "pull together" by juxtaposing different sources: one played an audio recording of a speech while showing photographs; another displayed a news article alongside an autobiographical piece offering a different account of the same event. Some students performed the role of museum guide, walking classmates through their "exhibit" by placing books, postcards, photos, food, and jewelry in different spots around the classroom. Another student turned the written portion of the assignment into a "brochure" and handed out copies to classmates. The varied approaches student-presenters used indicated their awareness that it is not just the sources we examine but the ways they are presented and framed that impact how we learn about and understand historical events and experiences.

In reflections on this assignment, students expressed that it "gave [them] a chance to look at history in a different way." Many students, including those who were already informed about their topic, were surprised by the information and perspectives encountered in their research. Students also appreciated the opportunity to research and write on topics relevant to their own identity or heritage. One student reflected that, "doing this project allowed me to learn more about what my ancestors went through and where they came from, and I got closer to my culture in this way, too." In addition, students learned a lot through the act of listening: many noted in reflections that classmates' presentations taught them about events that they had never heard of before. Others commented that classmates introduced them to new perspectives on topics that had always been covered the same way in their previous educational experiences. Students also discussed feeling passionate and empowered by the opportunity to share their projects with their classmates. As one student wrote, "I was extremely excited to present my museum on Tibet, because as a Tibetan, I wanted the others to know about the country and people's suffering under the rule of the Chinese government." Another student explained, "My topic is one that people are aware of but don't care enough to do anything about. I hope that, by sharing the unheard stories of the everyday people involved, I will inspire people to care." A student who did a project on global sex trafficking wrote that "the more I understood what people went through, it made me want to become active in my community and inform my fellow classmates." As part of the presentation, this student included information about organizations, including local organizations in New York City, to which individuals can donate or volunteer to help victims of sex trafficking. Because students were so enthusiastic about sharing their projects in ways that would raise awareness and move others to action, when I revised this assignment for future use, I added an extra credit option to "go public" with their work: students were encouraged to showcase their projects in and with larger communities, by, for example, submitting sections of their written work for the assignment to our campus newspaper. Students' interest in sharing their work with a broader audience suggests that they recognized the role storytellers and curators can play in sharing urgent (hi)stories with the public, raising awareness about historical and contemporary crises, and inspiring action within their communities.

Assessing the Unit: Successes and Challenges

I want to close by addressing some of the challenges and successful outcomes of the project and the unit. First, I was startled by students' lack of prior knowledge about the Holocaust. I had wrongly assumed that all students would have some understanding of Holocaust history, but class discussions and written reflections suggested that, at the start of the unit, most students did not know exactly when or where the Holocaust occurred. Many were also unaware that the Holocaust and World War II were interrelated events. Students' written reflections on what they knew about the Holocaust before the unit contained one-sentence responses such as "I don't really know anything about the Holocaust"; "I don't remember exactly what [the Holocaust] is"; and "I know it had to do with Jews and Germans, Hitler, and concentration camps." Some students thought the Holocaust had occurred centuries ago—the fact that many Holocaust survivors live in the United States today, and that we would have the opportunity to hear one such survivor speak, was quite surprising to them.

In post-unit reflections, however, students indicated how their knowledge had expanded, especially through hearing the survivor's talk, visiting the KHC, and conducting and exhibiting their own research. One student noted that he learned the words "pogrom" and "genocide"; another wrote that she had never heard of Kristallnacht before and now wanted to learn more about that night; still another wrote, "I never realized how much the Holocaust relates to things going on today. The Holocaust Center and my classmates' presentations revealed to me that things like this are still happening all over the world." Though this was not an intensive study of the Holocaust, for these community college students it was an important starting point for learning about an atrocity that many were uninformed about—or entirely unaware of—before this unit.

In part because of their limited prior knowledge, another challenge was to help students recognize connections between their topics and the Holocaust without overgeneralizing or oversimplifying. As this was only a five-week unit within a literature course, it did not allow for the more in-depth content-based instruction students would need to understand all of the cultural and historical specificities of how the Nazis rose to power and why Jews and other groups were targeted for persecution. At times, students made overly generalized or oversimplified connections between the Holocaust and their own topics. To help students make connections while also considering comparisons or distinctions, when I revised the unit for future use I designed some activities and discussion questions intended to help students be more attentive to the historical and contextual specificities of different instances of genocide and mass atrocity.

Nonetheless, despite these limitations, my experience suggests that it is worthwhile for educators to include Holocaust and genocide education in their courses, even if they may not be able to cover these topics in great depth. Because QCC offers courses such as "Holocaust Literature" and "History of Genocide in the Twentieth Century," students who gain some knowledge about the Holocaust and genocide through a creative unit in an introductory-level course may go on to study these topics in more depth in upper-level courses. Even if students do not study these topics in future courses, they gain some knowledge they take beyond the course—including something as simple as the kinds of Holocaust resources we have on our campus. As one student wrote in a post-unit reflection, "I actually had no idea that QCC even has a Holocaust museum [until our class visited the KHC]." Another student had thought students weren't allowed in the KHC without a professor, and she mentioned that since she now knew it was open to the public, she planned to visit on her own time. Introducing students to campus-based cultural resources, and making them aware of how they can pursue academic interests within and beyond the classroom, is also important work.

Another challenge specific to the assignment was that, at first, many students had trouble understanding why I was asking them to work with literature—especially fiction—as part of this project. Some students were initially resistant to the idea of using "made up" stories to understand and explore "real-life" events. Even when seeking out first-person perspectives, they often discounted novels, poetry, and short stories as less meaningful than autobiographies, memoirs, and primary source documents. However, throughout the research process, many students learned how fictional texts, while not "true stories," can still be useful for understanding some of the (hi)stories that "History" both hides and contains. As one student wrote while reflecting on the unit assignment, "we learn about History as it is filtered through the perspective of the elite, whoever has the most power and influence. Literature allows for different perspectives, both real and imagined, which invite us to consider history from different angles and points of view."

One of the challenges of teaching literature is to help students understand how fictional or "made up" stories can speak to real histories and be situated within real historical, political, and societal contexts. This project helped students to grasp these concepts and to recognize and appreciate how literature offers narratives that can counter, challenge, or complement official accounts of an event. One student wrote in the post-unit reflection that his research suggested that our collective memory of historical events is sometimes closer to "myth" because "people want to believe or remember the best parts of a story." Another student wrote in his essay that, "for centuries, the job of recording history fell to an elite few who could manipulate … or alter the truth by leaving out certain information or discounting certain perspectives." Since many students chose topics that they already knew something about first hand from personal or familial experience, they couldn't always accept the information that they found as fact: in some cases, students suspected that what they were reading was closer to "myth," suggesting people's desire to "believe or remember the best." Throughout their research, a few students questioned the credibility of sources they found: one student thought more people were killed in the Sikh genocide than an article reported; another thought sources minimized the difficult conditions for Korean comfort women. When they couldn't find certain perspectives in official accounts, students searched for those perspectives in literary works. As such, they saw how literature, including fiction, can speak to the existence of—and offer a response to—gaps and silences in historical narratives.

This was an outcome I was particularly pleased with, since it helped students think more critically about what literature is and why it matters. Although QCC students are required to take an Introduction to Literature course, many of them come in to class asking why they have to study literature at all, especially when it is "made up." Their creative, self-directed projects offered compelling answers to those questions, and many students gained an appreciation for literature that they did not have prior to this unit. Alongside, or in juxtaposition to, historical and non-fiction sources, the study of literature added complexity and nuance to how students researched, thought, and wrote about genocide and mass atrocity. By using literature as a means of understanding and exploring real-world experiences of genocide and mass atrocity, literary study took on new relevance for these community college students.

Appendix 1: Unit Outline

The unit described in this chapter was taught over a five-week period in a course that met twice a week for 110 minutes per session. The course was held in a lab classroom where each student had access to a computer for in-class writing and research. There were 24 students in the class. The weekly activities and scaffolded steps of this unit are briefly outlined here.

Week One

Class Session 1:

- Introduction to unit on "The Holocaust in a Global Context: (Hi)Stories of Genocide and Mass Atrocity"
- In-class writing: students reflect on their existing knowledge of the Holocaust and prior learning experiences with Holocaust history
- Full-class discussion of students' reflections on their knowledge of the Holocaust
- Class views and discusses several texts and sources on the Holocaust and instructor gives brief lecture on Holocaust history
- Assignment guidelines for the Multimedia Museum Curating Project are distributed and discussed (see Appendix 2)

Class Session 2:

- Students attend talk by Holocaust survivor
- Students take guided tour of the KHC
- For at-home work, students are assigned to write a one-page reflection on the Holocaust survivor's talk, their tour of the Holocaust center, and how both might help them think about topics and approaches for their museum projects

Week Two

Class Session 3:

- Students select a topic for the museum project by today
- Students complete a research preparation worksheet in class and begin in-class research
- Instructor works with individual students during class to consider effective research approaches and potential challenges specific to various topics

Class Session 4:

- In-class research continues
- Students begin locating and reviewing possible sources for inclusion in their museums

- Instructor and embedded librarian are available for consultations with students who may need help finding relevant sources or furthering their research

Week Three

Class Sessions 5 and 6:

- Students finalize sources for project and begin drafting project essays in class
- Each student has an in-class conference with instructor to discuss progress on the project

Week Four

Class Sessions 7 and 8:

- Students continue drafting and revising project essays
- Workshopping ideas for presentations: students work in small groups to discuss their projects with their peers and consider some of the creative ways sources and topics might be presented to the class

Week Five

Class Sessions 9 and 10:

- Students present their Multimedia Museum Curating Projects to the class

Class Session 10:

- Students submit final drafts of project essays and all other project components
- For at-home work, students are assigned to write a one-page post-unit reflection on their learning experiences throughout this unit and assignment

Appendix 2: Multimedia Museum Curating Project Assignment Guidelines

Task

Drawing upon our discussions about the Holocaust, genocide, and mass atrocity—as well as the role of literature in history and storytelling—to help you brainstorm, you will select an historical or current event, a social or political problem, a global crisis, or a similar topic or issue that you think deserves to be represented in a museum. You will then curate a multimedia "museum" on this topic using sources and artifacts of your own finding and choosing.

Your topic might be a past event or atrocity which you feel has been underrepresented or misrepresented throughout history, deserving more attention or a different representation. It might also be a current issue or problem that your museum can help to raise awareness about. You may wish to choose a topic that relates to your own personal interests or experiences or a topic that you are eager to learn more about.

You will use your research and analysis skills to find and choose the sources or "artifacts" that will form your museum. These will consist of informative/non-fiction sources as well as literary and creative works that represent, portray, or discuss your topic in different ways.

Required Project Components

1. **5-page essay about your museum and sources:** Think of this essay as a guide someone might refer to while visiting your museum and encountering its sources/artifacts. What is the background information you would want visitors to understand about the event or topic you are portraying? What would you want museum visitors to know about how and why you have curated the museum as you have and about the different types of sources included? See the essay guidelines later for more details on what to include in this portion of the assignment.
2. **Museum Sources/Artifacts:** You must have at least **five** different sources or "artifacts" in your museum: **two** literary works in different genres (e.g., poetry, short story, novel, play, memoir, autobiography, etc.); **two** non-fiction informational sources (e.g., newspaper

article, peer-reviewed essay, historical monograph, etc.); and **one** audio/visual source (photograph, painting, video clip, documentary, interview, song, etc.). You may have more than five sources, but you must meet the minimum requirements above to successfully complete the assignment.

3. **An eight to ten-minute multimodal presentation of your project**: During the final week of this unit, you will present your museum and its artifacts to the class. In this presentation, you should *show* us your sources in addition to *telling* us about them. This might mean displaying sources electronically and/or preparing photocopied handouts of print sources (at least enough for every two people to share one copy). Please feel free to be creative or interactive in how you present your museum and its sources to the class—there are a variety of ways you might approach this aspect of the assignment.
4. **A separate one-page reflection** on the events we will attend at the KHC (Holocaust survivor talk and KHC tour). Your reflection should discuss: (1) what you learned from or found interesting about these events; (2) what you noticed about how different artifacts and exhibits at the KHC were curated; and (3) how you drew ideas or inspiration from these events when working on your own project.

Writing Guidelines for Five-Page Essay

Please keep in mind that your essay for this project is not a "traditional" research essay that offers an objective report on your topic; instead, your essay should offer a comparative analysis on what we might learn about this topic by examining different sources and perspectives. Develop your essay by including the following:

- A brief explanation of your topic and some background information. What is the most important information that someone unfamiliar with this topic would need to know **before** looking at your sources and museum?
- A project rationale: explain **why** you chose this topic. Why is it important to you? Why is it important for others to learn about? What do you hope people who "visit" your museum will learn or take away from it?

- Discussion and analysis of your sources: explain why you chose to include each source and what you think makes it powerful or important to read, look at, or listen to. What perspective, point of view, or information does each different source provide? When possible, include **quotations** from sources to further demonstrate why that source is significant or what perspective it presents.
- A consideration of how the different written genres and other creative forms used in your project offer different ways of understanding your topic. How do your sources offer different insights or perspectives because they are different *kinds* of information, different *genres* of writing, or different *forms* of creative work?
- Discuss one or two sources you chose *not* to include in this project. As you do your research, you will likely come across many sources but will not include all of them. Why did you choose some sources over others? How might your project be different if you had used different sources? What perspectives might be unaccounted for in your project?
- Include a Works Cited page in Modern Language Association format citing all of the sources in your museum (this does not count toward the five pages you must write to meet the length requirement).

CHAPTER 13

Trust No Scorn on the Page and No Hate in the Frame: Deconstructing Hate Speech and Empowering Tolerance in English 101

Barbara K. Emanuele

"Why isn't this talked about? Why doesn't anyone talk about these camps?" These were two questions asked during an in-class discussion in the fall 2016 section of my English 101 course at Queensborough Community College (QCC). It was a question spurred by students' reading of Garett Hongo's essay "Kubota," wherein the author reflects on his grandfather's experiences being questioned by the US Government in the immediate days after Pearl Harbor and the lasting impact that these experiences had on him and his family. Over the course of the semester, such questions were matched by many other "Whys?" Why is the history of America's indigenous people minimized by Westerners? Why hasn't the Westboro Baptist Church had their religious tax-exempt status revoked? Why is "fat-shaming" allowed everywhere we look? Why did so many turn a blind eye to what the Nazi regime was doing? Why do genocides keep happening if we know about them from nearly the moment they begin?

B. K. Emanuele (✉)
Department of English, Queensborough Community College, CUNY, Bayside, NY, USA
e-mail: BEmanuele@qcc.cuny.edu

A. E. Traver, D. Leshem (eds.), *Humanistic Pedagogy Across the Disciplines*, https://doi.org/10.1007/978-3-319-95025-9_13

Even when students could generate a "because" answer to one of these questions, a verbal recounting of dates and facts didn't do enough to describe *how* minds could be driven to hate. In nearly every case, what we now call micro-aggressions (the casual degradation of any marginalized group) escalated into formalized hate speech distributed to the public through mass media and classroom curricula. Students were particularly horrified to realize that such hatred had been taught, and they were eager to learn what could be done in response. This chapter reviews one such response—a project that required students' close reading of some of the vilest hate texts ever written, their assessment of these texts for patterns in language and image composition, and their creative efforts to reframe them to promote tolerance and understanding.

Long before the fall of 2016, I began to investigate opportunities to teach hate media and creatively reverse its impact. Luckily, my participation in the 2013–2014 NEH Colloquium Series at QCC's Kupferberg Holocaust Center (KHC) provided the funding and sanction to introduce such texts in the classroom. This financing enabled the purchase and distribution of course materials, and the grant's faculty working group provided the peer support in pedagogy and praxis that adjunct instructors, like myself, are often denied. In working with colleagues, my personal goal was to find a way to empower students in their daily battles with intolerance. To do so meant unpacking hate texts and images to discover how they were created, why they were made, and what could be done to turn such bigotry into objects that uplift, inspire, and promote tolerance. While my fall 2016 students were confronted with many samples of hate speech throughout the course of the semester, this chapter focuses on their work with excerpts from *Der Giftpilz* (*The Toadstool*, 1938) and *Trau keinem Fuchs auf gruner Heid und keinem Jud bei seinem Eid* (*Trust No Fox on his Green Heath And No Jew on his Oath*, 1936), elementary school readers produced by the Sturmer Publishing House, a wing of the Nazi Propaganda machine. What follows is a reflection on how to best prepare students for such work, how to scaffold that work, and details about the work itself. It is intended to serve as a guide for collective engagement with the texts and mutual empowerment over prejudice.

How We Recognize Hate Speech: Preparing Students to Critically Analyze Hate Propaganda

Before beginning this work in any course, it is important to first understand the students enrolled in the course. Community college students are often referred to as "non-traditional" students.[1] Kennesaw State University (2004) defines a traditional student as: "one who enrolls in college immediately after graduation from high school, pursues college studies on a continuous full-time basis at least during the fall and spring semesters, and completes a bachelor's degree program in four or five years at the young age of 22 or 23. Traditional students are also typically financially dependent on others, do not have children, consider their college career to be their primary responsibility, and are employed only on a part-time basis if at all during the school year" (n.p.). Although this definition was written less than two decades ago, such a student is rare today. For example, while still employing the phrase "non-traditional," The National Center for Educational Statistics (2002) has a far more realistic definition of the contemporary college student, including those seeking associate degrees:

> Delays enrollment (does not enter postsecondary education in the same calendar year that he or she finished high school); Attends part-time for at least part of the academic year; Works full-time (35 hours or more per week) while enrolled; Is considered financially independent for purposes of determining eligibility for financial aid; Has dependents other than a spouse (usually children, but may also be caregivers of sick or elderly family members); Is a single parent (either not married or married but separated and has dependents); Does not have a high school diploma (completed high school with a GED or other high school completion certificate or did not finish high school). (n.p.)

One takeaway from these definitions is that many contemporary college students are busy subsisting in the very conditions that create a hothouse for hate: conditions of economic insecurity that leave little to no time for proper consideration of information; conditions of relative deprivation created by the media's promotion of unrealistic physical, mental, spiritual, and financial standards; conditions stymied by low-paid and often abusive work; conditions mediated by racism, including regular confrontations with members of law enforcement; conditions that restrict expressions of gender identity and sexuality; and conditions reflective of religious intolerance and fear.

Significantly, there is no reason to believe that students' previous education has accurately addressed how such conditions lead to organized hate, or what can be done to disrupt these impacts. For example, Medoff (1996, 167) describes how high-school level history textbooks have led many college students to adopt the popular misconception "that Americans were unaware of the Holocaust and therefore unable to alter the course of events." Additionally, community college students, whose lives weave together the responsibilities of work, school, and family, may feel too overwhelmed to learn more about the Holocaust or how to prevent similar events in the future. As a result, in order to prepare community college students to critically analyze hate propaganda, it is important to first teach them to think deeply about the context of their own lives, including their reactions to these conditions. In particular, they must learn to understand that hate is not something that humans are programmed to do; rather, it is a learned expression that stems from varied and often reinforcing sources, including the modeling process. This realization both readies and centers students in their learning about the Holocaust, while it also positions them as informed, empowered agents who can act against hate in their own lives.

Unfortunately, our era of assessment and rubrics is both a help and a hindrance to this type of learning. As a result of various standardization initiatives in public education today, most students are used to having an assignment laid out for them in a series of steps aligned with a grading grid or rubric. While this "tell me what to think and how to think it" mentality might not be appropriate training for critical thought—after all, it is how dictators have been able to create an environment groomed toward intolerance—it can be harnessed for the careful organization of students' creative work. For example, this project used multi-week assignments that gave students frequent, if not daily, opportunities to: (1) refine their critical thinking skills in reading, writing, and speech; (2) appreciate multiple value systems; and (3) make judgments on texts and other source materials. The following section outlines these scaffolding exercises, which aimed to prepare students for their careful, critical consideration of hate propaganda.

What We Experience Through Words: Scaffolding Students' Critical Analysis of Hate Propaganda

Consistent with an extended curriculum plan, my fall 2016 students began the term by reading essays that focused on self, family, and friends to comprehend the nature and impacts of our most primary connections with others. In small groups, they unpacked key points of the assigned texts to understand the particulars of the author's experience and general truths about how we gain an awareness of ourselves, how we maintain the self while melding with family, and how we create kin-like bonds with friends.[2] Students concluded the unit by writing a brief reflective essay on who they are and how they came to be, which helped to build their confidence by respecting and celebrating their stories. At that point, because their group work had created an environment in which they felt comfortable, students also shared their work with those classmates they knew and trusted.[3]

This learning was followed by students' engagement with essays about education and work—settings that introduce us to the outside world and also, quite often, to institutionalized hate. Students then analyzed their prior experiences for what they were, which helped to prepare them for future critical analyses.[4] In complement, they analyzed popular cartoons from *The Simpsons* (for its commentary on public schools) and *Dilbert* (for its commentary on the modern workplace). Drawing on their experiences and the aforementioned readings, students dug into each frame of the strips, asking: Where are the characters positioned? How are they drawn? What colors are used, and how? As many of my students were devotees of art, they emerged as discussion leaders; helping to reframe the classroom dynamic by encouraging more honest reactions to the cartoons rather than those presupposed to please the instructor.

Students then performed a similar exercise alongside the readings. Googling "Elementary School Students," "Elementary School Classrooms," "College Students," and "College Classrooms," they were introduced to the deliberate decision-making processes that constitute these images, including decisions about who/what is made visible and decisions about light/contour. As with students' analysis of *The Simpsons* and *Dilbert* cartoons, this exercise began as a large full-class discussion that segued into small-group analyses of specific images.

When breaking down a text, students need to learn to look beyond the message an author puts out there to *how* he/she sends the message. They need to learn to look at word choices, punctuation choices, and the use of space on the page—all of which combine to create a tone that guides a reader toward certain thoughts as they engage with a text. To promote this learning, I had students look at song lyrics and unpack their language; so students would not feel judged or picked on because of their musical preferences, I selected an array of musical references, including Robin Thicke's infamous "Blurred Lines," as well as songs that included ridiculous examples of anti-Asian sentiment (like "Turning Japanese" by the Vapors) and songs that encouraged domestic violence (like "Johnny Get Angry," most popularly performed by Joanie Summers).

While not all English 101 instructors will have such flexibility in choosing their course texts, I believe it is important to create at least two weeks' worth of similar low-stakes classroom activities before presenting students with hate propaganda. Through these activities, students gain confidence in their analytical skills and improve their ability to have frank discussions about sensitive topics like the Holocaust. As Charlesworth (1996, 128) notes, "(i)f such sensitivity is not shown, then the encounter with such horror can prove too much and students (will be) unable to intellectualize what they have experienced."

Yet, the argument can also be made that intellectualizing hate experiences and texts can lead to the rationalization of organized hatred. These reading and writing assignments helped my students develop the ability to think through hate without over-rationalizing it. More specifically, they encouraged them to examine the images that surround them, and that, in their sum total, begin to taint our minds toward intolerance. The assignments also primed students to critically unpack the text and images of hate propaganda, which is the focus of the following section.

This Is How We Break Down Hate: Students' Critical Analysis of Hate Propaganda

My fall 2016 course concluded with readings from elementary school readers produced in 1936 and 1938 by the Sturmer Publishing House, a wing of the Nazi propaganda machine. I provided students with these readers, explaining why certain sources, like the German Propaganda Archive and the United States Holocaust Memorial Museum, are reliable sources, and other venues, like *Third Reich Books,* are not.[5] I then projected the cover image from *Der Giftpilz* onto a large screen in the classroom, asking students to consider the image through the lessons learned in their earlier analyses of education and work-related cartoons. With this introduction, students began to unlock the code behind the cover image, considering the prominence of the Star of David on the central mushroom figure, as well as the main stereotypes applied in Anti-Semitism. As their eyes moved around the image, they noted each mushroom's facial features and worked through why something as innocuous as a large nose can be skewed into a tool of hate.

"How to Tell a Jew" (1938), another illustration from *Der Giftpilz*, is equal in size and terror to the simplicity of the reader's cover art. In this image, well-groomed young healthy blonde-haired men, taught by an equally attractive male instructor, populate a bright and sunny classroom. As they analyzed this image, students first noticed the absence of females in the classroom, which led them to acknowledge that the image lacked other manifestations of diversity, as well. Students' attention then turned to the writing on the chalkboard. Asked whether a respectful teacher would allow a student to draw someone to resemble an ape, or to tolerate a student's superstition around the numbers "666," my students described the image for what it was and continues to be: an instrument of hate designed to promote one physical aesthetic while using exaggerations to devalue another.

Repetition is key to the artwork and the text of *Der Giftpilz*. As Bytwerk's (2017a) translation of "How to Tell a Jew" is of a suitable length, students were organized into small groups to unpack the verse. In the process, they were introduced to an ear-worm—portions of a text that, when heard often enough, claims space in the mind and becomes a lens through which to view the world. For example:

> From a Jew's face
> The wicked Devil speaks to us,
> The Devil who, in every country,
> Is known as an evil plague.
> Would we from the Jew be free,
> Again be cheerful and happy,
> Then must youth fight with us
> To get rid of the Jewish Devil.

Armed with basic literary terms, students noticed that the word "devil" is used repeatedly in the text and that, in assonance and consonance, "devil" is linked to "evil." They also noted word choices, including the absence of words; they pointed to the relative lack of positive words like "cheerful" and "happy," which is consistent with the poem's focus on evil and how to fight it. They then identified and located other examples of earworms and began to track the process of brainwashing.

Bytwerk's (2017b) excellent translation of *Trau keinem Fuchs auf gruner Heid und keinem Jud bei seinem Eid* (*Trust No Fox on his Green Heath and No Jew on his Oath*) provided students with additional opportunities to review the readers' use of insidious repetition. For example:

> "We do not buy from Jewish shops!"
> Says the mother to the child.
> "'Tis only German goods we buy;
> Remember that, my darling."
> German women should only buy
> What's been made by German hands,
> By German industry and strength.
> That's why we only go
> To those stores with German goods,
> Here also we save more,
> For their wares are cheap and good.
> From Jews you get bad value!
> Hence take note of mother's words,
> Be sure you never buy from Jews.

To bring hand-eye coordination into play, I asked students to diagram each line of verse, underlining affirmative language, observing where a word fell in a stanza, and noting how closely words were tied together in placement and definition. Through this exercise, students discovered how positive words like "buy" and "goods" were tied to ideas of strength and value, and how negative words like "bad" were tied to Jews. Students also called attention to the fact that a mother had uttered these words, and how the text's visual and audio cues mimicked nursery rhymes.

Properly prepared, students continued to work in groups to unpack and assess additional readers. After two class sessions of analyzing the readers' illustrations, text, and tone, students were ready to respond creatively to their messages.

This Is How We React to Hate: Students' Creativity as a Mode of Empowerment

As students examined the readers for patterns in language and image composition, they began to make connections to texts and images that they are exposed to every day on social media. These links formed the basis of an assignment that asked students to not only unpack hate speech, but to respond directly to it by reversing it. Students were tasked with finding and responding to four instances of hate speech from social media in four to eight pages of writing.

In preparing their assignments, students were asked to include the original text, for comparison and assessment purposes, with their more positive and tolerant response text that mirrored the length, rhythm, rhyme (if present), word choice, and punctuation of the original. The assignment outline reminded students that "translating" or "reversing" hate texts involves line-by-line engagement with the original hate text, changing each hateful or malevolently intended word. It also encouraged students to transpose punctuation to accent empathic thinking and to use earworms, assonance, and consonance to affirm and uplift. In response, and for example, one group of students reworked the "proanalifestyleforever" blog's pro-Anorexia mantra into a series of "commandments" that promoted healthy living and a positive self-image.[6]

I also offered my more artistically inclined students the opportunity to focus on and recreate four hateful images. In this version of the same assignment, students modeled the style and era of the original image, but they used different colors and repositioned and/or rescaled persons and objects in their response. Those students who used photographs were encouraged to maintain the use or absence of color and to refrain from using Photoshop to alter the original. For example, one group of students used photos from segregated buses in the South during the Civil Rights era in contrast to modern buses and trains in a culturally and racially diverse New York City.

As students worked on their projects, I found it helpful to schedule a library session where, under the guidance of experts in research, the class lessons and conversations were reinforced. An additional benefit of this session was that the school's servers helped to assure that students' pursuit of texts and images was performed in a "safe space." The library visit also benefited students by providing assistance for their delivery of an annotated bibliography that described why they chose the sources that they did. While Manfra and Stoddard (2008, 263) describe how this type of work "calls on students to not only understand the concepts they have studied, but to articulate those understandings," I also found that students' preparation of an annotated bibliography gave them the opportunity to reflect on and account for the roots of their activism.

As students regularly benefit from the chance to draft and revise their work, and from opportunities to see how a peer has successfully tackled an assignment, I then organized an in-class workshop session. During that session, students engaged with each other's projects and received feedback from their peers. I was also able to step in and clear up any remaining confusion, where necessary, at that time.

Regardless of whether a student's project was text or image-based, it prompted them to engage in close reading, critical thinking, and creative work. As a result, grading necessitated a rubric, which is included at the end of this chapter as an Appendix. I distributed this rubric to students at the start of the project, and I used it as a guide for the quantitative assessment of the project's outcomes. Significantly, I have found these assessment results to be particularly valuable in my efforts to conduct talks, write papers, and consider grants that will perpetuate the work of the project.

Concluding Thoughts

I designed this project to give students a better understanding of their responsibilities to others on this planet. By moving from the interrogation of historical examples of hate propaganda to the reframing of contemporary examples of hate propaganda, the project helped students develop the skills necessary to address and dismantle hatred while investing in and taking ownership of their own ideas and expressions using the electronic tools available to them. In fact, students reported that the project had inspired them to take action outside of the classroom space. For example, they noted their ability to make better use of the limited character format of Twitter to respond to harmful lyrics with a "clapback" of their own. They also spoke of using Facebook's blog posts and video capabilities to respond to "fake news," and of using Instagram to promote healthier images of the self. Additionally, many students responded directly to hate speech plastered outside of the walls of QCC by reporting the incidents to campus police and replacing the hateful stickers and flyers with texts and illustrations of a tolerant and empowering nature. One student even went on to intern at the KHC and is now actively in the process of bringing the statue of the *Comfort Woman* by Kim Seo-kyung and Kim Eun-sung to campus.

Just as the project encouraged my students to embrace their place in the world, it also heightened my sense of my *own* responsibilities as a citizen in the twenty-first century. It is not enough for educators to teach facts, dates, and places. Words are empty without meaning—and meaning often comes from making a work one's own. To this end, and as an adjunct instructor, I am committed to continued connections with my dynamic faculty support group from the 2013–2014 NEH/KHC Colloquium Series, as these connections helped me to fine-tune my understanding of the role that we all play as "first responders" in challenging hate texts. My hope is that this project will inspire those on both sides of the instructor's desk in their own journey toward understanding.

Appendix: The Rubric for the Final Project

Hate text	*Hate art*	*Hate photos*	*Bibliography*	*Process essay*
Excellent: You have found a text that comes from a Hate group recognized by the SPLC or approved by me; your responding text uses the same amount of adjectives, descriptive nouns, repetition, and rhyme to symmetrically respond to the original text.	Excellent: You have found artwork that comes from a Hate group recognized by the SPLC or approved by me; your responding artwork is created by you and follows the style of the original art including positioning of the main object, number of objects and characters, while symmetrically using color, sharpness, and light.	Excellent: You have found a photographic image from a Hate group recognized by the SPLC or approved by me; your responding photo is taken and edited by you and follows the style of the original photo including positioning of the main object, number of objects and characters, while symmetrically using color, sharpness, and light.	Excellent: You have correctly cited the hate group's website following the current MLA template for web page citation; you have thoughtfully explained why you chose to address this hate group using creative and precise language.	Excellent: You have written a text that both creatively and precisely illustrates how you converted the hate text, art, or image through a detailed explanation of how you created your work.
Very good: You have found a text that comes from a Hate group recognized by the SPLC or approved by me; your responding text uses just about the same amount of adjectives, descriptive nouns, repetition, and rhyme to symmetrically respond to the original text.	Very good: You have found artwork that comes from a Hate group recognized by the SPLC or approved by me; your responding artwork is created by you but is not as precise in following the style of the original art including positioning of the main object, number of objects and characters as above, or your use of color, sharpness, and light is not as directly symmetric as above.	Very good: You have found a photographic image from a Hate group recognized by the SPLC or approved by me; your responding photo is created and edited by you but is not as precise in following the style of the original photo including positioning of the main object, number of objects and characters as above, or your use of color, sharpness, and light is not as directly symmetric as above.	Very Good: You have correctly cited the hate group's website following the current MLA template for web page citation; you have thoughtfully explained why you chose to address this hate group using creative and precise language, though it is not as creative and precise as above.	Very Good: You have written a text that uses some creativity and precision to illustrate how you created the hate text, art, or image. Your explanation contains the appropriate details but they are not communicated as creatively and precisely as above.

Sufficient: You have found a text that comes from a Hate group recognized by the SPLC or approved by me; your responding text uses adjectives, descriptive nouns, repetition, and rhyme to symmetrically respond to the original text though your word choice could have been tighter.	Sufficient: You have found artwork that comes from a Hate group recognized by the SPLC or approved by me; your responding artwork is created by you but does not follow as well as it could have the style of the original art including positioning of the main object, number of objects and characters, or your use of color, sharpness, and light is not directly symmetric.	Sufficient: You have found a photographic image from a Hate group recognized by the SPLC or approved by me; your responding photo is created and edited by you but does not follow the style of the original photo including positioning of the main object, number of objects and characters, or your use of color, sharpness, and light is not directly symmetric.	Sufficient: You have correctly cited the hate group's website following the current MLA template for web page citation; you have explained why you chose to address this hate group with appropriate though not creative and or precise language.	Sufficient: You have written a text that illustrates how you created the hate text, art, or image. Your explanation contains the necessary details, but they are provided without creativity or precision of language.
Insufficient: The text you chose does not come from an SPLC recognized group or was not approved by me; you have used less than four pages of hate speech; your response text does not correspond to the original text; your response text does not change the meaning of the original text.	Insufficient: The artwork you chose does not come from an SPLC recognized group or was not approved by me; your artwork is not created by you, or does not change the meaning of the original art.	Insufficient: The photo you chose does not come from an SPLC recognized group or was not approved by me; your photo is not created by you, or your photo does not change the meaning of the original image.	Insufficient: You did not follow the MLA template for citing a web site; you repeatedly neglected to explain why you chose to address the hate group; you fail to supply a bibliography.	Insufficient: You omitted this part of the final project; your process essay omits details that would fully illustrate how you created the hate text, art, or image.

Notes

1. The entire nomenclature of "non-traditional student" strikes me as a micro-aggression masked as academese that immediately sets up a dynamic of those students who are "supposed" to be in higher education and those students who are not.
2. In previous years, I have taught "The Myth of the Latin Woman: I Just Met a Girl Named Maria" by Judith Ortiz Cofer (2017). The group discussion associated with that text focused on three key anecdotes regarding serenades offered to Cofer, how they were received by her, and how they would be received by the students if they were in similar situations. The resulting conversation of how "innocuous" gestures are often masked acts of sexism and racism began the process of the students reassessing their engagement with society and, in effect, becoming "woke" to what is around them.
3. Two assignments that are particularly helpful in building classmates' confidence in themselves and each other call on the students to apply their new-found awareness to everyday occurrences. In the concluding low-stakes group project for this unit, students are asked to find an advertisement featuring family and friends and to attend to who is featured in the ad (e.g., the race, age, gender of the people picture) and how they are situated around the product. With just a few guiding questions—Who is the center of the ad? What are the dominant colors?—they immediately see the social expectations that have long dominated societal roles and contributed to indoctrinated hate.
4. John Gatto's (1990) "Why Schools Don't Educate" is an ideal text for this critical reading because it is easily accessible and, given its eight-point format, easy to unpack. I recommend asking students to review his arguments in light of the context of when the essay was written, the modern moment, which students are addressed in his arguments, and which students are not.
5. The German Propaganda Archive provides translations of some Sturmer readers, as well as high-quality scans of their artwork (visit http://research.calvin.edu/german-propaganda-archive/).
6. This blog has since been deleted from the Internet.

References

Bytwerk, Randall. 2017a. How to Tell a Jew. *The German Propaganda Archive*. http://research.calvin.edu/german-propaganda-archive/story3.htm. Accessed 21 Mar 2017.

———. 2017b. We Do Not Buy from Jewish Shops. *The German Propaganda Archive*. http://research.calvin.edu/german-propaganda-archive/fuchs.htm. Accessed 21 Mar 2017.

Charlesworth, Andrew. 1996. Teaching the Holocaust Through Landscape Study. In *New Perspectives on the Holocaust: A Guide for Teachers & Learners*, 174–185. New York: New York University.

Cofer, Judith Ortiz. 2017. The Myth of the Latin Woman: I Just Met a Girl Named Maria. In *Queensborough Reads*, ed. The Department of English Queensborough Community College, 36–40. Originally published in *Latin Deli: Prose and Poetry*, Athens: University of Georgia Press, 1993.

Gatto, John Taylor. 1990. Why Schools Don't Educate. In *Queensborough Reads*, ed. The Department of English Queensborough Community College, 75–77. Originally presented at the New York City Teacher of the Year Award, New York, New York, January 31.

Manfra, Meghan McGlinn, and Jeremy D. Stoddard. 2008. Powerful and Authentic Digital Media and Strategies for Teaching About Genocide and the Holocaust. *Social Studies* 99 (6): 260–264.

Medoff, Rafael. 1996. *"Teaching about International Responses to News of the Holocaust: The Columbus Dispatch Project at Ohio State University," New Perspectives on the Holocaust: A Guide for Teachers & Learners*, 167–173. New York: New York University.

Kennesaw State University Center for Institutional Effectiveness. 2004. *A Fresh Look at Traditional and Nontraditional Undergraduates at KSU*. Center for Institutional Effectiveness. http://eimirvic.kennesaw.edu/AnalyticStudies/Students_2004_Traditional_Nontraditional_Undergraduates.pdf.

CHAPTER 14

"I thought Natives were all living an idyllic country life…": Students Reconsider North American Indigenous Peoples' Lives Through Speech, Gender, and Genocide

Franca Ferrari-Bridgers

According to Lindquist (2006) and Bergen (2003), the gravity of the Holocaust becomes apparent through its framing within considerations of Hitler's rise to power, the Nazi state, and World War II. It is essential, they argue, for students to understand all of the factors that lead to genocide including identification of a target, isolation, deportation, mass incarceration, and extermination. In this way, the specific unfolding of events during the Holocaust can be generalized into phases or stages and compared to other historical instances of genocide, mass violence, ethnic cleansing, or cultural genocide. However, this type of nuanced consideration of history and society seems to have diminished in American primary and secondary social studies education. Hence, as an Italian immigrant to this country, I have been shocked by my students' relative lack of knowledge

F. Ferrari-Bridgers (✉)
Department of Speech and Theatre, Queensborough Community College, CUNY, Bayside, NY, USA
e-mail: FFerrari@qcc.cuny.edu

A. E. Traver, D. Leshem (eds.), *Humanistic Pedagogy Across the Disciplines*, https://doi.org/10.1007/978-3-319-95025-9_14

of their own, American, history, particularly in regard to the experiences of North American Indigenous Peoples.[1] This became my challenge during the 2015–2016 programming of the National Endowment for the Humanities (NEH) Colloquium Series, "Gender, Mass Violence and Genocide," at Queensborough Community College's (QCC's) Kupferberg Holocaust Center (KHC): how can I provide a perspective to my students on North American Indigenous Peoples' experiences within a colloquium series focused on mass violence and genocide when they lack a basic understanding of what those experiences were?

In various forms, this question has long mediated my work in Public Speaking at QCC, particularly as students in that course prepare informative speeches about different topics of North American Indigenous Peoples' history. With each passing semester, I have become more and more aware that students' mental imagery of Indigenous Peoples is very different from the reality of Indigenous Peoples' lives. In fact, that imagery is typically a kaleidoscope of pieces from Disney movies like "Pocahontas" or "Peter Pan," memories of high school textbook readings, and unrealistic representations of Indigenous Peoples' living conditions today. For instance, at the outset of the course, many of my students believe that North American Indigenous Peoples are dead; completely integrated into American society (and that tribes no longer exist); rich because of casinos; or, echoing Rousseau's "bon sauvage" myth, living a carefree, peaceful, and idyllic life immersed in nature, fishing, hunting, and smoking the pipe.

Significantly, this imagery and lack of knowledge is not specific to QCC students; rather, it is endemic to most American college students because of what is taught about Indigenous Peoples' histories in American public schools. According to Lee (2015), Shear et al.'s (2015) and Shear's (2015) analyses of the primary and secondary education guidelines for teaching "Native American" history in all 50 states, 87% of these guidelines depict North American Indigenous Peoples as an extinct population that existed only prior to 1900. Most of these guidelines also lack information about contemporary issues relevant to populations of Indigenous Peoples, including ongoing conflicts over land, water rights, and sovereignty.

As a result, when confronted with the contemporary realities of Indigenous Peoples' lives on reservations—realities illustrated, for instance, by alarming statistics from the United States Census Bureau's 2014 study on Pine Ridge reservation in South Dakota[2]—my students often grow upset and question why they didn't learn these facts in school. In addition, most are taken aback by the realization that Indigenous Peoples' current living conditions are often interpreted as the end result of processes of genocide, ethnic cleansing, mass violence, and cultural genocide. Recognizing the many factors that weaken these claims of genocide (i.e., colonialism, war, virgin-soil epidemics, and the lack of a premeditated plan to intentionally and simultaneously eliminate entire tribes of North American Indigenous Peoples), my students still can't believe that this is our history and reality in the United States, a land that, for many, as first- or second-generation immigrants, represents freedom, justice, and dreams of success and wealth.[3]

It was this gap between what students knew about the history of the United States and the current status of Indigenous Peoples that led me to align my Public Speaking course with the fall 2015 programming of the NEH/KHC Colloquium Series, "Gender, Mass Violence and Genocide." This program offered the perfect historical and social sciences forum through which my students could learn about gender violence, genocide, mass violence, and ethnic cleansing directly from experts in the field. In this way, it also provided my students with the opportunity to gain the necessary intellectual tools to understand and evaluate the connections between the past and contemporary realities of North American Indigenous Peoples' lives.

In this chapter, I describe the project that grew out of this alignment. I begin with an exploration of my efforts to contextualize North American Indigenous Peoples' history. I then segue into a review of the pedagogical decisions that informed the project design. Following this, I describe the assignments that constituted the project, and I review students' work on those assignments. I conclude the chapter with a discussion of how students' participation in the project helped them to better understand North American Indigenous Peoples' histories and develop important communication and public advocacy skills.

The Contextualization of North American Indigenous Peoples' History and the Controversy of Genocide

Coming to understand North American Indigenous Peoples' history as one of possible genocide is difficult for students given that, despite a few notable exceptions, the majority of American public schools deal with this history from a narrow Euro-American perspective that excludes all indigenous narratives.[4] According to Shear et al. (2015), most social studies textbooks describe the killing of North American Indigenous Peoples as part of an inevitable war that needed to be won at all costs to form the United States. In fact, with the exception of Washington State, the vast majority of states' social studies textbooks avoid the word "genocide" when referring to the historical experiences of North American Indigenous Peoples.

Coming to understand North American Indigenous Peoples' history as one of possible genocide can also be difficult for students because of the controversy that surrounds this framing. Olster (2015) grounds this controversy in the federal government's lack of genocidal intent in its interactions with all tribes. Yet, Madley (2015) suggests that the dramatic reduction of the population of North American Indigenous Peoples—from 5,000,000 or more in the pre-colonial times to 240,000 individuals in 1880–1900—needs historical explanation. In doing so, he invites us to consider "statements of genocidal intent, massacres, state-sponsored body-part bounties, and mass death in government custody," together with the "breaking of treaties, forced removal, (and) confinement to reservations," as factors "for locating, evaluating, or ruling out possible instances of genocide" (Madley 2015, 98–99).

As a result of their limited prior knowledge and the complexities of the aforementioned controversy, I decided that students' work in my Public Speaking course needed contextualizing. The first step of that contextualization was aligning the course with a fall 2015 event in the NEH/KHC colloquium series, which provided students with a framework through which to analyze the relationship between gender violence and instances of genocide, mass violence, and ethnic cleansing. In that aligned event, "Gender and the Future of Genocide Studies," (2015) Dr. Elisa von Joeden-Forgey discussed the relationship between gender violence and genocide, noting how instances of sexual violence can be interpreted as red flags signaling the unfolding of genocide. In her list of examples of the types of sexual violence that can accompany genocide, Dr. von Joeden-Forgey referred to the forced sterilization and past/current removal of children from North American Indigenous Peoples' families in Canada and the United States.

The second step of this contextualization was students' reading of "The Convention for the Prevention and Punishment of the Crime of Genocide" (1948), which states that genocide is a crime committed by the killing and/or bodily/mental harm of members of a specific ethnic group with the deliberate intent to bring about the physical destruction of that group. This destruction can be wrought through the direct killing of members of the group, through the prevention of births within the group, and through the forcible transfer of children to another ethnic group. To these forms of destruction, I asked students to add cases of "environmental racism," a term coined by Benjamin Chavis, an African American civil activist, in the 1987 environmental report, commissioned by the Commission for Racial Justice (1987), "Toxic Wastes and Race in the United States," to describe "the concentration of hazardous waste disposal sites in or near areas with a relatively large ethnic minority population." Many of the cases of "environmental racism" that we considered spoke to the unequal health risks borne by minority populations in the United States (e.g., higher rates of risk for asthma, lead poisoning, cancer, birth defects, and infertility).

The third step of this contextualization was students' analysis of scholarship that explores North American Indigenous Peoples' history through the lenses of gender violence, genocide, mass violence, and ethnic cleansing. Building on Dr. von Joeden-Forgey's lecture, students were directed to engage with a mix of primary and secondary sources, including at least two peer-reviewed articles from scholarly journals. Additionally, they were asked to watch Dr. Andrea Smith's 2011 online lecture, "Sexual Violence and American Indian Genocide," which explores four materializations of sexual violence among North American Indigenous Peoples: (1) environmental racism and genocide; (2) sterilization and genocide; (3) medical experimentation programs and genocide; and (4) boarding schools for North American Indigenous Peoples and sexual violence. Students were also asked to watch Aaron Huey's (2010) Ted Talk, "America's Native Prisoners of War," which links the current third-world living conditions of residents of the Pine Ridge Reservation to a sequence of historical events starting with the 1824 creation of the Bureau of Indian Affairs and ending with the 1980 Supreme Court ruling about the Black Hills land claim.

Pedagogical Rational: Public Speaking, Civic Engagement, and Social Justice

Traditionally, Public Speaking courses focus on topics very different from gender violence, genocide, mass violence, and ethnic cleansing. As the typical learning objectives of a Public Speaking course include writing and performing informative and persuasive speeches, students are typically encouraged to learn about and present on topics of their own choosing.

Pedagogically, my creation of a Public Speaking course in which students write and perform informative speeches about North American Indigenous Peoples' histories, lives, and cultures reflects Soley's (1996) rationale for the inclusion of controversial subjects in college courses. According to Soley (1996, 9), when faculty include controversial subjects in their curricula, they encourage students' understanding of society and help them to "make thoughtful decisions and judgments," "sustain democratic principles and participate in democratic processes," and "(create) habits that will fortify continued learning." By integrating the study of a controversial subject into a course focused on the development of students' communication and public advocacy skills, I sought to provide students with opportunities to learn how to speak effectively and take action on a variety of social justice issues and concerns.

More practically, my creation of a Public Speaking course focused on North American Indigenous Peoples' histories, lives, and cultures also stems from the novelty of the topic. According to an informal survey that I conduct every semester at QCC, most students have only a superficial understanding of North American Indigenous Peoples' histories, and few of them have ever met an indigenous person or visited a reservation. Yet, this lack of historical, cultural, and personal knowledge often advantages students' speech writing and performance. For example, it tends to encourage them to evaluate historical events related to instances of genocide, mass violence, and ethnic cleansing from a neutral perspective, that is, a perspective free from preconceived ideas, personal biases, and negative stereotypes. This, in turn, fosters their understanding of that history and its current ramifications, while it also motivates them to communicate their informed opinion much like public advocates do—with objectivity, independence, genuine interest, and empathy.

As I considered the best way to structure students' learning in the course, I drew on Newmann and Wehlage (1993, 8) to design a sequence of assignments that encouraged students to perform "authentic intellectual work." These assignments aimed to develop students' "higher-order thinking skills" as they learned to: construct knowledge; interpret, analyze, and summarize sources; engage in conversations with experts and with their peers; and "(make) connections to the world beyond school." For example, by using Dr. von Joeden-Forgey's, Dr. Andrea Smith's, and Aaron Huey's talks as primary sources, students were given the opportunity to develop higher-order thinking skills by engaging in "conversations with experts." Likewise, in writing their speeches, students were asked to "interpret, analyze, and summarize sources" that they would later use in communications with "their peers."

Finally, in developing the course and its assignments, I drew on Kolb's (1984) and Kolb et al.'s (2001) work on experiential learning. According to Kolb (1984, 41), experiential learning is "the process whereby knowledge is created through the transformation of experience," and it is characterized by concrete experience, abstract conceptualization, reflective observation, and active experimentation. While participating in this project, students were asked to combine the concrete experience of engaging primary and secondary sources with the abstract conceptualization of the topic through the acquisition of new knowledge and its comparison with their prior knowledge. Reflective observation was achieved through students' answering of topic-specific reflection questions and their creation of speeches. Additionally, active experimentation occurred when students had the opportunity to perform their speeches in front of an informed audience, engage in lively discussions with their peers in the post-speech Q&A sessions, and propose feasible and practical solutions to issues that North American Indigenous Peoples currently face.

The Assignments

Students were asked to complete two assignments comparing their prior knowledge about North American Indigenous Peoples' history with the knowledge that they constructed through the course contextualization. The first assignment was to write an informative speech, which integrated information from the Colloquium Series, online lectures, and credible sources, for performance in front of the class. To complete the first two points of their speech, students were asked to summarize the content of their readings. For the third point of their speech, students were asked to share their informed opinion about whether Indigenous Peoples' experiences could rightly be linked to processes of gender violence, genocide, mass violence, and/or ethnic cleansing.

Once students wrote and performed their speeches, they completed the second assignment, a reflection paper about what they had learned. Informed by the Association of American Colleges & Universities (AAC&U) Global Learning VALUE Rubric, the assignment's questions asked students to consider their newly acquired knowledge and how it relates to their family and community life; evaluate whether what happened to North American Indigenous Peoples was somehow justifiable from a cultural, political, and/or ethical point of view; and contemplate the global consequences of what happened to North American Indigenous Peoples.[5] Such structured prompts encouraged students to view Indigenous Peoples' history through the lens of their own personal experiences, which both Totten (1987) and Lindquist (2006) recommend as an effective strategy for helping students understand the gravity of mass violence.

Insights from Students' Reflection Papers

A review of students' reflection papers reveals the project's impact on their learning. First, the majority of students wrote that the project had helped them to better understand gender violence, genocide, mass violence, and ethnic cleansing as frameworks for interpreting North American Indigenous Peoples' histories. For instance, one student wrote that he didn't know what genocide was until he attended von Joeden-Forgey's lecture and wrote his speech. Since then, he had come to understand genocide as "acts intended to eradicate a specific ethnicity" and to apply a genocide framework to incidents of gender violence, mass violence, and ethnic cleansing around the world—including the experiences of North American Indigenous Peoples. Further evidence of this understanding can be found in the work of those students who wrote about the central role of the state in historical and contemporary incidents of mass violence. For example, in reflecting on the federal government's treatment of North American Indigenous Peoples, one student wrote that our government continues to fail "on a social responsibility level when it comes to the treatment of the Native Americans." He then connected this opinion to another central insight of genocide scholarship—the role of dehumanization in mass violence: "the government had a one sided relationship with Native Americans," considering them "almost non humans." Significantly, such insights led many students to reflect on the importance of studying history using impartial and unbiased sources. In the words of one student, history should serve as "a living reminder of evil atrocities" committed against human beings so that such atrocities never occur again.

Second, most students reflected on the extent to which they now see North American Indigenous Peoples' history as the primary cause for the substandard living conditions on many reservations today. For instance, one student wrote about the historical removal of Indigenous children from their families as he considered the current rate at which indigenous children are placed in foster care: "The traumatic effects on the families and the perpetuation of the history of abuse that began with colonialism ... still lasts today." Another student considered this history as she wrote about contemporary rates of interpersonal violence and substance abuse among North American Indigenous Peoples: "The patterns of decay affect all of us locally and globally in the form of talents lost." Condensing this learning, another student described how he had come to view North American Indigenous Peoples' experiences as an *ongoing* struggle: "Currently Native Americans face great challenges to deal with the shortcomings that history has given them and continuing circumstances of discrimination."

Third, many students described—and evidenced—how the study of a controversial subject had improved their communication and public advocacy skills. In fact, in most of their reflective writings, students seemed to position themselves as allies in the aforementioned struggle. For example, many students wrote of their desire to participate in the democratic process by proposing practical and doable solutions aimed at supporting Indigenous Peoples' communities. These solutions included: the creation of grassroots organizations; the deliberation of stricter laws against environmental pollution; the creation of monuments and museums dedicated to North American Indigenous Peoples; and the establishment of class action lawsuits against those who abuse(d) children in boarding schools and state care. Students also wrote of wanting to petition federal, state, and church authorities to publicly apologize to North American Indigenous Peoples, describing a desire to, in the words of one student, "acknowledge and call (out) these crimes against humanity by confronting the political and social systems" responsible for their history and current reality. At a pedagogical level, students' proposed solutions and calls to action represent the active experimentation phase of the experiential learning process: after experiencing and conceptualizing new knowledge, students sought to actively apply their learning through the proposal of concrete and feasible solutions to the problems identified (Kolb 1984; Kolb et al. 2001). As many students went beyond the scope of the assignment to actually make contact with leaders of indigenous communities and to interview them online, their work also illustrates a desire to connect their learning to "the world beyond school" (Newmann and Wehlage 1993).

Conclusion

To conclude, this project not only helped students gain a better understanding of a tragic chapter in American history, it also helped them to develop awareness of a significant social justice issue: the contemporary reality of North American Indigenous Peoples' lives. In particular, by coupling the history of indigenous people in the United States with the NEH/KHC Colloquium Series, "Gender, Mass Violence and Genocide," this project encouraged students to tackle a controversial topic through multiple lenses, including primary/secondary sources. Likewise, hearing directly from Indigenous Peoples like Dr. Andrea Smith helped students build a more realistic perspective on the role Indigenous People played and still play in American history, as well as the impact that history has had on structuring their current reality. This newly acquired knowledge caused a clash between students' old and new imagery of Indigenous Peoples, and it inspired in them a curiosity to learn, understand, and change the world. In fact, because this controversial learning occurred within a Public Speaking course that asked students to write and perform an informative speech for an audience, students were able to develop the communication skills necessary to actually advocate for and make that change.

Appendix: Informative Speech Assignment

Informative Speech: Body of the Speech

Please follow the steps below to complete the body of your informative speech.

STEP 1: Consult background information about the general topic of your speech.

- Watch "Andrea Smith: Sexual Violence and American Indian Genocide" lecture (https://www.youtube.com/watch?v=Neg-RIbi764)
- Read "Andrea Smith: Sexual Violence and American Indian Genocide" lecture script
- Watch "Aaron Huey's Ted Talk America's Native Prisoners of War" (https://www.ted.com/talks/aaron_huey)

STEP 2: Select one of the following as the specific research topic for your informative speech:

- Environmental racism and genocide
- Sterilization and genocide
- Medical experimentation programs and Native community genocide
- Boarding Schools for Native Americans and sexual violence

STEP 3: Select and consult appropriate sources.

- Search and read one peer-reviewed article about your research topic.
- Search and read/watch one newspaper article, web page, or YouTube video reporting one specific fact/event related to your topic.
- Attend the event, "Gender and the Future of Genocide Studies," on Wednesday, September 30, 2015.

STEP 4: Write the main points of the body of your speech.

- Write a summary of your event/fact source. (400 words) (Main Point 1)
- Write a summary of your peer-reviewed article. (400 words) (Main Point 2)
- Use your summaries to write the three main points of the body of your speech:
  - Main Point (1)
  - Main Point (2)
  - Main Point (3): Relate your knowledge from Main (1) and Main (2) to your understanding/notes/intake of the "Gender and the Future of Genocide Studies" lecture and the "Andrea Smith: Sexual Violence and American Indian Genocide" lecture. (300 words)

STEP 5: Complete speech outline

- Complete your speech outline by writing the INTRO and CONCLUSION of your speech.

STEP 6: Deliver your speech and participate in the Q&A session after your speech.

Informative Speech: Reflection Assignment

In order to complete the reflection assignment associated with your informative speech, please respond to the following prompts. You will find the AAC&U Global Learning Value Rubric, Dr. Andrea Smith's lecture, Dr. Elisa von Joeden-Forgey's lecture, and your readings helpful in this regard. (400 words)

1. Effectively address the significant issues you became familiar with while writing your informative speech. (50 words)
2. Briefly explain how these issues relate to your life, your community, and the natural environment. (50–100 words)
3. Are these issues justifiable from a cultural and/or political perspective—why or why not? (50 words)
4. Are these issues justifiable from an ethical perspective—why or why not? (50 words)
5. Evaluate the consequences of these issues at the local and global levels. (50 words)
6. What ethical, workable, and interdisciplinary solutions would you propose to solve this global complex problem? (50–100 words)

Notes

1. The author's decision to refer to Native Americans as "Indigenous Peoples" stems from Smith's (1999) article, which traces the origin of the term "Indigenous Peoples" to the civil rights movement of the 1960s, when it was used to acknowledge Indigenous activists' fight for self-determination
2. Examples of these alarming statistics include: an 80%unemployment rate; more than 52% of residents living below the poverty line with a yearly median individual income of US$ 4000; 80% of residents affected by alcohol addiction; and a life expectancy of 48 years for men and 52 years for women.
3. The majority of Queensborough Community College (QCC) students are members of ethnic or racial minority groups, and most QCC students are first-generation college students. At last count, QCC students hail from 139 countries and speak 87 different languages.

4. For an example of one such exception, see *The Montana Education Act for All* published by the Montana Office of Public Instruction (2004), which mandates that all Montana schools include curricula about Indigenous Peoples' histories, cultures, languages, and contemporary status.
5. To access a copy of the AAC&U Global Learning VALUE rubric, please visit: https://www.aacu.org/value/rubrics/global-learning.

References

Bergen, Doris, L. 2003. *War and Genocide: A Concise History of the Holocaust*. Lanham, MD: Rowman and Littlefield.

Commission for Racial Justice. 1987. *Toxic Wastes and Race in the United States*. New York: United Church of Christ.

Huey, Aaron. 2010. America's Native Prisoners of War—Ted Talk. Filmed [September 2010]. YouTube video, 15:34. Posted [September 2010]. https://www.ted.com/talks/aaron_huey.

von Joeden-Forgey, Elisa. 2015. Gender and the Future of Genocide Studies. Lecture, from Queensborough Community College, Bayside, NY, September 30, 2015.

Kolb, David, A. 1984. *Experiential Learning: Experience as the Source of Learning and Development*. Englewood Cliffs, NJ: Prentice-Hall.

Kolb, David A., Richard E. Boyatzis, and Charalampos Mainemelis. 2001. Experiential Learning Theory: Previous Research and New Directions. In *Perspectives on Thinking, Learning, and Cognitive Styles*, ed. Robert J. Sternberg and Li F. Zhang, 227–247. Mahwah, NJ: Lawrence Erlbaum.

Lee, Tanya, H. 2015. The Native American Genocide and the Teaching of US History. *Truthout*, April 1, 2015. https://www.truth-out.org/news/item/29954-the-native-american-genocide-and-the-teaching-of-us-history.

Lindquist, David H. 2006. Guidelines for Teaching the Holocaust: Avoiding Common Pedagogical Errors. *Social Studies* 97 (5 (September)): 215–221. https://doi.org/10.3200/TSSS.97.5.215-221.

Madley, Benjamin. 2015. Reexamining the American Genocide Debate: Meaning, Historiography, and New Methods. *American Historical Review* 120 (1 (February)): 98–139. https://doi.org/10.1093/ahr/120.1.98.

Montana Office of Public Instruction. 2004. *Indian Education for All*. Helena, MT: Montana Office of Public Instruction. http://opi.mt.gov/programs/indianed/IEFA.html.

Newmann, Fred M., and Gary G. Wehlage. 1993. Five Standards of Authentic Instruction. *Educational Leadership* 50 (7 (April)): 8–12.

Ostler, Jeffrey. 2015. *Oxford Research Encyclopedia of American History*. "Genocide and American Indian History." Oxford: Oxford University Press. http://americanhistory.oxfordre.com/view/10.1093/acrefore/9780199329175.001.0001/acrefore-9780199329175-e-3?rskey=Bk30Gg&result=1.

Shear, Sarah B. 2015. Cultural Genocide Masked as Education. In *Doing Race in Social Studies: Critical Perspectives*, ed. Prentice T. Chadler, 13–40. Charlotte, NC: Information Age Publishing INC.

Shear, Sarah B., Ryan T. Knowles, Gregory J. Soden, and Antonio J. Castro. 2015. Manifesting Destiny: Representations of Indigenous Peoples in K–12 U.S. History Standards. *Theory & Research in Social Education* 43 (1): 68–101. https://doi.org/10.1080/00933104.2014.999849.

Smith, Linda T. 1999. *Decolonizing Methodologies: Research and Indigenous Peoples*. New York, NY: Zed.

Smith, Andrea. 2011. Conquest—Sexual Violence and American Indian Genocide. Lecture, CMC Media and Democracy Lectures Wealthy Theatre, Grand Rapids, Michigan. https://www.youtube.com/watch?v=Neg-Rlbi764.

Soley, Mary. 1996. If It's Controversial, Why Teach It? *Social Education* 60 (1): 9–14.

Totten, Samuel. 1987. The Personal Face of Genocide: Words and Witnesses in the Classroom. *Social Science Record* 24 (2): 63–67.

CHAPTER 15

Echoes of Exile: Genocide and Displacement Studies in the Undergraduate Music Curriculum

Mirna Lekić and André Brégégère

Addressing the growing anti-refugee sentiment and rhetoric, rising xenophobia, and general public bewilderment evident in the United States and abroad at a time when world-wide displacement hit a record high, the eight programs of the 2016–2017 NEH Colloquium Series at Queensborough Community College's (QCC) Kupferberg Holocaust Center (KHC), titled *Fleeing Genocide: Displacement, Exile and the Refugee*, amplified the voices of those with personal exile experience and those professionally acquainted with the many challenges facing migrant and refugee populations.[1] The series coordinators enabled college-wide participation in the colloquium by promoting multidisciplinary curricular alignment; faculty were invited to develop assignments or short units of study around one or more of the program(s), request mandatory student attendance at the event(s), and share the resulting student artifacts with the coordinators.[2] Members of the QCC Music Department participated

M. Lekić (✉) • A. Brégégère
Department of Music, Queensborough Community College, CUNY,
Bayside, NY, USA
e-mail: MLekic@qcc.cuny.edu; ABregegere@qcc.cuny.edu

A. E. Traver, D. Leshem (eds.), *Humanistic Pedagogy Across the Disciplines*, https://doi.org/10.1007/978-3-319-95025-9_15

by aligning several academic- and performance-based music courses and by performing in the seventh program of the series, "Echoes of Exile," a concert of chamber, vocal, piano, and jazz works that traced genocide and refugee experiences through multiple generations.

Performed by the music faculty, guest artists, and the QCC student Jazz Ensemble, "Echoes of Exile" presented works of refugee composers (Frédéric Chopin, Dino Rešidbegović, and Hanns Eisler), pieces written on the theme of exile or in response to mass violence (songs by Franz Schubert and Robert Schumann and chamber music by Dmitri Shostakovich and Ramin Heydarbeygi), as well as jazz standards (by Billy Strayhorn, Gerald Marks, and Seymour Simons) that were performed in the Japanese internment camps.[3] The selections chosen for "Echoes of Exile," many of which were written or preserved by refugees, invited students to consider attempts at cultural genocide and to explore the survival of threatened cultures and peoples through music. The program's commissioned work, by composer Dr. André Brégégère, incorporated songs of Holocaust refugees to demonstrate to students—both through performance and through in-class discussions with the composer—that a modern musical language can reflect the pervasive sense of homelessness that characterizes our time, that real-world artifacts live on in creative work, and that the act of listening to music invites us to consider different individual perspectives. The featured musical selections, in which students participated as performers, listeners, and writers, highlighted the human dimension of displacement; showed cross-cultural experimentation; advanced learning through the study of different genres, styles, and forms; and emphasized tradition and fluidity present in all music. Additionally, spoken introductions for each piece provided information on the creation, significance, and rationale for its inclusion in the program.

In this chapter, we provide an overview of several assignments and activities used in both academic and performance courses by the participating music faculty, all of which were grounded in the "Echoes of Exile" event.[4] We also examine and evaluate course and series learning outcomes on the basis of various student artifacts, including performance preparation, post-performance reflections, and written reports of different kinds. Knowing that looser classification and broader framing would foster more creative assignment design, members of the music faculty were invited to incorporate the concert or other events of the series into their curricula in any way they deemed suitable. The authors of this chapter participated in several roles. Dr. Brégégère wrote the commissioned composition, offered in-class presentations and discussions of his work, and assessed the effectiveness of the traditional Concert Report assignment in teaching about the Holocaust, genocide, and displacement. Dr. Lekić performed in the "Echoes of Exile" concert, served as the concert's artistic director, and examined the outcomes of studying relevant solo piano repertoire, as well as the CD Liner Notes Project (see Appendix), both of which she used in her classes.

Activities and Assignments in Academic Courses

The majority of music faculty at QCC teach *Introduction to Music*—a music appreciation course that functions both as an introduction to the basic concepts and vocabulary of music and a historical survey of the Western art-music tradition from Monteverdi to the present. The class does not require any previous musical background, and, for most students, it represents their first exposure to Western classical music. This course is also "Writing Intensive," which signifies its role in a university-wide effort to improve students' literacy and communication skills. Thus, a significant portion of the student's evaluation in this course is based on writing assignments.

Introduction to Music courses aim to prepare students to listen, learn, and engage with music on a deeper level; to address the narrow and highly subjective experience of a typical student who takes such a course as a general education requirement; and to build on the students' previous experience and knowledge as they learn to speak about music, place it into context, and make further connections. For faculty who teach survey courses based largely on Western musical traditions, there is an ever-present concern with keeping the content relevant and relatable. Knowing the proven success of the contextual, as opposed to the historical and analytical, approach to teaching music history, the NEH/KHC Colloquium Series provided a perfect opportunity to further emphasize this approach and thus enhance the learning experience of everyone involved. This section provides an overview of the composer-led in-class presentation and discussion and an assessment of two writing assignments used to align *Introduction to Music* courses with the NEH/KHC Colloquium Series, in particular with the "Echoes of Exile" concert, the CD Liner Notes Project (assigned in Dr. Lekić's class), and the Concert Report (an assignment employed by Drs. Brégégère, Gliere, Lekić, and Litroff).

CD Liner Notes Project

As "Echoes of Exile" offered a selection of music reflecting Dr. Lekić's expertise, the CD Liner Notes Project (see Appendix) served as a means of building on the content of the concert and enlarging the relevant repertoire through the multicultural lens of the QCC community. Guided by the lessons learned from the research on teaching the Holocaust in a variety of settings, this assignment put to use music's particular power to recognize individual stories—a guiding principle in creating a deeper and better understanding of the Holocaust, mass violence, and the resulting displacement. Additionally, the CD Liner Notes Project provided a means of unifying many diverse styles, languages, and perspectives, across time and through a common theme, while at the same time humanizing the artists, the composers, and the subjects of their work.

The goal of the assignment was to create a class compilation of music dealing with displacement, exile, and refugees—accompanied by detailed liner notes for each selection. Each student was asked to contribute two pieces or songs inspired by these themes. The selections could be in any language and any musical style, and they were to be drawn from the music students already knew or be new discoveries. Students were to use the skills acquired in class to peel away and examine the many layers of their selections (instrumentation, form, text, harmonic/rhythmic/melodic language, and motives, etc.) and to write about this and the researched cultural context of the selected music in the form of CD liner notes.

In prior classes, students were presented with examples of exile-inspired classical repertoire, examples of Grammy-winning CD liner notes (a style of writing with which many are unfamiliar), and various current and past refugee populations whose musical testimonies they might be interested in researching further. Earlier writing assignments had also prepared students to provide commentary on musical action as well as text-sound relationships.

Throughout this project, students learned to listen actively and in context, all the while translating the general history of genocide and mass violence into personal stories told through music. Students' selections were compiled and preserved on the Colloquium Series' online library guide.[5] This website, an archive of musical responses to the experiences of mass violence, displacement, and exile, now stands as a resource that will enrich other courses and create opportunities for exploration of multiple musical traditions at QCC and beyond.

Because the choice of selections was not limited to a certain period or style, students' own preferences and previous knowledge were recognized and they were empowered to trust and also challenge themselves. They were asked to apply what they had learned in and outside the class to newly discovered repertoire and to selections with which they might have been familiar, but to which they were now listening with new ears. Most importantly, through this process students were hearing and experiencing historical events through the perspective of an individual. The project also provided students with the opportunity to engage with primary and secondary sources, which fostered their critical and analytical commentary. This listening and writing exercise, like much of our course work, was aimed at creating better, more engaged listeners who were capable of understanding different perspectives and listening in context.

The resulting class playlist reflected the diversity of the QCC student body both in terms of the students' heritage and their interests. It included music addressing the Holocaust, conflicts and mass displacement in India/Pakistan (during the partition), Iran (after the 1979 Revolution), Ireland, Cuba, Colombia, and Syria, as well as exile experienced by African Americans and the Roma in their home countries. The playlist also featured a variety of styles, including classical, pop, and world music. The liner notes revealed students' developing historical perspective, their willingness to explore difficult topics and tackle more complex compositions (such as Arnold Schoenberg's *Survivor from Warsaw*), their new or renewed concern for current issues, and their felt expressions of empathy, understanding, respect, and responsibility. For example, in the liner notes that accompanied his selections, one student wrote: "The phenomenon of a man in exile will always attract listeners because each individual has been faced with adversity and the sense of exile in being removed from his comfort zone."

Most song choices were highly personal. A student included a well-known Pakistani refugee song featuring lyrics written by her grandfather, once a refugee himself.[6] She chose songs that depicted the pain of displacement resulting from the partition of India, a topic to which she wished to bring more attention. Other students reflected on the feeling of being exiles within their own country as a result of racism, which even the greatest of sacrifices (such as those of the fallen "Buffalo" soldiers) could not overcome. Students also commented on the music's role in combatting and/or offering alternative perspectives to the misconceptions advanced by the media and politicians, providing a "new and clearer lens through which the world can understand a [foreign] culture." As one student wrote, the role of the artists was "to tell the story, implant it in the minds and hearts of their audience, and remind them of their history and responsibility."

Some students described how the lyrics (and subsequent research) proved informative and important in providing different perspectives and addressing the dangers of prejudice, while others described how the music itself helped to unify communities through universal experiences. Even students who had not personally experienced displacement or exile wrote liner notes that expressed a profound understanding of the anger, hopelessness, pride, and strength felt by those seeking to rebuild their lives in a new place. Many also expressed hope and willingness to engage in the discussion with a new multicultural and historical perspective. One student commented: "I am impressed by people from around the world. Many are helping refugees and there are many campaigns happening at the moment… I am planning to find out more campaigns near me and volunteer." The class playlist and the accompanying notes revealed a student body ready to listen, to be challenged, and to participate as responsible citizens.

In-Class Presentation

An in-class presentation by Dr. Brégégère was added to two sections of the *Introduction to Music* course, focusing on the commissioned piece he wrote for "Echoes of Exile."[7] The presentation aimed to bridge the gap between the compositional process, its performance, and the listener's experience. At the time of the commission, Dr. Brégégère had been asked by the colloquium coordinators to employ, in some way, material from the Stonehill Jewish Song Collection, an online archive of more than 1000 songs performed by Holocaust survivors and recorded by Ben Stonehill in New York City only a few years after the end of the war, in 1948.[8] After listening to several of these songs, Dr. Brégégère decided to use *Treblinke dort* ("Treblinka is there"), a version of a song written "when the Warsaw ghetto inhabitants had begun to discover the fates of those who were being deported during the summer of 1942" (Gilbert 2005, 51). This choice was made for musical and thematic reasons: the melody of the song, based on a popular tango, is quite beautiful and haunting and the lyrics are almost unbearably poignant in their very direct description of unthinkable events—families torn apart, human beings herded into wagons taking them to an extermination camp. The trio that resulted from this effort is a five-movement composition for violin, cello, piano, and tape (i.e., prerecorded sounds) named after its titular song, *Treblinke dort*.[9]

Incorporating the original song into the commissioned piece posed the challenge of integrating traditionally "tonal" material within a modern compositional language and doing it in a way that was both dignified (i.e., not turning into a parody, or a pastiche), and approachable—honoring the more didactic aspect of this project, which endeavors to promote awareness and remembrance of the Holocaust. Dr. Brégégère decided to employ the song in two ways: first, as a simple instrumental setting of the melody for violin and cello, with piano accompaniment, in the third movement of the trio (which counts five movements). In this first appearance, the song appears like a moment of peaceful relief within the more dissonant, angular context of the piece as a whole. This statement of the song and its nostalgic Tango melody can be understood as a momentary glimpse into a happier past, before the tragic events of the Holocaust. The song reappears at the end of the piece, in the fifth movement, in a very different light: Dr. Brégégère directly employed the original recording from the Stonehill collection, which emerges through loudspeakers (in musical parlance, i.e., the prerecorded, "taped" part) from the dying sound of the last notes from the piano, while the song's poignant lyrics, in the original Yiddish and in translation, are projected on to a screen. As the song progresses, we hear the sound of a train emerging in the background; this sound gradually becomes louder, as the song becomes softer. At the end, only the sound of the moving train remains, symbolizing the fateful journey of those sent to Treblinka, as well as the extinction of their voices, and in most cases, their lives.

Dr. Brégégère's class-based presentations of this piece were followed by an open discussion with the students. Some of the students' first questions, in both classes, revolved around the context of the song. While many students displayed a general awareness of the Holocaust (i.e., that European Jews were persecuted for their religion by the German Nazi regime during World War II), none of them knew about the specifics of the extermination camp at Treblinka. Thus, the presentations offered opportunities to reinforce the students' historical perspective on the period. Other questions touched upon the relationship between the musical work and its subject matter. This is often an elusive relationship, especially in the case of a work for instruments alone, and the examination of it forms an important topic in any music appreciation course. Finally, some other student questions focused on more practical topics, such as the relation between composer and performers, the rehearsal process, and the technical preparation of the prerecorded "taped" part.

The Concert Report

The Concert Report is a consistent assignment in all music appreciation courses at QCC, as it is at many other institutions. It requires students to attend a concert of live classical music and to write a three-to-five-page essay describing the event with the objective of developing their critical evaluation of the music they heard based on the concepts that they learned during the class. In the case of the music appreciation courses aligned with the NEH/KHC Colloquium Series, students were free to attend any concert that would later serve as the basis for their report, but most chose to attend the "Echoes of Exile" event. The sample statements below are quoted directly from students' Concert Report assignments, with minimal editorial edits indicated in square brackets:

1. "The concert opened my mind as to how music [...] can have an underlying meaning to it. Even though the pieces played at the concert had to do with people going through extreme hardships, [...] it made me realize how even in the darkest moments, people still tend to create a form of beauty out of it."
2. "The piece called 'Ethnic Cleansing' is the one that stood out to me the most [...] because it was explaining a lot of the traumatic experiences that took place during that time. [It] stuck out to me because I cannot imagine being harmed because of my lifestyle and religious [beliefs]."
3. "My overall feelings of the concert were that it had opened my mind to different global and social issues that people in the world currently face. It also taught me not to ever sit down and expect everyone's life to be the same as mine. [...] This concert [...] taught me that when I start to believe times are hard I can make it through."
4. "The concert achieved its purpose because the performers gave useful information about the history of the world, the composer, and the music. [...] For example, the [pieces] about the Holocaust made me think about what Hitler did to the Jewish people, and made me feel very sad. I remembered all the things that I had read about the Holocaust in the book *Night*, and in *The Diary of Anne Frank*."

5. "Music can [be] a reflection of people longing for home. For example, when my parents and I hear music from our country, we feel proud and happy because it awakens emotions, [...] a feeling of going back home."
6. "I learned about how music represented the story and struggles of a person, community, country, or the world. [...] It is important to learn history but it is not one of my strongest subjects, and music just made history more fun and enjoyable to learn."
7. "[*Treblinke dort*] demonstrated how real world artifacts that survived genocide through refugees can live on in a new, creative [work] in honor of the memory of the victims."
8. "One lyric of [the song *Treblinke dort*] I remember deeply [is]: 'sisters and brothers went in there, but they never came out.' Refugees should live in safety like us. [...] I hope my college organizes more educational events like this concert, making people aware of issues or problems around the world."
9. "The fifth movement [of *Treblinke dort*] had the biggest impact on me. It was a tape recording of a man singing, with the lyrics projected on the screen. [...] it made me realize that the whole point of the program was to understand what life was like in the Jewish concentration camps and the Japanese-American internment camps. That out of one nation's fear, these people were taken away from their homes and sent away to places where they were treated as less than human. Although those people went through horrible times that I couldn't even begin to imagine, [they] were able to find joy in music. *Echoes of Exile* was an amazing concert that gave me a different look into the history of these two tragic events."
10. "The instruments and the music could be considered the voice of the people who had to endure these horrors. [...] The concert was a great way to spread the message and enlighten the audience on what was happening during [times] of exile, displacement, and discrimination."

These sample statements illustrate five themes represented, in one form or another, in most of the assignments: Music and Meaning (student samples #1, 6); Music and Empathy (#2, 3, 8, 9); Music and Hope (#1, 3, 7, 9); Music and Memory (#5, 7, 10); and Music and Learning (#4, 6, 10).

The excerpts also demonstrate the impact of the "Echoes of Exile" concert on a wide array of learning outcomes, both relating to music appreciation courses and to the more general domain of the Humanities (i.e., outcomes related to the development of concentration and communication skills, an aesthetic appreciation, an informed historical perspective, knowledge about contemporary social issues, and an informed appreciation of other cultures). Furthermore, the sample statements also illustrate the benefit of framing the "Echoes of Exile" concert through the lens of the Holocaust/refugee theme, modeling how, through music, one can address history and issues of society and identity across the disciplines.

Activities and Assignments in Performance Courses

Throughout the semester, the participating music faculty sought to apply music as a way to promote discourse, explore the self and the other, and elicit empathy. In performance classes, the instructors' choice of repertoire demonstrates their course alignment with the colloquium. For example, members of the QCC Jazz Ensemble were asked to prepare for and perform in the "Echoes of Exile" event and thus demonstrate knowledge of jazz performance practice and its significance as applied to historical accounts of jazz in World War II Japanese internment camps in the United States. The inclusion of this repertoire, as it related to the internal displacement of Japanese Americans, served to bring the many themes of the Colloquium—themes of exile, social injustice, prejudice, fear, and hysteria—closer to home.

Piano students enrolled in Dr. Lekić's Instruction in Piano III and IV courses (a combined section class) were assigned early and late intermediate classical repertoire written by refugee composers, as well as popular pieces with a relevant social message (works by Frédéric Chopin, Béla Bartók, György Ligeti, Ruth Schonthal, Antonín Dvořák, and Michael Jackson). In addition to developing technical and expressive skills and applying theoretical knowledge, students examined the experiences that compel the creation of art by researching the life of the composer and the historical context of the work and by considering the ways in which such knowledge and/or the work's apparent political message is and can be manifested in the composition and its performance. While searching for creative solutions to technical and musical challenges, students explored the many ways compositional content can be brought to life, and they considered the changes that could be made to clarify a work's message in a performance. The folk elements and innovations present in the studied compositions were identified as manifestations of the composer's identity, heritage, and memory, as well as of the individual creative genius. The pieces studied also drew attention to the refuge that art and music provide for the composer, performer, and listeners; to music's role in preserving history and tradition; and to the innovations that come about as a result of displacement.

At the end of the semester, students presented live in-class performances and were asked to complete a reflective questionnaire summarizing their experiences of the project as a whole. An analysis of students' questionnaires reveals that, in shifting the primary focus away from learning notes and mastering technical challenges, the project piqued student interest and increased their motivation, allowing them to think critically and experience historical events and the refugee experience from the perspective of an exiled individual. For example, in their responses to researching and playing assigned repertoire, students commented on the role of music as a "witness" and a "time machine" that allowed them to vividly live someone else's story and revisit the world and its problems at different times throughout history. They also noted music's particular effectiveness in expressing psychological and emotional states, and its power of persuasion. Additionally, students observed that, as a unique form of sensory and communal experience, music presented effective coping mechanisms for the composers, and provided a place for healing and reflection for all involved (the composers, student performers, and listeners).

Students also wrote that the project and the selected repertoire provided a learning opportunity or a reminder of why we must work to avoid mass violence and genocide at all costs. Touching upon the potentially devastating role of silence and indifference during times of war and genocide, they described music as an invitation to look inward and "change ourselves in order to change the world." For instance, one student wrote: "Music is a platform to bring cognizance. People would speak more on all socially conscious topics if they were more aware of what's happening in the world. Performing and studying such music is a great way to keep these topics relevant." Another noted: "We must study music not only for its beauty, but to understand how this world was and how it is seen by others. Only by acknowledging the experiences and feelings of others and those who came before us, in addition to our own, can we move forward." Finally, students described this repertoire as being especially valuable in promoting understanding, conjuring ways to recover, and as a mirror that could hold mankind and individuals accountable.

Conclusion

Incorporating the topics of the 2016–2017 NEH/KHC Colloquium Series into academic and performance music courses served to expand our course learning outcomes and to enrich students' class experiences. The inclusion of the themes of genocide, mass violence, and exile complemented students' development of discipline-specific skills by providing a broader historical perspective and contextualizing powerful personal stories as told through music. Normally tangential to music course material, these topics enabled an understanding of music not only as a means of creative self-expression but as a historical and social document and an art that illuminates both propaganda narratives, as well as forgotten and suppressed voices distant and near, past and present. Students' reflective work demonstrated an increased awareness of music's role in society, as a medium that both informs and moves people to consider and reconsider their roles and obligations as global citizens.

Appendix: Class CD and Liner Notes Assignment

This assignment aligns with the 2016–2017 NEH/KHC Colloquium Series, "Fleeing Genocide: Displacement, Exile and the Refugee." The goal of the assignment is to create a class compilation of music dealing with displacement, exile, and refugees, accompanied by detailed liner notes for each selection.

Assignment Description

Each student is asked to select two pieces or songs that deal with or are inspired by the themes of exile, displacement, and refugee life, and to write CD liner notes for the two selections. These can be in any language and any musical style, and can be drawn from the music you already know or be new discoveries.

Guidelines

STEP 1. Find two musical compositions/songs written on or inspired by the themes of exile, displacement, or refugee life. Note the title, composer, lyricist, and date of composition or release.

STEP 2. Provide an Internet link or an mp3 file (emailed to me) for the selected pieces. If your selections are songs, include the text/lyrics. In case of texts in languages other than English, provide both the original and the translation. Texts and lyrics do not count toward the four-page (two-page per piece) minimum.

STEP 3. Research the background of the pieces and their creators. You are looking for information that is significant in terms of the message/content of the piece. Keep in mind that everything you write must be in your own words and that all your sources should be listed in a separate bibliography page (not counted in the required number of pages). The bibliography page should follow the Chicago Manual of Style format.

STEP 4. Listen to the music many times, and comment on the relationship between music and text. In your commentary, describe how the composer achieves certain emotional effects or how the music gets the intended message across. Consider different elements of the music, such as: mood/character; structure/form; mode (major/minor); rhythmic/melodic/harmonic characteristics; instrumentation; texture; dynamics; range/register; and tempi.

STEP 5. Combine information from steps 1–4 in the format of liner notes (about two pages per composition). The lyrics and bibliography page should appear after the liner notes for each selection. You can use the sample liner notes provided on Blackboard for inspiration and as a guide.

Notes

1. United Nations High Commissioner for Refugees (UNHCR) data indicates that in 2015, there were more than 65 million displaced persons, 21 million of whom were refugees (UNHCR 2015).
2. *Fleeing Genocide: Displacement, Exile and the Refugee* was organized as the 2016–2017 NEH/KHC Colloquium Series by Drs. Aliza Atik, Kathleen Alves, and Mirna Lekić of Queensborough Community College (QCC), CUNY.
3. "Echoes of Exile" performers included members of QCC's music faculty (soprano Jennifer Gliere, pianist Mirna Lekić, saxophonist Scott Litroff, and violinist Karen Rostron), guest artists (cellist Marta Bedkowska-Reilly and soprano Sara Paar), and members of the Queensborough Jazz Ensemble (Lei Han, Frankelyn Hernandez, Jameel Nicholson, and Justin Pierre). A recording of the concert is available here: https://qcc.libguides.com/c.php?g=532288&p=3719527

4. Participating music faculty included Drs. Brégégère, Gliere, Lekić, and Litroff.
5. The 2016–2017 NEH/KHC Colloquium Series' library guide can be accessed at: http://qcc.libguides.com/KHRCA_Fleeing_Genocide2016-17.
6. "Chaandi Raatein" (Starlit Nights) by Feroz Nizami and Musheer Kazmi.
7. The composer talk took place in *Introduction to Music* sections taught by Drs. Lekić and Brégégère.
8. The Stonehill Jewish Song Collection is available at http://www.ctmd.org/stonehill.htm.
9. *Treblinke dort* can be viewed via the following link: https://youtu.be/2kAxPYyUbaI.

Reference

Gilbert, Shirli. 2005. *Music in the Holocaust: Confronting Life in the Nazi Ghettos and Camps*. Oxford: Clarendon Press.

CHAPTER 16

Using Campus Resources and Problem-Based Learning to Prepare Students to Become Global Citizens

Danny Sexton

Over the last 20 years, there have been major shifts in the way that college English professors teach composition. An earlier model, which was the focus of my own training and my composition classrooms for a number of years, centered on instructing students how to write in the various rhetorical modes: narrative, description, exposition, and argumentation. These objectives were partly met by having students read model essays that treated mainly personal issues, such as education, family relationships, and social issues. Significantly, these social issues tended to be of a local nature, dealing with prevalent issues in the United States. What these models neglected, however, was the larger global community in which our students lived.

First, let me clarify my usage of two terms that appear consistently in this chapter: global education and global citizenship. While they are related, they are not identical. My usage of global education relies largely on a definition put forth by Kenneth A. Tye: "Global education involves

D. Sexton (✉)
Department of English, Queensborough Community College, CUNY, Bayside, NY, USA
e-mail: DSexton@qcc.cuny.edu

A. E. Traver, D. Leshem (eds.), *Humanistic Pedagogy Across the Disciplines*, https://doi.org/10.1007/978-3-319-95025-9_16

learning about those problems and issues that cut across national boundaries, and the interconnectedness of systems—ecological, cultural, economic, political, and technological" (Tye 1990, 5). The emphasis here is on acquiring knowledge about the world that extends beyond a student's individual and local communities. Global citizenship, however, moves beyond knowledge to an active participation. Oxfam offers a good working definition that aligns with my usage in this chapter: "a global citizen is someone who … take[s] an active role in their community, and work[s] with others to make our planet more equal, fair, and sustainable" (Oxfam UK). The connection, then, is that through global education, we can prepare students to become global citizens.

To some, the call for global education in American schools might appear a fairly recent development. However, Sadiq Abdullahi traces it back to "the [1968] publication of the Foreign Policy Association's report entitled *An Examination of Objectives and Priorities in International Education in U.S. Secondary Schools.*" This report drew attention to the need for "students to become active participants in changing their communities and the world" (Abdullahi 2010, 25). Abdullahi details the slow and arduous integration of global education in American schools, focusing on how some groups saw it as "un-American." Not until the 1990s, when many state departments of education and "national professional organizations, such as the National Council for the Accreditation of Teacher Education and the American Association of Colleges for Teacher Education" issued mandates and position statements, did American schools start to take seriously the need to incorporate global education into the curriculum (Abdullahi 2010, 27).

In this chapter, I first offer a brief history of the theory and practice of global education in American higher education before focusing specifically on the challenges faced in community colleges and gateway courses, such as English Composition. Then, I outline how I utilized the campus resources available at my institution to design and implement a problem-based learning group project that raised student awareness of the global refugee crisis by requiring them to evaluate current solutions and create their own solutions based on research and classroom discussions. I conclude with final thoughts on the ways in which the project allowed for a social justice component in the classroom while preparing students to become global citizens.

School Context and Author's Positionality

A number of factors can affect how global education is incorporated into the curriculum—the institution, the needs of the students, the particular course, and the availability of resources. I am an assistant professor of English at Queensborough Community College (QCC), one of seven community colleges within the City University of New York (CUNY) system, the largest urban public university in the United States, and the first major institution to implement an open-admissions policy. CUNY also boasts a very diverse student body (City University of New York Master Plan 2012–2016, 2014). In fact, QCC is "one of the most diverse colleges in the nation … [composed of] students from 129 countries and [who] speak 78 different languages [with] twenty-four percent of the students … born outside the USA" (QCC Office of Institution Research and Assessment 2016–2017, 18). For a number of our students, English is often a second or, in some cases, a third language.

The academic needs of QCC students are as diverse as the student body itself. Some students are highly prepared for college courses while others require foundational skills. Furthermore, students attend QCC for a variety of reasons. A number of them will end their post-secondary education with the completion of the associate degree while many more will transfer to a four-year institution, either within or outside the CUNY system. No QCC, or CUNY, professor can walk into a classroom on the first day of classes assuming that all students are at the same level or are there for the same ends. Furthermore, introductory core courses, such as English Composition, serve—for better or worse—as gateway courses designed to familiarize students with a set of skills necessary for continued success in their academic and professional endeavors. The dilemma that many of us who teach these so-called gateway courses at any institution of higher education often face is how to structure our courses to provide core competencies while also creating a space for global education. While QCC does have a global student body, there is a major difference between a diverse campus and one that is critically aware of its diversity. The aim is to give students the tools to analyze and discuss intelligently what they see and experience but may not have the words to express.

On my composition syllabi, there are always two sets of objectives—one focuses on course objectives, and the other focuses on general education objectives. Significantly, these general education objectives include many of the elements that we associate with global education: using historical or social sciences perspectives to examine the formation of ideas, human behavior, social institutions, or social processes; using analytical reasoning to identify issues or problems and evaluate evidence in order to make informed decisions; and differentiating and making informed decisions about issues based on multiple value systems. At the end of each semester, I conduct a self-evaluation and reflection to gauge if my composition courses have successfully met both sets of objectives. While the course objectives are met through the lessons provided and the assignments completed, the general education objectives are typically only marginally met. For a number of semesters, I experimented with various programs and projects to help achieve these objectives, but none worked as effectively as I would have desired.

At QCC, we are fortunate to have three campus resources available to promote students' general education, especially around topics such as social justice and global learning: the QCC Art Gallery, the Queensborough Performing Arts Center (QPAC), and the Kupferberg Holocaust Center (KHC). These types of campus resources are the ones that Maxine Greene advocates we use to encourage what she calls aesthetic education: "the intentional undertaking designed to nurture appreciative, reflective, cultural, participatory engagements" (Greene 2001, 6). While I have used these resources for my own research, I had not taken full advantage of them for my students until I learned that one of my English department colleagues used the KHC to structure a semester-long group project in which students worked in teams to create a strategic plan for a fictional NGO tasked with solving a specific development problem in a country of their choice. In their strategic plans, students identified and investigated previous solutions, offered a new solution informed by research and a stipulated budget, designed a built-in assessment for that solution, and proposed avenues for further research.

My colleague's semester-long project is one example of problem-based learning (PBL). PBL dates back to the 1950s when medical schools put it into practice as a response "to the criticism that traditional teaching and learning methods fail to prepare medical students for solving problems in clinical settings" (Hung et al. 2008, 486). During the 1990s, other disciplines began to adopt PBL, acknowledging that "learning from problems is a condition of human existence [and when we] solve the many problems we face every day, learning occurs" (Barrows and Tamblyn 1980, 1). A connection can be drawn between the benefits of PBL and the mission of the KHC, which is "to use the lessons of the Holocaust to educate current and future generations about the ramifications of unbridled prejudice, racism, and stereotyping" (Kupferberg Holocaust Center). While my colleague's PBL was not directly related to the Holocaust, his students did use the KHC's archives to learn and engage with issues of "unbridled prejudice, racism, and stereotyping"—the same issues that are behind many of the global problems we have faced in the past and continue to face in the present.

The Refugee Program Project: Design and Assignment Layout

After hearing of my colleague's use of PBL in his composition courses, I began to develop my own model that would allow me to utilize QCC's campus resources. Ultimately, I aligned my course with the 2016–2017 National Endowment for the Humanities (NEH)/KHC Colloquium Series, "Fleeing Genocide: Displacement, Exile and the Refugee." Comprised of eight events, the series aimed "to put the past in conversation with the present by exploring the history of genocide and refugees … [and] to move our students and community past abstract compassion, into an investigation of the reality of genocide and the trauma of displacement" (QCC Library Guide 2017). The colloquia addressed one of the most pressing issues facing us as a society—the global refugee crisis. The United Nations High Commissioner for Refugees (UNHCR) reports that, "we are now witnessing the highest level of displacement on record". Given the current refugee crisis and the focus of the NEH colloquia for the 2016–2017 year, I decided to organize a PBL group project around issues facing refugees.

In the fall 2016 semester, I divided my two composition courses in half, dedicating the first part to more typical course activities. Students read, discussed, and wrote personal essays on various texts, such as *The Declaration of Independence*, Henry David Thoreau's "Civil Disobedience," Martin Luther King's "Letter from Birmingham City Jail," and Erich Fromm's "Disobedience as a Psychological and Moral Problem." These works provided students with foundational texts that address issues of social engagement, responsibility, and equality. At the beginning of the second half of the semester, I introduced and explained the group project. Students were assigned to a group whose goal was to create a fictional program that assists refugees to the United States. Similar to my colleague's

NGO assignment, the finished project required that each group demonstrate a thorough awareness of the refugee issue, understand and evaluate solutions that other organizations have proposed, and develop their own solution and argue why it would be effective.

Given the number of tasks that students had to accomplish during the project, I created a Refugee Program Project Guide that outlined and described the key components of the project, provided students with a plan/paper outline, and indicated the point distribution. Since this Guide was instrumental to the success of the project, I have included it as an Appendix to this chapter.

The Refugee Program Project in Practice

The first goal of the Refugee Program Project was to introduce students to the refugee issue, which was accomplished by a library orientation. Ahead of time, I provided the librarian with the same Guide the students had received. After a general introduction to the library databases and resources, students were given nearly 50 minutes to do individual research on refugees. During our next class session, students had their first group meeting where they discussed the refugee issue in general and brainstormed issues that they wanted to address in their project, such as assisting men to find work, helping refugee children adjust to schooling in the United States, or creating safe spaces for women in refugee camps. In this brainstorming phase, I limited my participation because I did not want students to be influenced by my recommendations; however, I did ask questions to help them focus. For instance, one group wanted to concentrate on children, and I asked if it would be helpful to be more specific, such as thinking about an age range, gender, and/or the children's country of origin. I then left the students to discuss among themselves various options. During students' second meeting, their goal was to decide on the specifics of their project and to submit a progress report.[1]

Two lectures that were held in the fall 2017 semester as part of the "Fleeing Genocide" Colloquium Series related directly to the group project. The first lecture, "Building a Better Future: Educating Refugee Youth," was delivered by Sara Rowbottom, the Education and Learning Manager at the International Rescue Committee, and it highlighted relevant issues relating to the education of refugees. The second lecture, "Current Refugee Crisis and Refugee Polices," was delivered by Stefan Feller, United Nations Police Advisor in the Department of Peacekeeping

Operations, and it introduced the current refugee crisis and related UN policies and programs. Students were required to attend one of these lectures and then write a reflection in which they answered the following questions: (1) What were the relevant points of the lecture? (2) Did the lecture relate to your group project, and if so, how? (3) Did the lecture change any ideas that you had about refugees or related issues? For bonus points, students were given the option to attend the other lecture and to write that reflection as well. In most of the groups, students were able incorporate information that they learned from the lecture into their final project.

Equipped with information from their library research, group discussions, and the colloquia, students had another research day, this time using a computer lab where they searched for sources related to their specific refugee population, issue, and the solutions that were currently in place. As with the brainstorming process, I took a hands-off approach and watched how students constructed their research day. In some groups, all members searched independently; in others, students decided that each member would do a limited search on one particular component of the project. In subsequent group meetings, students met to evaluate the solutions that other organizations had suggested. In evaluating the solutions, students were asked to consider the following questions: (1) What was successful about the solution? (2) In what areas could the solution be improved? The goal was that, in evaluating what other organizations have done, students would come to devise their own solution, which would echo the success of other organizations while also working to remedy their weaknesses.

The final stages of the project included both a group presentation and individual papers. In both, students needed to: (1) give a general overview of the refugee issue; (2) specify their targeted group and issue; (3) explain and evaluate at least two solutions that other organizations have developed; and (4) identify/explain their own solution and clarify what measures they would use to test its effectiveness.

Self-Evaluation and Reflection

At the end of the fall 2016 semester, I once again conducted a self-evaluation and reflection. In an effort to focus on the global orientation of QCC's general education objectives, I concentrated on features that have been identified as imperative to "new movements in education," particularly: (1) knowledge should have a social purpose to ameliorate the human condition; (2) the curriculum should include the study of major global issues; and (3) learning requires an action dimension (Hicks 2008). In prompting students' learning about the global refugee crisis, and by encouraging their development of programs to address that crisis, the Refugee Program Project met all of these aims.

An analysis of student artifacts from the project (i.e., group progress reports and final presentations, as well as individual final papers and personal reflections) revealed a high level of student engagement with the issues raised. The most interesting artifacts were the student reflections on the NEH colloquia that they attended. I reviewed all students' reflections and selected the comments that appeared most often. Many students commented that the lectures were "informative," "enlightening," "attention-grabbing," and "impressive." The two most common student comments concerning the entire group project experience included how much they had learned and the need to raise awareness of the refugee issue.

What I also noticed was that students seemed to enter the refugee issue from two vantage points. As I stated earlier, QCC has a very diverse student body with a significant number of students being either immigrants or direct descendants of immigrants. Thus, for many students, the project allowed them to view their family history in a new light. One student exemplified this connection in the following opening paragraph of her reflection:

> It's easy to take for granted what it's like to be a natural-born citizen of the United States. Despite being the child of immigrants, the process of coming to the U.S. is not something that I've given much thought to—my mom came first together with my brother, and then my dad joined them a few months later, and then I was born. It sounds simple, but doesn't go into the details of what it was like for my brother to move to a whole other school system, or for my father to go from a respected university professor to a delivery boy. And even then, my family was fortunate enough to have the support of their relatives back home and to have a nest egg to kickstart their future. Refugees and asylees are not often so lucky.

On the surface, this student's reflection might appear to miss the mark since it reads the refugee issue in comparison to her own life; however, Peter McLaren (2013, 13) reminds us that "the individual, a social actor, both creates and is created by the social universe of which he or she is a part. Neither the individual nor society is given priority in analysis: the two are inextricably interwoven, so that reference to one must by implication mean reference to the other."

Among those students who lacked a more personal connection to the issue, the project fostered awareness of an issue that impacts so many across the globe. For example, one student ended his reflection by identifying what he labeled as the "four heinous and horrible crimes—genocide, crimes against humanity, war crimes, and crimes of aggression"—and arguing that "[every one] of these crimes is leading to massive victimization of large parts of [the] population, to their displacement inside or outside their respective count[ries], to a large number of threatened people seeking refuge and to migration."

Challenges

Although the project was successful, there were two challenges that emerged in its implementation. First, students initially met the group component of the project with a collective sigh of dissatisfaction. A few students even asked if they could do it as an individual project, which would have defeated the "transformational approach to learning, [that happens when] a group of people who share a concern, set of problems, or a passion about a topic and who deepen their knowledge, and expertise in this area by acting on an ongoing process" that the project was designed to achieve (Wenger and Synder 2002, 4). I knew that offering students this definition would not allay their concerns, so I stopped and asked them to explain their reluctance to work in groups. Many of them shared experiences of working in groups where one or two students did most of the work, or experiences where their group assignments had always seemed like "busy work" with no clear connection to the course objectives. To address this concern, I pointed each student to the part of the Refugee Program Project Guide that clearly connected the project to the course objectives and outlined what each student was expected to contribute.

Second, a number of students indicated that although they had heard news of the refugee issue, they had never fully considered the seriousness of the issue or the complexities of life as a refugee. Conducting research, attending lectures, and discussing the issue with their peers raised their level of awareness and began to deepen their understanding of the challenges faced by displaced people. During many of the final presentations, students showed clips of refugees and the hardships they faced—and these clips often brought them to tears. Students showed various clips focusing on refugees from certain countries (e.g., Haiti and Syria) and/or a certain population (e.g., children and women). This emotional reaction led to a difficult, but necessary, teachable moment. While I reminded students that our project had been constructed around fictional solutions, I asked them to consider how we could act in the real world. Students suggested that they could begin to put into practice some of the solutions that they had proposed as part of the project, such as writing letters to people in positions of power, volunteering time to tutor refugee children, or donating clothes and canned goods.

Moving Forward: Empathy, Social Justice, and Preparation

In addition to the aforementioned challenges, several pedagogical issues emerged as I constructed, administered, and reflected on this project. The one that persistently reared its head was the question of teaching empathy. In his seminal essay, "The Servant as Leader," Robert Greenleaf defines empathy as "the imaginative projection of one's own consciousness into another being" (Greenleaf 1970, 10). Empathy, however, is not content matter that can be taught; it is a practice. While one of the goals of any educator should be to create classroom spaces where students can practice empathy, we must be careful here because there are various types of empathy, such as "passive empathy," which "seeks an emotional reaction but absolves the learner from reflection or responsibility through the denial of pure relations" (Bourn 2015, 112). This issue was a primary concern for Greenleaf. He saw that institutions, particularly universities, had often unconsciously severed a bond between the institution and the community: "By extending education for so many so far into the adult years, the normal participation in society is effectively denied when young people are ready for it. With education that is preponderantly abstract and analytical it is no wonder that there is a preoccupation with criticism and that not much thought is given to 'what can *I* do about it?'" (Greenleaf 1970, 4).

One significant way that we can foster students' practice of empathy is through the incorporation of social justice components in our classrooms. Social justice in the classroom is defined as "recognizing and acting upon the power that we have for making positive change" (Dell' Angelo 2014). In other words, education must not stop at raising students' awareness of issues; it must also encourage them to embrace a problem-solving perspective. The Refugee Program Project outlined in this chapter met this definition by encouraging students to see that there is something that they can do about the problems facing us as a global society.

Nicholas Michelli defines civic preparation as one of the primary purposes of public education in the United States. Such preparation stands to restore students' connections to each other, and to help them integrate into our even larger global community. Yet, while many American institutions now incorporate global education as a part of their curriculum, we cannot accurately assess if the global education they have received will lead them to become global citizens. However, my belief is that when our students leave our classrooms more aware of global issues and problem-solving techniques, they are more equipped to put into practice these skill sets semesters and years later when they are no longer our students. The Refugee Project is one designed to raise awareness of issues beyond students' local communities and give them the tools to become global citizens. For me, our most immediate goal as educators is *to prepare* students "to see the problematic and to act on it" and to "be active, not passive; engaged, not bored" (Michelli 2005, 7). Regardless of the size, demographics, or campus resources available at our institutions, there are numerous opportunities to raise students' awareness of larger global issues and to create lessons that encourage our students to become active and responsible members of a larger global community.

Appendix: Refugee Program Project Guide

Project Overview

Each student will be randomly assigned to a group whose goal is to create a program that assists refugees to the United States. The group will conduct research on refugees and then select a particular issue that the group will address. The finished project requires that each group demonstrate a thorough awareness of the refugee issue, understand and evaluate solutions that other organizations have proposed, and develop the group's own solution and argue why it will work.

Blackboard Group

Each group will have its own Blackboard group page that will allow members to communicate with one another outside of class and to share thoughts, research, and other relevant information with one another.

Progress Reports

Each group will be supplied with a progress report form. At the end of each class group meeting, the group is required to submit the form detailing the work they have done. Additionally, each group should also outline their plans for the next meeting. The reports are a collaborative effort and the responsibility falls equally on each group member. The task of writing these reports should be shared among the group members with each member doing at least one of the reports.

Project Steps

Below are the components required for this project. While each group will work on these components together, each group member's individual research paper must also include all of these elements.

Research Annotated Bibliography

As the name suggests, an annotated bibliography has notes for each entry. These notes are specifically geared toward using the source in your research paper. Each entry should cover the following points:

- The kind of source
- The thesis, if there is one
- If it is substantiated by evidence
- How it might fit into your research
- Possible references to other valid research

For this project, the annotated bibliography must include at least three scholarly sources. As a group, you may collaborate on the sources and drafting the annotated bibliography, but each member is responsible for submitting an individual annotated bibliography. This will be turned in two weeks before the paper is due.

History/Previous Solutions

The history/previous solutions outline the current history of the refugee issue. It will start with a general summary that provides a historical overview of the refugee issue, and then it will move to the particular issue that you are addressing, such as education, medical coverage, children, or so on. After the introduction of the issue, there should be a summary of at least two solutions that have already been proposed and an evaluation of their effectiveness (their strengths and weaknesses). For the research paper, this section should be two to three pages in length.

Targeted Solution

The targeted solution is your plan to address the particular issue that you have identified. It should state clearly what your solution is, how it is different than previous solutions, and a rationale as to why it will be more effective than previous solutions. As targeted solutions will vary widely among groups, there is no set way in which this information needs to be presented. You should, however, answer the following questions in your representations of your materials.

- What are you going to do?
- Why are you doing things the way you are?
- What other alternatives have you ruled out?

In essence, you are giving a detailed plan with a justification that anticipates possible criticism. For the research paper, this section should be at least two pages in length.

Plan/Paper Outline

12-point Times New Roman font, double spaced

A. Introduction

1. Broad overview of the refugee issue (general)
2. Explanation as to why this issue needs to be addressed
3. What particular issue is the focus of the plan/paper?

B. History

1. A more detailed look into the issue (specific)
2. Overview of the challenges posed by the issue

C. Previous Solutions

1. First solution
    a. Explanation
    b. Its strengths
    c. Its weaknesses
2. Second solution
    a. Explanation
    b. Its strengths
    c. Its weaknesses

D. Targeted Solution

1. Who are you targeting and why?
2. What are the benefits of your plan?
    a. How does it continues to build upon what has worked successfully in previous solutions?
    b. How does it address the weaknesses of previous solutions?
3. What objections do you think others might raise to your solutions (at least one), and how do you address those objections?

E. Conclusion

1. How will you measure your solution's effectiveness?
2. If your solution works, what do you expect to see?
3. Ways that the solution can be improved after the first year

Works Cited Page

After the last page of the research paper, there must be a Works Cited page that accurately lists all the sources that were quoted within the body of the paper.

Presentations

At the end of the project, your entire group will give a presentation on your targeted solution. This presentation has the dual function of showcasing your research and pitching your targeted solution. Your group must, therefore, aim to strike a delicate balance between being informative and engaging in showmanship. How you choose to do this is up to you; however, I suggest that you spend about 20 percent of your presentation on your foundational research, pivot toward your targeted solution for about 60 percent of the presentation, and close with your evaluative measures and conclusion. Resist the temptation to include *everything*. There will be questions at the end, and an opportunity to explain your project more thoroughly in that format. The group presentation must be a minimum of 10 minutes and no more than 20 minutes. During the presentation, you may use any media that you see fit: flyers, video, audio, PowerPoint, Prezi, and so on.

Point Distribution

The Refugee Program Project is worth a total of 40 percent of your final course grade. The grade breakdown is as follows:

Group Meeting Progress Reports 5 percent

There will be seven of these reports due, one after each group meeting. The grade will be determined based on the following: the submission of all seven reports and the thoroughness of forms submitted. This is a group grade, and all members of the group will receive the same grade.

Research Annotated Bibliography 10 percent

While group members may work together on the bibliography, each student will receive an individual grade based on how well she or he has completed the assignment.

NEH Reflection Assignment 5 percent

Each student must attend at least one of the NEH events hosted this fall. Both are held on Wednesdays during club hours. The first is on November 16, and the second is on December 7. After attending an event, students will have a reflection assignment to complete. This is an individual grade.

Refugee Program Project Presentation 10 percent

This grade is based on the thoroughness of the group presentation. Each member of the group will receive the same grade. If a group member is not present during the presentation, that member will receive a 0 for this component unless the rest of the group who did present writes a one-page argument explaining why the absent group member should receive credit. The argument must explain the absent member's level of participation in preparing the presentation and what grade, if any, the member should receive. The final decision, however, is that of the instructor.

Paper 3 (Research) 10 percent

This is an individual grade based on the quality of the research paper that each student will submit on December 1.

Group Bonus Points

Students may earn up to 10 bonus points to be added to each group member's Refugee Program Project grade (this excludes the research paper grade) if they devise a name and a logo for their organization. If the group does decide to satisfy this option, the name and logo must be presented during the presentation.

Individual Bonus Points

If a student attends a second NEH event and completes the associated reflection assignment, the student may earn up to 15 additional bonus points. These points may be added to any grade over the course of the semester.

Note

1. Students had to submit progress reports after every group meeting. While these reports varied somewhat depending upon the students' goals, most recorded the group discussion, the major decisions reached, and the group's plan for their next meeting. As students had to submit progress reports throughout the semester, and because they were asked to rotate who completed those reports, each student completed at least one report over the course of the project.

References

Abdullahi, Sadiq A. 2010. Rethinking Global Education in the Twenty-First Century. In *Global Pedagogies: Schooling for the Future*, ed. Joseph Zajda, 23–34. Dordrecht, Netherlands: Springer.

Barrows, Howard S., and Robyn M. Tamblyn. 1980. *Problem-Based Learning: An Approach to Medical Education*. New York: Springer.

Bourn, Douglas. 2015. *The Theory and Practice of Development Education: A Pedagogy for Global Social Justice*. New York: Routledge.

City University of New York Master Plan 2012-2016. 2014. Investing in Our Future. PDF. Accessed 12 Mar.

Dell' Angelo, Tabitha. 2014. Creating Classrooms for Social Justice. *Edutopia* Blog September 14. https://www.edutopia.org/blog/creating-classrooms-for-social-justice-tabitha-dellangelo

Greene, Maxine. 2001. *Variations on a Blue Guitar: The Lincoln Center Institute Lectures on Aesthetic Education*. New York: Teachers College Press.

Greenleaf, Robert. 1970. *The Servant as Leader*. Indianapolis: Robert Greenleaf Center.

Hicks, David. 2008. Ways of Seeing: The Origins of Global Education in the U.K. Paper presented at the UK ITE Network Inaugural Conference on Education for SustainableDevelopment/Global Citizenship. London, July 2008.

Kupferberg Holocaust Center. http://www.qcc.cuny.edu/khc/index.html. Accessed 12 Mar.

Hung, Woei, David H. Jonassen, and Rude Liu. 2008. Problem-Based Learning. *Handbook of Research on Educational Communications and Technology* 3: 485–506.

McLaren, Peter. 2013. Critical Pedagogy. In *Transforming Practice: Critical Issues in Equity, Diversity and Education*, ed. Janet Soler, Christopher S. Walsh, Anna Craft, Jonthan Rix, and Katy Simmons, 3–18. London: Institute of Education Press.

Michelli, Nicholas. 2005. Education for Democracy. What Can It Be? In *Teacher Education for Democracy and Social Justice*, ed. Nicholas M. Michelli and David Lee Keiser, 3–30. New York: Routledge.

Oueensborough Community College CC Office of Institutional Research and Assessment. *2016–2017 Fact Book*. Accessed 12 Mar.

Oxfam UK. What is Global Citizenship? http://www.oxfam.org.uk/education/who-we-are/what-is-global-citizenship. Accessed 12 Mar.

QCC Library Guide. 2017. KHRCA Colloquia 2016–2017: Fleeing Genocide: Displacement, Exile, and Refugee: Introduction. Last modified August 30, 2017. https://qcc.libguides.com/KHRCA_Fleeing_Genocide2016-17

Tye, Kenneth A. 1990. *Global Education: From Thought to Action*. Alexandria, VA: Association for Supervision and Curriculum Development.

UNHCR. Figures at a Glance. http://www.unhcr.org/en-us/figures-at-a-glance.html. Accessed 14 Mar.

Wenger, E. McDermott, and W.M. Synder. 2002. *Cultivating Communities in Practice*. Boston: Harvard Business School Press.

CHAPTER 17

The Power of Images: Enhancing Learning Outcomes in a History of Photography Course Through an Understanding of Genocide and the Refugee Experience

Kathleen Wentrack

As an art historian at Queensborough Community College (QCC), I understand the power of images in our society and the impact they can have on our students. As a result, when I teach QCC's History of Photography course, I include an analysis of war photography, which inevitably leads students to consider recent conflicts as well as a photographer's motivation to capture the devastating circumstances of the human condition. Through participation in the 2016–2017 National Endowment for the Humanities (NEH)/Kupferberg Holocaust Center (KHC) Colloquium Series, "Fleeing Genocide: Displacement, Exile, and the Refugee," I was able to deepen this analysis, prompting students' consideration of current conflicts, the plight of refugees, and the role that images—such as the iconic photograph of the drowned Syrian child floating up on a beach in

K. Wentrack (✉)
Department of Art & Design, Queensborough Community College, CUNY, Bayside, NY, USA
e-mail: KWentrack@qcc.cuny.edu

A. E. Traver, D. Leshem (eds.), *Humanistic Pedagogy Across the Disciplines*, https://doi.org/10.1007/978-3-319-95025-9_17

Turkey—have on society. By aligning the course with the colloquia, essays, and documentaries on the global refugee crisis, I aimed to instill in my students a sense of empathy, an understanding of genocide and the refugee experience, and a need to act as engaged twenty-first-century citizens. To assess the impact of, and student learning from, this addition to my curriculum, students wrote pre- and post-reflections on their understanding of multiple facets of the refugee crisis. After a brief exploration of my pedagogical background, this chapter focuses on my experience incorporating this material into my course and the ways in which it benefited my students' learning.

Academic Pedagogy Experience

I have been teaching for almost 17 years in The City University of New York (CUNY), 15 of them at QCC—one of the most culturally and ethnically diverse campuses in the United States. Having lived, worked, and studied for eight years outside of the United States, I understand what it feels like to be a "foreigner" and to, at times, not know what is going on around me. My experiences as a teacher and a learner outside of the United States taught me that there are different ways of learning that depend on the individual student's skills, aptitude, and educational background. The students at QCC come with diverse experiences, education levels, and skills. To meet their needs and my learning objectives, I combine a variety of approaches and assignments in my courses to allow for each student to learn and develop.

In 2011, I became involved in two different pedagogy initiatives on campus. The first was Students Working in Interdisciplinary Groups (SWIG), which is aligned with the Association of American Colleges & Universities (AAC&U) designated High Impact Practice (HIP) of Collaborative Assignments and Projects (Kuh 2008; Association of American Colleges & Universities 2013). SWIG collaborations bring two or three faculty together to develop interdisciplinary projects in which students from different disciplines collaborate in a wiki and/or create a digital story or other projects to disseminate to the class, the college community, or the public at large (Fractus Learning 2014). SWIG students use a range of technologies to collaborate and exchange ideas asynchronously, and they learn to recognize and apply different disciplinary lenses in their thinking. The SWIG pedagogy moves the participating classes to a student-centered space where peers are the audience for learning and dialogue. Reflection activities are an important component to the SWIG pedagogy, as they guide students toward metacognition of that learning (Yancey 2016; Yancey 1998; Dewey 1956; Dewey et al. 1947). The SWIG leadership team developed training for new faculty on pedagogy, assignment creation, and assessment tools that include rubrics for collaboration, assignment execution, and digital projects. Since 2011, I have participated in two or three SWIG collaborations every semester.

The second QCC pedagogy initiative in which I became involved was Moving Ahead with ePortfolios (MAeP), which is part of larger efforts of faculty at several CUNY campuses to enhance ePortfolio integration into teaching practice. MAeP trained QCC faculty to use ePortfolios to post student assignments that were modified incrementally over four semesters using the Integrative Learning VALUE Rubric, one of 15 rubrics developed by the AAC&U (Wentrack and Pincus 2014; VALUE Rubric 2009). For example, in the first semester, QCC faculty adopted level one ("Connections to Experience") of the Integrative Learning VALUE Rubric by adding to writing assignments reflective components that asked students to make connections between the assignment and their previous experiences and academic knowledge. Likewise, in the following semester, the second level of the rubric ("Connections to Discipline") was added to the reflection components of writing assignments to encourage students to make connections across disciplines and coursework. Since my involvement with SWIG and MAeP, I have continued to use reflection as an important component in my students' learning.

My activities on pedagogy at QCC were discussed with other art historians who, like me, work in a field that has traditionally placed little value on teaching. In 2013, Karen Shelby and Michelle Millar Fisher, colleagues from CUNY's Graduate Center, established *Art History Teaching Resources* (*AHTR*), an open-access resource for lesson plans and innovative pedagogy in art history. In 2015, I was invited to become a contributing editor. After a literature review and survey through our professional organization, the College Art Association, this collective of art historians noted that, in the field of art history, the Scholarship of Teaching and Learning (SoTL) was sorely overlooked and that we needed a resource for educators concerned with pedagogy. In the fall of 2016, we launched a peer-reviewed, open-access journal hosted at the Graduate Center, entitled *Art History Pedagogy and Practice (AHPP)*, to help fill this lacuna.[1]

These pedagogical activities encouraged my pursuit of additional opportunities for student learning and faculty collaboration at QCC, as well. In the 2015–2016 academic year, I aligned my History of Photography course with the NEH/KHC Colloquium Series, "Gender, Mass Violence, and Genocide." Through this alignment, students' study of photography was conducted in an historical and cultural framework that included consideration of representations of gender and race during different time periods and specifically gender during mass atrocities and genocide. Additionally, students' study of war photography, which was embedded in a unit on Photography in Print, was also enhanced through this alignment. As participants in the series, my students read Jasmina Dervisevic-Cesic's memoir, *The River Runs Salt, Runs Sweet*, which recounts her experiences living through war in Bosnia, and they attended her talk on campus. The written and spoken details of her life story complemented and expanded student learning of violence and genocide in the war photography that was studied in class. To supplement this learning, they also visited the Metropolitan Museum of Art's exhibition, "The Aftermath of Conflict: Jo Ractliffe's Photographs of Angola and South Africa." Students' reflections about these learning experiences astounded me in their thoughtfulness. For example, in addition to reflecting on their course-specific learning, most students wrote that they learned not to stereotype or judge too quickly people who are different from themselves. Such responses prompted me to continue linking my class with events in the NEH/KHC Colloquium Series and to further align my pedagogical efforts with the KHC's mission "to use the lessons of the Holocaust to educate current and future generations about the ramifications of unbridled prejudice, racism, and stereotyping." More specifically, they solidified my desire to enhance my fall 2016 History of Photography students' learning through their participation in the 2016–2017 Colloquium Series, "Fleeing Genocide: Displacement, Exile, and the Refugee."

The History of Photography Course at QCC

I have taught History of Photography at QCC every semester for the past 12 years. The enrolled students are roughly half Art and Design majors with the remainder coming from different disciplines at the college who take the course out of interest or to fulfill the arts requirement in their curriculum. The course is a semester-long survey of the history of photography that moves chronologically through the various periods of its experimental roots and earliest developments in the nineteenth century up through today. We study photography through an historical and cultural framework that includes an analysis of individual images and processes. By doing so, we aim to understand why and how images are made, what they tell us about the cultures that made them, and how the photographs can be analyzed to understand the period and culture.

History of Photography is informed by a number of course outcomes and goals. For example, a primary learning outcome of the course is that "students learn vocabulary specific to techniques of photographic production and the study of photography, and apply it during classroom discussions and on exams." Additionally, my course goals include "providing students with a multicultural education to foster an awareness of their role as global citizens" and "fostering students' abilities to connect course content to experiences outside the classroom and of relevance to their lives." I also aim to provide my students with a variety of experiences to meet the different learning styles of the diverse range of learners in my classroom and to address two of QCC's General Education Outcomes: (1) "use analytical reasoning to identify issues or problems and evaluate evidence in order to make informed decisions" and (2) "make ethical judgements while recognizing multiple perspectives, as appropriate in the program of study."

As noted in the previous section, I now understand reflection to be a significant means by which to structure and measure community college students' achievement of course outcomes and goals. Thus, I begin and conclude each semester of History of Photography with a reflection assignment. The purpose of the course's pre-reflection, which is administered at the beginning of the semester, is to prompt students to make connections between their lives and their education and to encourage students to consider how the upcoming course could be beneficial to their lives beyond the classroom. The purpose of the course's post-reflection, which is administered at the end of the semester, is to capture students' learning and to encourage their application and transfer of that learning to other courses across the disciplines, different areas of their education, and family and work contexts. Once the semester concludes, I regularly compare students' pre- and post-reflections to assess their learning.

In general, both moments of reflection parallel my own intentions to scaffold a slowing-down process for my students, to get them to look and process what they are seeing, learning, and experiencing while they develop the skills necessary for critical thought in our Internet-dominated, socio-historical moment. In addition, these reflective moments also aim to encourage students' awareness of themselves as learners. In particular, students' post-reflections function as a tool to develop their metacognition. Finally, these moments also help students become more conscious of how the work that we are doing in class relates to the goals and objectives of the course.

Aligning History of Photography with the 2016–2017 NEH/KHC Colloquium Series, "Fleeing Genocide: Displacement, Exile, and the Refugee"

In the fall of 2016, History of Photography students completed a pre-reflection before they initiated participation in that year's Colloquium Series, "Fleeing Genocide: Displacement, Exile, and the Refugee." This reflection asked them to consider the following questions: What does it mean to provide students with a multicultural education, and how has it played a role in your learning? Do you believe that it's important for students to receive a multicultural education, and if so why? What does genocide mean to you? Have you or anyone you know ever been displaced? What do you know about refugees in the world, and why do you think people become refugees? What experience have you had with conflict? How did you diffuse these conflicts, explain yourself, and/or change minds? Have you or your family ever had an experience with war? If so, how has this experience influenced your understanding of other cultures?

Halfway through the semester, students were introduced to the course unit on twentieth-century and contemporary war photography, which included references to photographers like Robert Capa, Donald McCullin, and James Nachtwey. As part of this unit, students were assigned a textbook reading (Hirsch 2008, 254–294), and they were asked to view the PBS Frontline documentary "Children of Syria" (2016). We also had open class discussions about war, genocide, and the mass killing of citizens, what it must feel like to be separated from loved ones, and experiences of fleeing home under such dire circumstances.

Students were then asked to consider these issues more formally, in two parts. For the first part, students read/listened to a poem, a short article, and a podcast about refugees and the refugee experience, and then they wrote a four-to-six-sentence response. For the second part, students attended the Colloquium presentation, "The Current Refugee Crisis and Refugee Policies," by Lieutenant General Stefan Feller, Police Adviser to the United Nations who serves as a Director in the Department of Peacekeeping Operations. At that event, Lieutenant General Feller discussed the current refugee crisis, current and past incidents of genocide, and United Nations policies and programs designed to address these conditions.

After these experiences, students completed the post-reflection, which asked them to integrate our class-based learning with insights from the aforementioned poems, essays, podcasts, and Colloquium. To best structure their responses, students were asked to respond to the following questions: Given your course learning, and the current cultural climate in the United States, do you think it's important for students to receive a multicultural education—why or why not? What does empathy mean to you, and how is it relevant to this assignment and society? What have you learned about refugees in the world, and how has your understanding of displacement, conflict, and refugees changed as a result of this assignment?

Insights from Students' Reflections

During almost two decades of teaching, I have learned that efforts to engage issues outside of the art history classroom, to make connections with contemporary events, and to encourage skill development and metacognition have helped to improve student learning. My analysis of fall 2016 History of Photography students' pre- and post-reflections provides further confirmation of this assessment. In general, and as indicated along the themes later, students' responses on the post-reflection were much more thorough, thoughtful, and insightful than were their responses on the pre-reflection. The following sections summarize student responses and highlight select examples of representative and insightful comments from students.

A Multicultural Education

On QCC's diverse campus, multiculturalism is not just a lens through which students learn to view experiences and conflicts around the world, it is also a perspective that students engage as they interact with and learn from one another. Moreover, in a History of Photography, multiculturalism is a meaningful analytic tool that students can use to better understand difference and multiple perspectives in their analyses of photographs. Thus, I was pleased to find that, in their reflections, all students expressed the belief that a multicultural education is an important element of life today. Significantly, however, students' responses in the post-reflections were more developed and specific in their ability to convey the *beneficial effects* of a multicultural education. For example, in her pre-reflection, Student A wrote the following in response to a prompt about the topic: "What it means to provide students with a multicultural education is to provide students with an education where there are different viewpoints. Students with differing races, socioeconomic backgrounds, experiences, and the like." Later, in her post-reflection, Student A built on this definition, demonstrating an increased awareness of the global reach, impacts, and actions inspired by a multicultural education: "I believe it is extremely important for students to receive a multicultural education because students need to know what is going on in the world. Of course, we all might share different views and beliefs, but that is how you learn, by exposure to new ideals… Additionally, a multicultural education ensures that everyone can speak from personal experiences, and use those experiences to empathize with another, and work together for a bigger cause."

As indicated by this example, students' cumulative learning, including their attendance at an NEH/KHC Colloquium, brought them closer to reaching my teaching goals of preparing global citizens and imparting the relevancy of my course to their lives. More specifically, students moved from expressing a general knowledge about what a multicultural education is to expressing a more active awareness of the effects of such an education in their communities and the world.

Displacement, Genocide, and Refugees

Other reflection questions addressed students' understanding of the refugee experience and circumstances of displacement and genocide in our world. In their pre-reflection responses, most students were able to convey a basic definition of a refugee as someone who has chosen to flee or had to flee from their home due to social, political, religious, or ethnic reasons. For example, in his pre-reflection, Student B wrote: "I do not have much knowledge on refugees. I believe they are people who do not agree with their community and laws and are forced to leave. I think people become refugees in search of a better place to live where they are accepted and respected." When asked about the phenomenon of displacement, most students' pre-reflections focused on immigrants, including their own experiences, as immigrants, of navigating different cultures.

Yet, when prompted by the same or similar questions in their post-reflections, students conveyed a more nuanced understanding of the complex political and social environments that bring about refugee crises, conditions of displacement, and genocide. They also reflected on their previous lack of knowledge, as well as their appreciation for the ways in which the course readings, lectures, discussions, and the Colloquium presentation had deepened that knowledge. For example, in his post-reflection, Student B wrote:

> When my professor first asked the class to write down what we thought a refugee was, I was stuck. I cannot deny, I was not very much informed on the subject. I had this certain stereotype in my head of what a refugee was. I knew it was someone on the run, running away from home. This stereotype I had quickly disappeared once we watched a documentary as a class, "Children of Syria." From the title alone I learned that a refugee could be any age, race, gender, there was no filter. It was difficult for me to watch this documentary, especially in class trying to hold back tears. Witnessing the day-to-day life of this particular family was heartbreaking... I am impressed by the strength and heart in these people who have been through so much and continue to suffer.

Such reflections provide direct evidence of the project's alignment with the outcomes and goals of this History of Photography. For example, and related to the two previously mentioned General Education Outcomes, students used analytical reasoning and critical thinking skills to assess new information on refugees in combined media. Along the way, they developed the critical and visual thinking skills that, for the History of Photography students, are both essential to the analysis of photographs and linked to course outcomes.

Likewise, while most students were able to provide a basic definition of genocide in their pre-reflections, their post-reflections evidenced a keener understanding of genocide as a process. Several students also made links to the past; for instance, in the following post-reflection excerpt, Student C connects the plight of Syrian refugees to the experiences of Jews during the Holocaust, noting how the American government was less than willing to accept refugees in both cases of mass atrocity: "Government officials seem to have no idea what it is like to fear for your life, to be hypervigilant, to not have stability... These victims' lives have been turned upside down and they want basic human rights: to have shelter, to have an education, to feel safe."

The campus event, "The Current Refugee Crisis and Refugee Policies," by Lieutenant General Feller had a significant impact on students' understanding of genocide, its history, and their ability to make these connections. For example, Student D reflected: "General Feller's presentation really opened my eyes and made me see the horrific event of genocide and that the well-being of innocent refugees is very sporadic. A genocide can happen any day and at any time in these areas of the world." Overall, the students' post-reflections indicated that the Lieutenant General's presentation impressed upon them historical moments of modern genocide, as well as the relationship between mass violence and displacement. His talk made genocide tangible for the students and increased their understanding of the images of refugees and war that were studied in class.

Also relevant to students' learning about refugees, displacement, and genocide was their development of empathy. To understand how they connected empathy to the experiences of refugees *and* their course learning, the post-reflection included a prompt that asked students to both define and apply the concept. In response, Student E wrote: "Empathy is what everyone should be feeling before rejecting others or shutting them out. Empathy is to put yourself in someone else's shoes, it is defined as the ability to understand and share that feeling of others. I put myself in (the refugees') place and honestly don't know how they are strong enough to go through what they have to go through, it's truly awful."

Demonstrating how this empathic learning is directly connected to course goals, particularly my desire to "foster students' awareness of their role as global citizens," Student F wrote: "Empathy is a strong emotion of understanding the feelings of others. I feel that not enough people attain this trait. People are not aware of the crisis going on, so they do not share feelings because they cannot relate. I believe more people should be educated on the reality of this war going on and its consequences. As a whole, we should take responsibility and stand up for the values, not only of ourselves, but of others."

Conflict and Resolution

In their pre-reflections, students wrote at length about experiences of conflict at home, with friends, and in the workplace. In recounting these experiences, some noted how difficult it is to change people's minds once they have a strong opinion about something. Others described the lengths to which they go to avoid conflict. Few students, however, revealed a macro-level understanding of conflict and resolution in their pre-reflections. As a result, it was heartening to see evidence, in students' post-reflections, of their development in this regard.

Again, Lieutenant General Feller's presentation seemed to most profoundly impact students' thinking along these lines. For example, Student G offered the following nuanced macro-level commentary in his post-reflection:

> (It) is a saddening reality that the United Nations and their mission exist on the periphery of geopolitical conflicts and politics. It is not good that there is limited funding and personnel available for such noble causes, the fact that General Feller pointed out that there is no unified training system leaves a lot to be desired. I know from personal military experience with the United States Armed Forces that the security situation in Afghanistan and subsequently the Afghan United Nations personnel and police are woefully inadequate for the task they are assigned. This combined with the not nearly enough funding and the complexities of law, sovereignty, and rules of engagement will mean that United Nations police will always have there [sic] mission hampered by external forces and the will of nation states.

Students were also struck by the devotion Lieutenant General Feller, and his colleagues, have to protecting people in conflict zones. In fact, like Student H below, several students included a version of General Feller's memorable quote—"We go where others do not"—in their post-reflections on the event:

> Listening to guest speaker Lieutenant General Stefan Feller made me realize that there are good people out there who won't stop fighting for a change. The fact that Lieutenant General Feller makes it his priority to ensure refugees in the poorest and most dangerous countries like Haiti, the Central African Republic, Rwanda, Palestine, Afghanistan, Bosnia, etc., the right to freedom and safety amazes me. I was shocked to hear that there are about 120,000 people working for the peace operations. These police officers and military officials risk their own safety to protect these refugees from wrong doings and help them get their lives back on track. The bravery of these UN peacekeepers exemplifies Lieutenant General Feller's saying, "We go places others don't."

Lieutenant General Feller's presentation provided information that made the images of global conflict and displacement more understandable and impactful. In doing so, it encouraged my efforts to "provide students with a multicultural education to foster an awareness of their role as global citizens" and to "foster students' abilities to connect course content to experiences outside the classroom and of relevance to their lives."

Conclusion

By aligning the learning outcomes and goals of a History of Photography with the 2016–2017 NEH/KHC Colloquium Series, and by integrating a diverse range of learning modalities that included visual, textual, and oral information, I was able to enrich students' analytic skills, make the course more relevant to students' lives, and cultivate students' awareness of themselves as global citizens. Pre- and post-reflection activities helped students, and me, to both gauge their learning from a different perspective and document that learning along a number of significant outcomes, including those specified for the course and the college.

Appendix: Poetry, Essay, Podcast, and Resource Recommendations for Students in Formal Writing Components

Auden, W.H. 1939. Refugee Blues. http://www.ppu.org.uk/learn/poetry/poetry_against1.html. Accessed 1 Dec 2016.

"Children of Syria." 2016. Produced by Marcel Mettelsiefen. Frontline PBS Documentary. Boston: WGBH Educational Foundation. https://www.pbs.org/wgbh/frontline/film/children-of-syria/. Accessed 18 Mar 2018.

Goldberg, Michelle. 2016. If You Want to Live Here, You Need to Live by the Rules Here. *Slate*. http://www.slate.com/articles/news_and_politics/cover_story/2016/07/sexual_assault_case_involving_refugees_in_idaho_in_the_age_of_donald_trump.html. Accessed 1 Dec 2016.

International Center of Photography. *Robert Capa*. https://www.icp.org/browse/archive/constituents/robert-capa?all/all/all/all/0. Accessed 18 Mar 2018.

Lee, Li-Young. 2008. *Immigrant Blues*. https://www.poetryfoundation.org/poems-and-poets/poems/detail/52210. Accessed 1 Dec 2016.

Originally published in Li-Young Lee *Behind My Eyes*. W.W. Norton & Company, Inc.

McCullin, Donald. *Don McCullin*. https://donmccullin.com/. Accessed 18 Mar 2018.

Nachtwey, James. *Witness: Photography by James Nachtwey*. http://www.jamesnachtwey.com/. Accessed 18 Mar 2018.

New York Times. *War Photography*. https://www.nytimes.com/topic/subject/war-photography. Accessed 18 Mar 2018.

Nye, Naomi Shihab. 2016. *The Traveling Onion*. https://onbeing.org/blog/the-traveling-onion-a-poem/. Accessed 1 Dec 2016.

Robbins, Liz. 2015. 11th-Hour Detour Puts Family in Connecticut as Indiana Bars Syrian Refugees. *New York Times*, November 17. http://www.nytimes.com/2015/11/18/nyregion/11th-hour-detour-puts-family-in-connecticut-as-indiana-bars-syrian-refugees.html?action=click&contentCollection=U.S.&module=RelatedCoverage&region=EndOfArticle&pgtype=article. Accessed 1 Dec 2016.

Saunders, Beth. *Nineteenth-Century Photography*. http://arthistoryteachingresources.org/lessons/nineteenth-century-photography/. Accessed 18 Mar 2018.

———. *Twentieth-Century Photography*. http://arthistoryteachingresources.org/lessons/twentieth-century-photography/. Accessed 18 Mar 2018.

"This American Life: Episode 592, 'Are We There Yet?'" 2016. http://www.thisamericanlife.org/radio-archives/episode/592/are-we-there-yet. Accessed 1 Dec 2016.

"This American Life: Episode 593, 'Don't Have to Live Like a Refugee.'" 2016. http://www.thisamericanlife.org/radio-archives/episode/593/dont-have-to-live-like-a-refugee. Accessed 1 Dec 2016.

Victor, Daniel. 2015. Comparing Jewish Refugees of the 1930s with Syrians Today. *New York Times*, November 19. http://www.nytimes.com/2015/11/20/us/comparing-jewish-refugees-of-the-1930s-with-syrians-today.html?_r=0. Accessed 1 Dec 2016.

Note

1. *Art History Teaching Resources* (AHTR) and *Art History Pedagogy and Practice (AHPP)* were generously funded by the Samuel H. Kress Foundation, with additional support from the City University of New York (CUNY) Graduate Center.

References

Association of American Colleges & Universities. 2013. High Impact Educational Practices. https://aacu.org/sites/default/files/files/LEAP/HIP_tables.pdf. Accessed 2 Apr 2017.

———. 2009. VALUE Rubric Development Project. http://www.aacu.org/value/rubrics. Accessed 2 Apr 2017.

Art History Pedagogy and Practice. http://academicworks.cuny.edu/ahpp/.

Art History Teaching Resources. http://arthistoryteachingresources.org/.

Fractus Learning. 2014. Bloom's Taxonomy for the Digital World. https://www.fractuslearning.com/2014/08/18/blooms-taxonomy-digital-print-table/. Accessed 28 May 2017.

Children of Syria. 2016. Produced by Marcel Mettelsiefen. In *Frontline PBS Documentary*. Boston: WGBH Educational Foundation.

Dewey, John. 1956. *Experience and Education*. New York: Macmillan.

Dewey, John, et al. 1947. *Art and Education*. 2nd ed. Merion, PA: Barnes Foundation Press.

Hirsch, Robert. 2008. *Seizing the Light: A Social History of Photography*. 2nd ed. New York: McGraw-Hill.

Kuh, George D. 2008. *High Impact Educational Practices: What They Are, Who Has Access to Them and Why Do They Matter?* Washington, DC: AAC&U.

"Moving Ahead with ePortfolios." Queensborough Community College. http://www.qcc.cuny.edu/eportfolio/maep.html.

Wentrack, Kathleen, and Dion Pincus. 2014. Moving Ahead with ePortfolios, (MAeP). In *Queensborough Community College: Reflective Practice MAeP. Catalyst for Learning: ePortfolio Research and Resources*. http://qbcc.mcnrc.org/maep/.

Yancey, Kathleen Blake. 1998. *Reflection in the Writing Classroom*. Logan, Utah: Utah State University Press.

———. 2016. *A Rhetoric of Reflection*. Logan, Utah: Utah State University Press.

Index[1]

[1]Note: Page numbers followed by 'n' refer to notes.

A. E. Traver, D. Leshem (eds.), *Humanistic Pedagogy Across the Disciplines*, https://doi.org/10.1007/978-3-319-95025-9

I

FSC
www.fsc.org
MIX
Papier | Fördert
gute Waldnutzung
FSC® C083411

Kolibri 360 GmbH
Ferdinand-Jühlke-Straße 7
99095 Erfurt, Deutschland
produktsicherheit@kolibri360.de